ENDURING EPICS

Indian Art Series

ENDURING EPICS

Raghupati Bhat

MOSA
MUSEUM OF SACRED ART

NIYOGI BOOKS

MOSA
MUSEUM OF SACRED ART

Director
Martin Gurvich
Curator
Sushma K. Bahl
General Manager
Raymond Hoogenboom
Collections
Anushka Hoogenboom
Publishing
Phelelani Mdabe
Website
Dario Knez

Belgium
General Manager
Raymond Hoogenboom
Reception
Maria Grison • Patience Offei • Bergita Gjergjaj
Château de Petite Somme, B-6940, Septon (Durbuy), Belgium
t: +32 (0)86 43 30 22 • *e*: info@mosabelgium.com • www.mosabelgium.com

Italy
General Manager
Patrizio Landolfi
Via Scopeti 106/108, San Casciano in Val di Pesa, 50026, Florence, Italy
t: +39 (055) 82 00 54 • *e*: info@mosaitaly.com • www.mosaitaly.com

Catalog
Texts
Sushma K. Bahl
Designer
Phelelani Mdabe
Photography
Param P. Tomanec • Sushma K. Bahl

ISBN: 978-93-83098-44-6

Marketed world wide by
NIYOGI BOOKS
D-78, Okhla Industrial Area, Phase-I, New Delhi-110 020, INDIA
Tel: 91-11-26816301, 49327000, Fax: 91-11-26810483, 26813830
Email: niyogibooks@gmail.com, Website: www.niyogibooksindia.com

CONTENTS

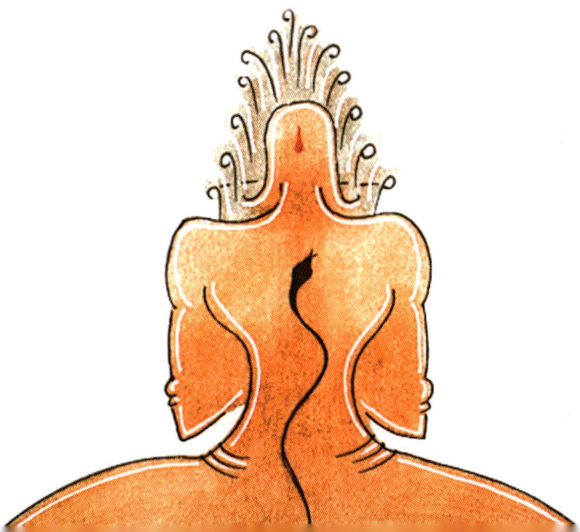

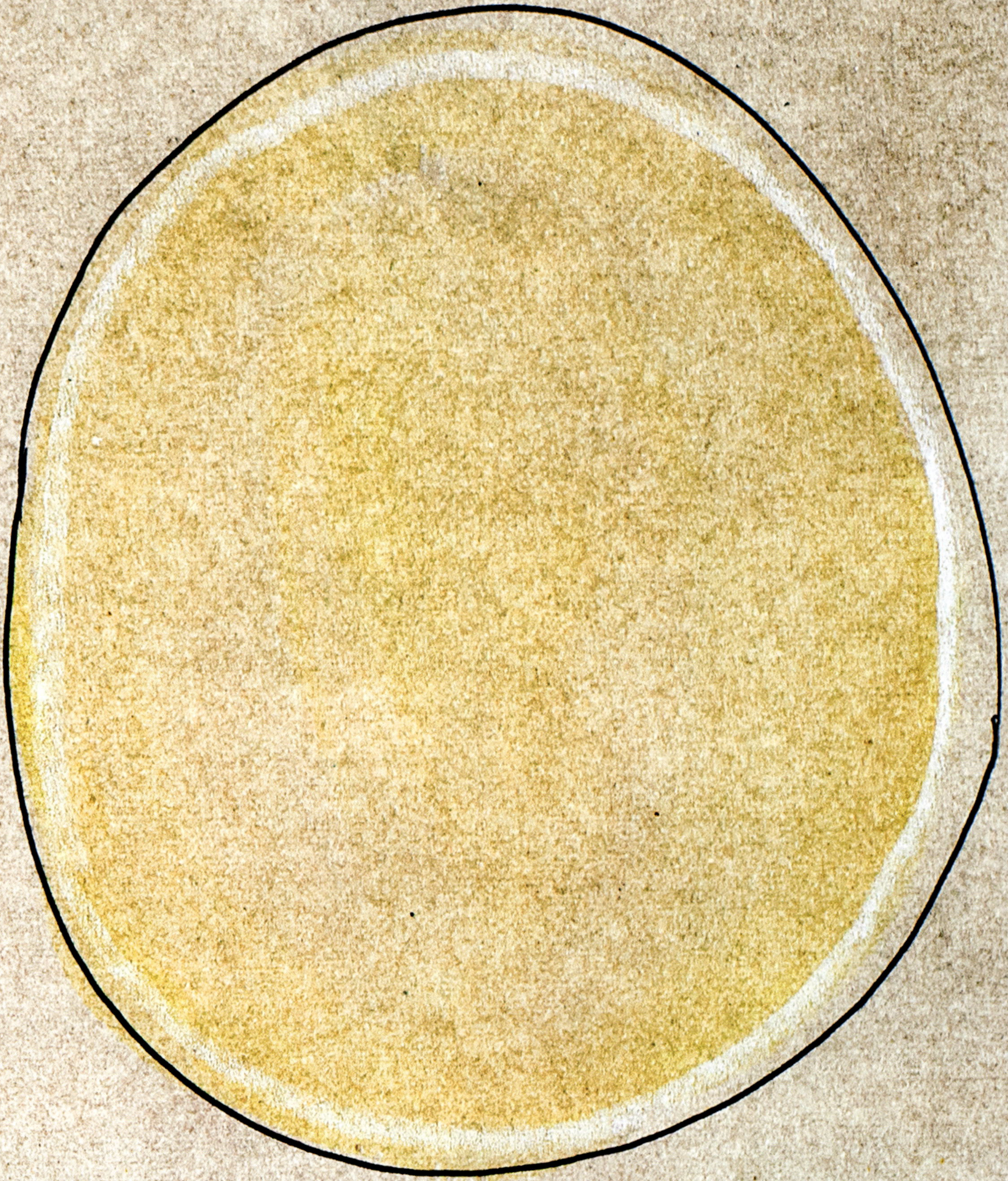

FOREWORD

Ambassador

सत्यमेव जयते

भारतीय राजदूतावास
EMBASSY OF INDIA
CHAUSSEE DE VLEURGAT, 217
1050, BRUXELLES
TEL. 640 91 40
FAX 648 96 38

March 10, 2014

MESSAGE

"I am delighted that the prestigious Museum of Sacred Art is organizing exhibitions of three prominent Indian artists in Belgium aimed at amalgamating different forms of spirituality associated with diverse global faiths through fine arts.

The theme of the exhibitions—Forms of Devotion—is apt in the context of the expositions that celebrate the multiplicity, diversity, creativity and vibrancy of devotional art of India in varied hues and forms. The unique paintings and calligraphic works of the Indian artists--Posapati Parameshwar Raju, Raghupati Bhat and Shobha Broota—transcend faiths and genres—figurative, mythological, abstract, Hindu, Muslim, Christian, Sikh, Buddhist, Jain etc – and showcase the dynamic multi-religious and multi-cultural life of India to the west.

The antiquity of Indian civilization matched by the vastness of its geographical extent has contributed to the rich and multiple art forms of India. These art forms have been successfully presented by the Museum of Sacred Art not only in Belgium, but also in the whole of Europe over the last five years since its inception. I deeply appreciate the initiative of the Museum to encourage interfaith dialogue through fine arts as manifested in these upcoming exhibitions.

I am confident that the Indian art- loving people of Europe would once again have the opportunity to witness Indian mythology, icons and folk tales through the forthcoming exhibitions and that too after the just concluded Europalia-India Festival.

I convey my best wishes to the Museum of Sacred Art of Belgium for a successful organization of the forthcoming exhibitions".

(M.S. Puri)

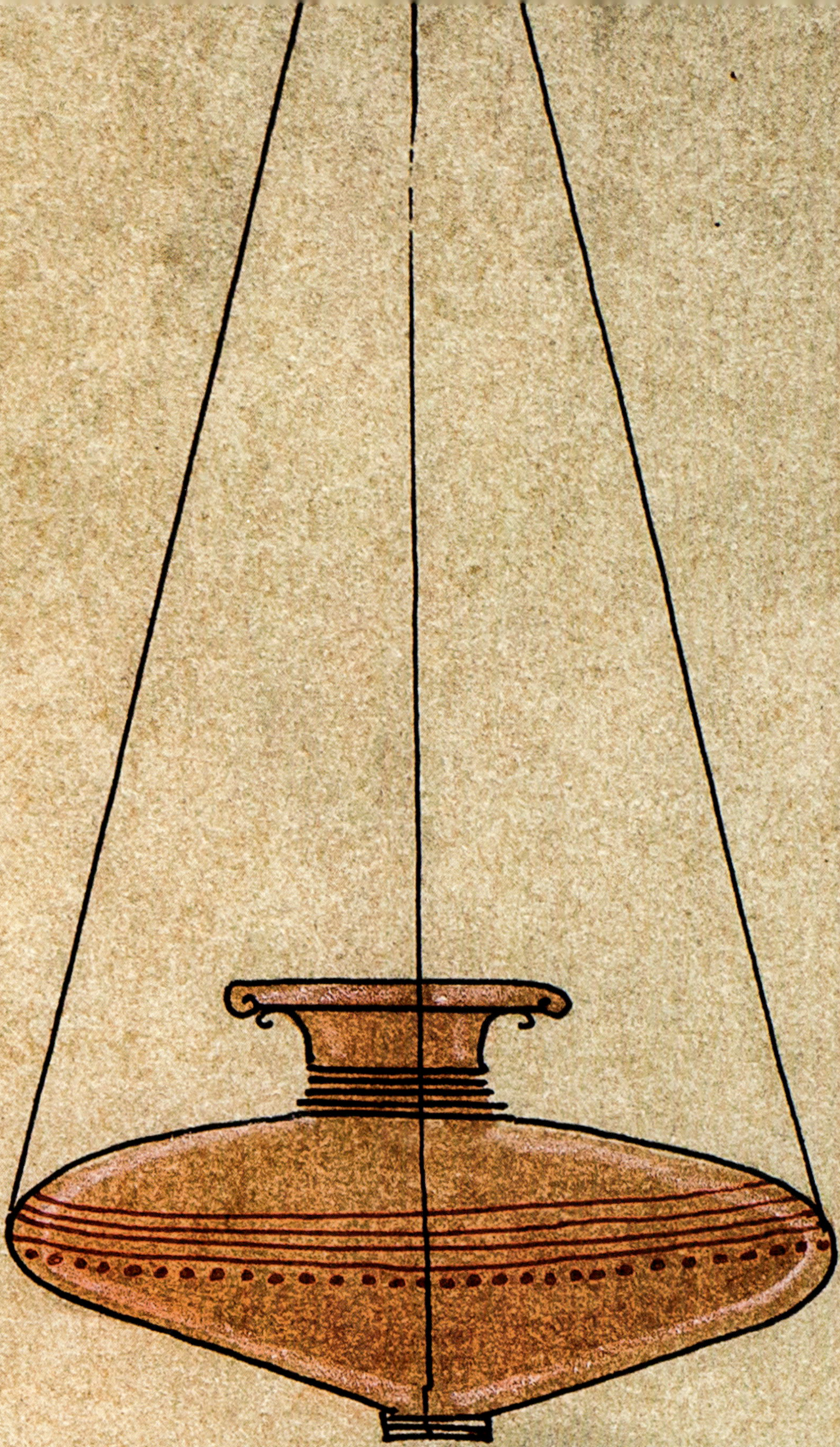

PREFACE

The prospect of inaugurating the 2014 art exhibits at MOSA with such outstanding, accomplished artists as Shobha Broota, Raghupati Bhat, and Poosapati Parameshwar Raju fills me with profound joy.

The inauguration will be attended by our guest of honor His Excellency M.S. Puri, ambassador of India to Belgium and the EU, and art curator Sushma K. Bahl, who has written the texts about all three artists. Moreover, this festive event will be graced by musical performances by celebrated flautist Panditji Hariprasad Chaurasia and renowned sitar player Subrata De. Our exhibition program for Indian and International artists working on spiritual, devotional and sacred art is quite dynamic and our galleries in Belgium (Radhadesh, Durbuy) and Italy (Villa Vrindavan, Florence) will be showcasing many of them in the upcoming years.

MOSA's goal is to bridge the cultural divide between India and Europe and between material and spiritual life. Art is a perfect medium to do so, and we hope that many Europeans will discover the excellent Indian artists who try to convey a spiritual message. We are convinced that MOSA's visitors will come to appreciate and enjoy the currently exhibited work of all three artists.

Raghupati Bhat's exhibit shares gallery space with Parameshwar Raju's. The two complement each other rather nicely. The Ramayana has been told and retold as well as depicted in the arts for millennia, and human society never tires of hearing these wonderful pastimes of the Lord. The Lord is eternal and so are His pastimes. We only inhabit this planet for a short time, and the greatest achievement obtainable by a human being is not wealth, fame, power, beauty, or material intelligence but devotion for the Almighty and making solid progress on the spiritual path.

In the paintings presented in this volume, Raghupati Bhat expertly fuses the traditional with the contemporary and offers a new interpretation of the great Indian classics: the Ramayana, the Mahabharata, and the Bhagavata Purana. These series are exquisitely composed with touches of calligraphy. Raghupati carries us to other times and plunges us in the bittersweet stories of Lord Rama and Sita Devi, the tragic and heroic pastimes of the Pandavas, and the exploits of the various avatars (incarnations) of Lord Krishna.

Let us reflect on those wonderful pastimes, and let us imbibe the high ethics and morality they contain. Lord Rama and Hanuman; Lord Krishna and Arjuna — the Lord and His dedicated servants will eternally continue to enlighten and inspire human society, no matter how materialistic it becomes. May the artistic renderings of classical texts in this catalog bring out in all onlookers feelings of genuine devotion to the Lord, of brotherhood to other human beings, and of compassion to animals and nature.

Martin Gurvich,
Director

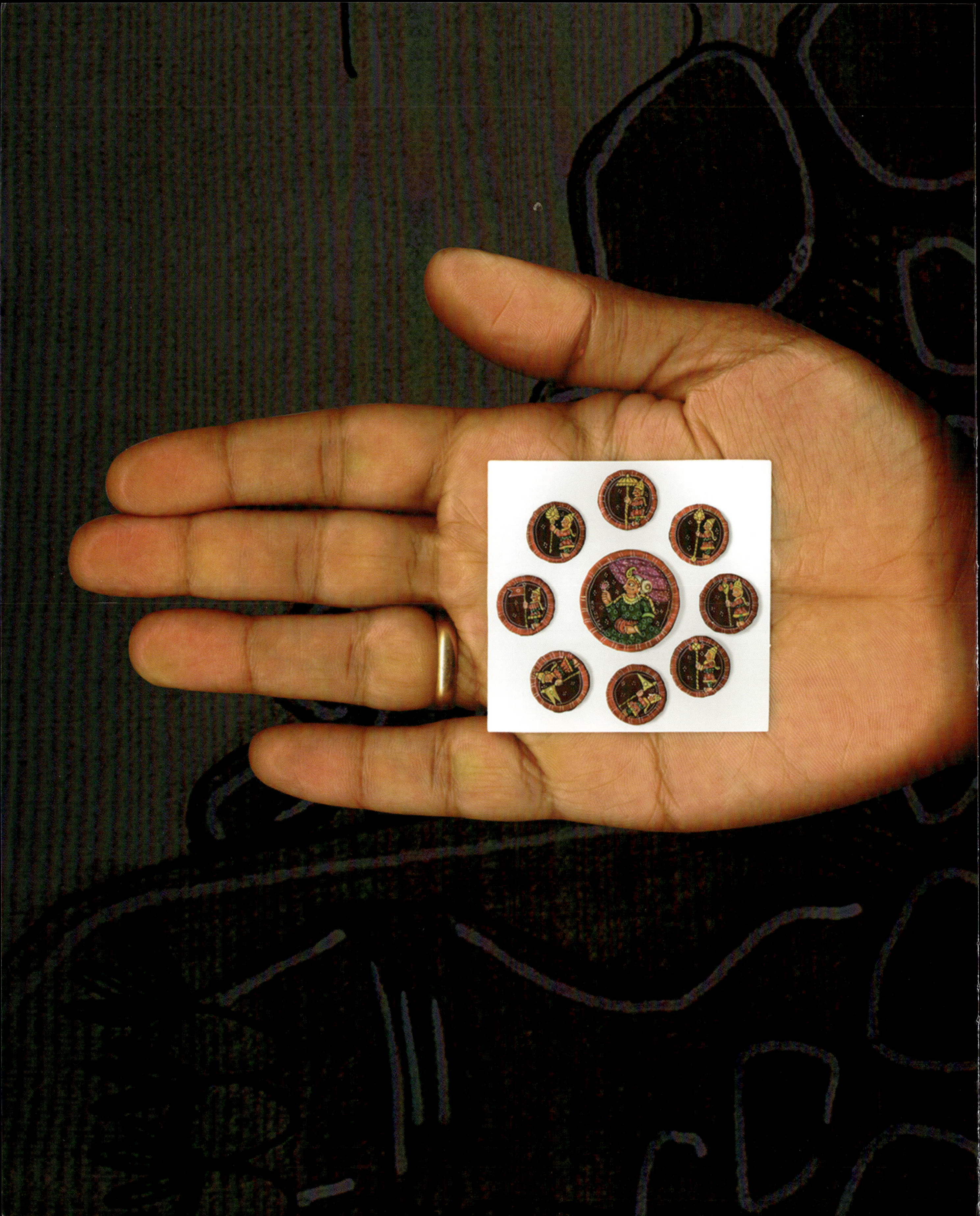

TRANSCENDENT IMAGERY

Sushma K. Bahl

A transcendent imagery in petite renderings and fine re-creations of mythological narratives mark Raghupati Bhat's artscape. Raghupati's vast creative repertoire includes imaginative re-presentations of characters and episodes from literary works, such as Ramayana and Mahabharata, and an expanse of Ganjifa work (intricate paintings on small playing cards) that have earned him the honorary title Ganjifa Raghupati Bhat. His drawings and paintings, metaphysical in their ethos, bring alive the pantheons and narratives described in classical and folk literature. Evocative of timelessness, Raghupati's art is adorned with a meditative streak.

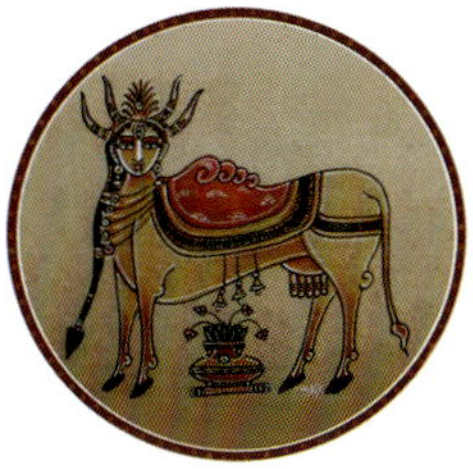

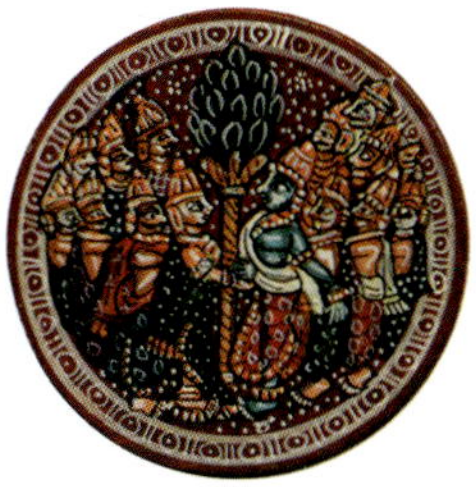

The Artist

Raghupati's interest in painting and passion for ancient Indian culture can be traced back to his early childhood. At first he lived in temple villages in Udupi, where his father was a priest for the local shrine. Later, for schooling, he was sent off to the temple city Nagamangla, where he lived in his sister's home. Although the family wasn't wealthy, the lad spent a carefree and happy childhood in the vicinity of temples and forests. He recalls his daily visits to the Ganesha temple, where he would sit and watch the sculptures for hours and visualize the mantras (sacred utterances) chanted by the priests. Gradually, as he continued sketching and painting forms and figures, his talent got noticed.

After Nagamangla, Raghupati moved to Bangalore to study art at Chitrakala Parishath under the careful tutelage of its Founder-Secretary, the legendary Prof. M. S. Nanjunda Rao. Raghupati's passion for art and urge to learn more about ancient Indian culture and artistic techniques took him to Kottayam, where he attended short courses and was

Sushma K. Bahl MBE is an independent arts adviser, writer, and curator of cultural projects, based in Delhi. She is the author of 5000 Years of Indian Art, and former head of the Arts and Culture, British Council, India. Amongst other projects Bahl was the guest director for XI Triennale-India 2005, the project consultant for Bharat Rang Mahotsav X11, and jury member for the 14th Asian Art Biennale Bangladesh 2010,and the curator of India-ASEAN artists' residency and exhibition in 2012. Ways of Seeing won her the best-curated group show IHC Art India Award. Bahl is both editor and contributor for catalogs and artists' books, including those on Thota Vaikuntam, Paresh Maity, Satish Gupta, Sarla Chandra, and Shuvaprasanna. She is also a trustee and advisory board member of cultural institutions both in India and abroad.

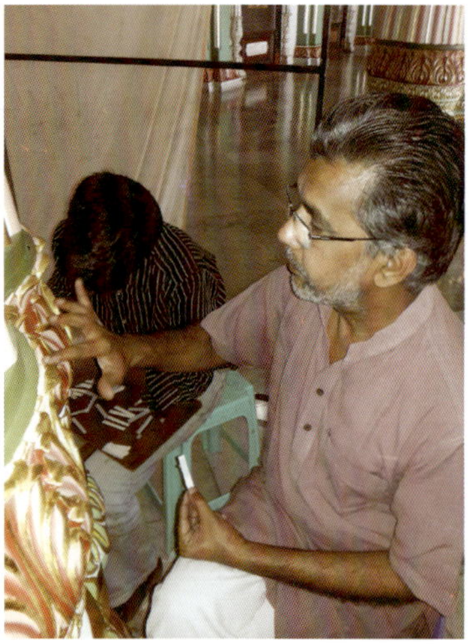
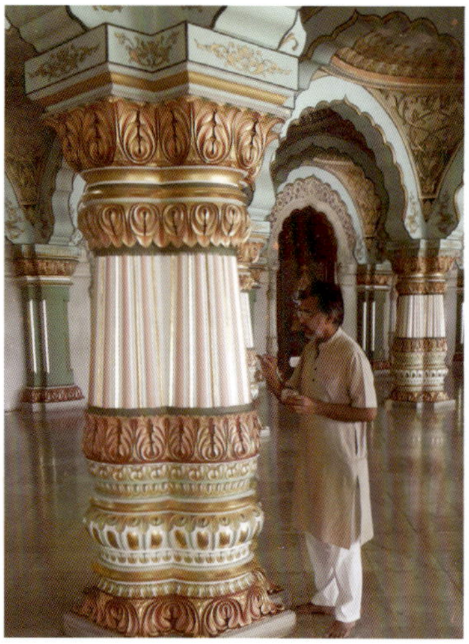
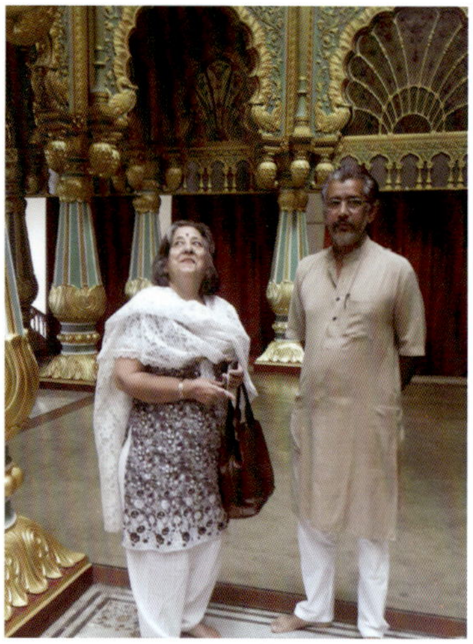

Restoration work at the Amba Vilas Palace.

trained in mural painting and folk tattoo art. There he also learnt how to make and work with natural colours and materials. "Temple sculptures were my school," says the devout artist whose work reflects the latent impressions that got etched into his mind and soul at a young age. The years spent amidst sculptures and paintings of gods and demons in temples proved inspirational for his immaculate work in miniature format on cards and on other renderings in his own unique style. "I like to create my own symbols, inspired by ancient Indian culture," the artist explains.

Raghupati's interest and belief in nature has also impacted his art. Fond of gardening and a strict vegetarian, he prefers natural vegetables and raw fruit to cooked meals. "Man is the only living being that cooks to eat; even animals eat what grows naturally," he says. To enjoy nature and the clean air, he gets up before sunrise and starts the day with a long walk, often uphill to the Chamundi temple, along with a couple of like-minded friends to discusses various Upanishads and artistic matters. After that, rituals like bathing, reciting mantras, and reading scriptures are followed by two or three long sessions of drawing and painting through the day with music playing in the background.

Like many of his contemporaries, he struggled hard in the beginning and survived by doing portrait paintings, temple murals, billboard paintings, and illustrations. Following his marriage in 1986, he moved from Nagmangla to Srirangapatana in 1990. His fascination with Ganjifa art prompted him not only to take up painting on small playing cards but also collecting old ganjifas and setting up Chitra Saale, a Ganjifa museum in Srirangapatana. Sadly, he had to close the museum in 1992 when he shifted his base to Mysore. This city has been kind to Raghupati.

He's doing well now and peacefully lives with his family in a house of his own design which features an image of the sun god with twenty-four gayatri mantras (Vedic hymns and chants) inlaid in the central roof.

Repertoire

The collection here includes over eighty-six mostly small paintings. There is a series on Krishna in his various avatars (incarnations). For instance, in one painting the much-adored deity appears as a playful baby next to Balarama and his mother, and in another as the charming and virtuous Rama. And in the Mahabharata section, Krishna is also depicted as a philosopher friend advising Arjuna on the battlefield. In yet another painting, chariots dash over the battlefield with flags fluttering in the air. Such works tell the multilayered story of the Mahabharata in engaging visuals, some of which have been published in books. The sketched and painted renderings also include episodes from the Ramayana. In one composition we see the four little brothers (Rama, Lakshmana, Bharata, and Shatrugna) born of king Dasharatha's three wives (Kaushalya, Sumitra, and Kaikeyi) in their baby swings. And in Kalyana the wedding of Sita and Rama is re-played, and dozens of people are shown squeezed into 36x27 cm of space! The depiction of the Battle of Sri Lanka similarly features numerous figures within a small frame, which, of course, speaks volumes about the artist's expertise in handling minute details with finesse. And the scene that shows Rama and Lakshmana protecting a yajna (ritual offerings to fire accompanied by Vedic chants) from demons, highlights the artist's imagination and his ability to present familiar episodes in different settings. A set of his sixty painted cards (7 cm diameter each), portraying stories of love and valour from the great Ramayana, is housed at the Victoria & Albert Museum in London. Raghupati's fascination with nature is especially evident in images showing little birds flying in the sky. Other works feature trees, lotuses, flowers, ponds, mountains, and other ecological symbols along with the sun and the moon. Noteworthy is the horse emitting fire in one painting and the detailing of the costumes and jewellery worn by men and women in several others. The seated guru and his prayerful follower standing in obeisance with the clouds and marquee above evoke familiar narratives and mythological episodes. Finely rendered within limited space, Raghupati's works offer a glimpse into the artist's talent to compose and create layered narratives in austere imagery.

The bodily contours of the naked sage Rishabhadeva in the Avatara section display Raghupati's mastery in portraiture, as does the painting of the half-animal, half-human Kamadhenu in the Ramayana section. There are finely etched black-and-white drawings in pen on paper, while in others a dash of subtle palette is added for enhanced visual impact. The paintings featuring the arrival of the sages at the hermitage or those depicting Krishna in his various incarnations — Kurma, Matsya, Narasimha, Vamana, and others — all evoke celebrated narratives.

As a devout Hindu, Raghupati has studied the Ramayana, Mahabharata, Bhagvad-gita, and the Upanishads. Though the episodes and characters he creates, on paper and on canvas, are drawn broadly in accordance with these sacred texts, they also reveal his imaginative touch. Contemporary elements are added to metaphysical themes, and icons are painted and drawn with sharp-pointed features as against the highly ornate voluptuous forms of the tradition. The artist has also drawn and painted deities that are worshipped outside of Hinduism, such as Buddha.

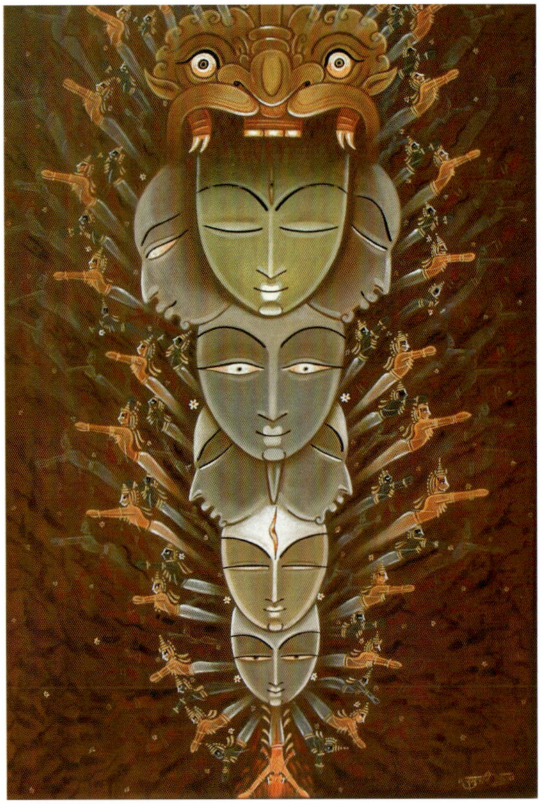

Vishwaroopa darshana

The prefix "Ganjifa" has been added to Raghupati's name to honour his pioneering work that helped revive this almost extinct art of miniature painting on tiny cards, also known as Chadh. Kings and nawabs (nobles of the Mughal and British eras) used ganjifas for playing card games, a favourite pastime of, for instance, Krishna-raja Wadiyars III of Mysore. To evolve his own style, Raghupati researched and interacted with the royals of Mysore and travelled through Karnataka, Orissa, Bihar, and other parts of India — wherever the form was practised. Painting the cards in different shapes and intricate designs, he is credited for revitalizing the Karnataka Ganjifa painting.

His work in this format includes various series on Dhammapada, Durgasaptasati, Basavanna's Vacanas, Vedas, Purusasukta, Raga-ragini (paintings based on Indian musical modes), yoga, Ayurveda (a system of traditional medicine), and, of course, the Visvarupa that won him the coveted National Award. Although Raghupati's focus has now shifted to painting on paper, with 330 Ganjifa cards of Chamundeshwari Chadh, 120 cards of Dasavathar, ninety-six leafs on Ramayana, and ninety-six on other epics, he has built a large repository of Ganjifa work.

Technique

Initially taking up a job with Kaavi Kale in the early '80s, Raghupati traversed tough terrains, working and experimenting with a variety of subjects and techniques to get to where he is today. From line drawings, painting portraits, posters, milestones, murals, and hoardings, he moved on to the fine art of painting traditional characters and narratives from scriptures. But before Raghupati took up Ganjifa work, he had already completed a series of miniature paintings of gods and demons on paper.

Raghupati takes time to develop his concept and thinking it through. Research and study of various literary classics and discussions with experts precede most of his artistic attempts. Based on those discussions, he produces intricate drawings and elaborate paintings on paper, card, cloth, walls, and canvas. He first sketches the imagery before he takes to painting with brush, though some of his miniature work is painted directly onto the paper. It takes him two to four weeks to finish one small painting. Raghupati began with individual figures but has now mastered the art of painting massive scenes with hundreds of figures on tiny surfaces. Some of his figuration is so minute that he needs to draw and illuminate it with a brush made of a single hair. And one needs a magnifying glass to see the finely-drawn divine deity in his or her full glory.

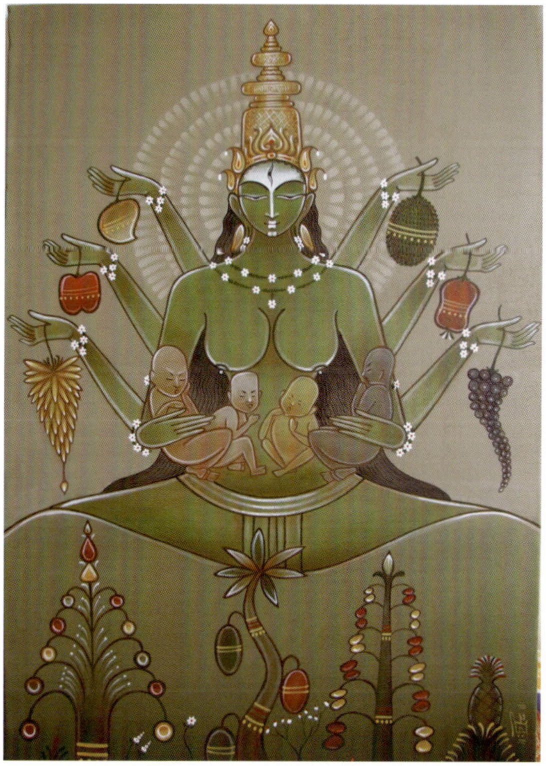

Mother Earth

Raghupati believes the human body is a compound of pancha-tattva (five natural elements) and follows the yogic discipline of painting as described in the Chitra Sutra from the Vishnu-dharmottara Purana. He has finished a number of drawings for an edition of Kumaravyasa Bharatha, a medieval epic in Kannada. Inspired by such concepts and Sanskrit texts, the aesthetics of his art evoke the viewer's imagination and meditative aptitude. Most of his work is produced in water colour and drawings on 36x27 cm paper. His Ganjifa works on cards, however, can be as small as about three or five square centimetres each, sometimes featuring hundreds of finelyetched tiny figures.

Invited by the last Wadiyar scion of the Mysore royal family, Raghupati has been working on the restoration of the murals and gold-foil work on the walls and pillars of the Durbar Hall and Kalyana Mantapa at Mysore palace. Leading a group of artists and art students, he is trying to bring the palace walls back to their original glory. Using organic materials and traditional techniques, he has been working there with over sixty young artist and art

students, including his own daughter Vidya, to complete this project. Under the master artist's supervision, the trainee artists learn to prepare the base and work with organic sources.

Raghupati prefers home-made materials, such as natural colours, paper, and cloth for all his work. He makes his own brushes, gums, varnishes, colours, and related accessories. Grinding minerals and mixing vegetables with flowers, leaves, roots, mud, and other organic materials, he gets his desired colours and palette "Minerals and vegetable colours are rich and give a subtle glow to the work," says the artist who essentially works with the three primary colours plus black and white. And his brushes are made of squirrel hair, which are "supple and especially suited for Ganjifa paintings." To prepare the base, he sticks old newspaper and cloth (up to seven layers) on wood with tree glue and animal gum.

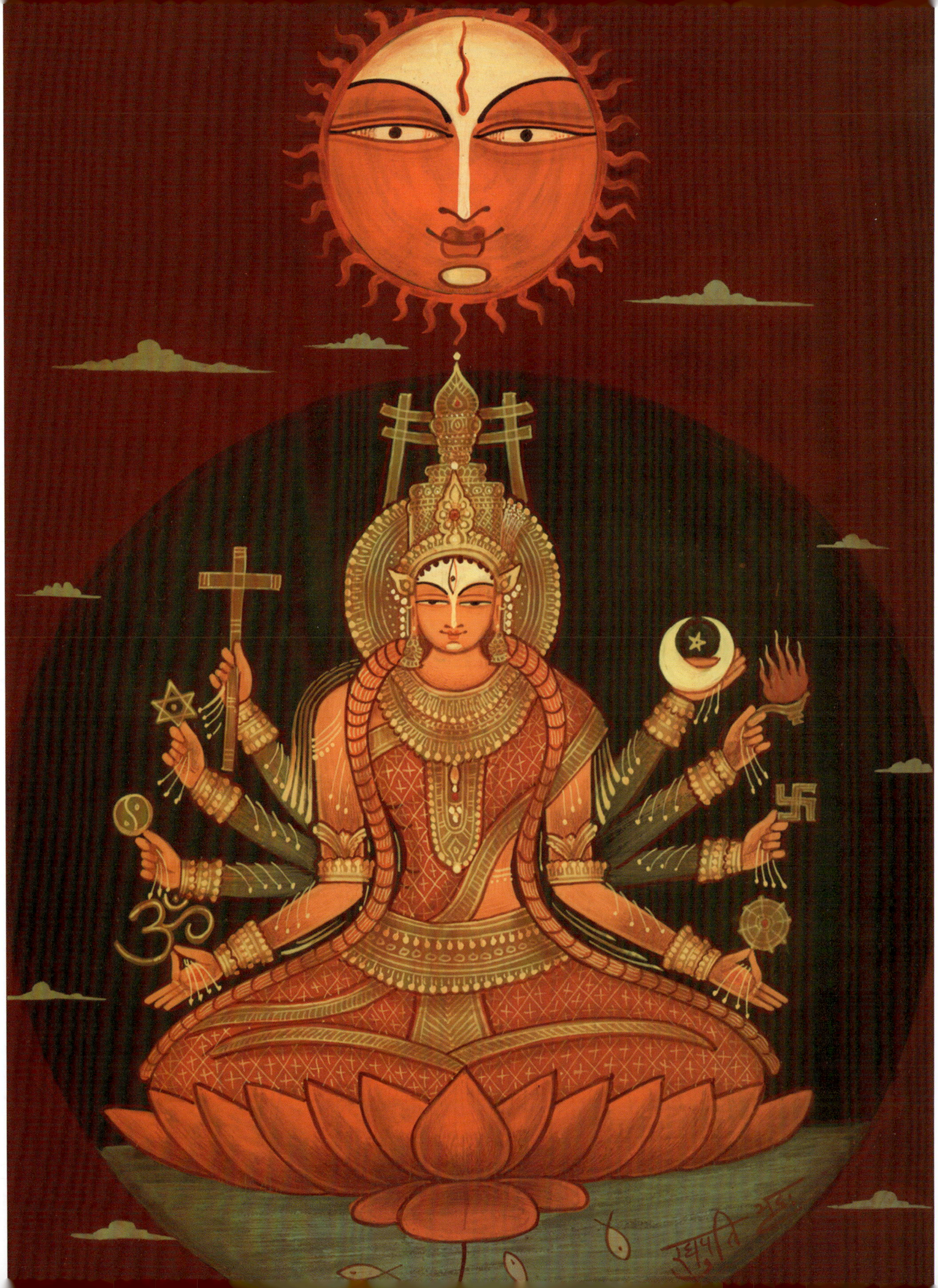

After the painting, the work is given a lacquer coating for added effect and longevity. The lacquer, too, is home-made and is prepared from honey, plants, and other natural materials. For works on paper, Raghupati prefers watercolours, but on canvas he uses acrylic. He has made several small line drawings with just pencil and pen, while others come with a touch of paint. Still others have their entire surface bathed in colour. Some compositions are adorned with calligraphic markings. "Inspired by my visit to Japan and China," Raghupati is currently experimenting with Kannada calligraphy to get text and form to coalesce in the images. "Gain and loss are two sides of the same coin," declares Raghupati, who sees life as a mixed blessing. He appears at peace with himself and communicates that tranquillity and inward gaze through his remarkable artistic creations. Engaging in conception and amazing in execution, the transcendent imagery by Raghupati Bhat presents a visually delightful and spiritually uplifting artscape.

< Jaganmatha – World's Mother

AVATARS

Sanaka, Sanandana, Sanatana, and Sanatkumara >
Watercolour and pen on paper, 36 x 27 cm

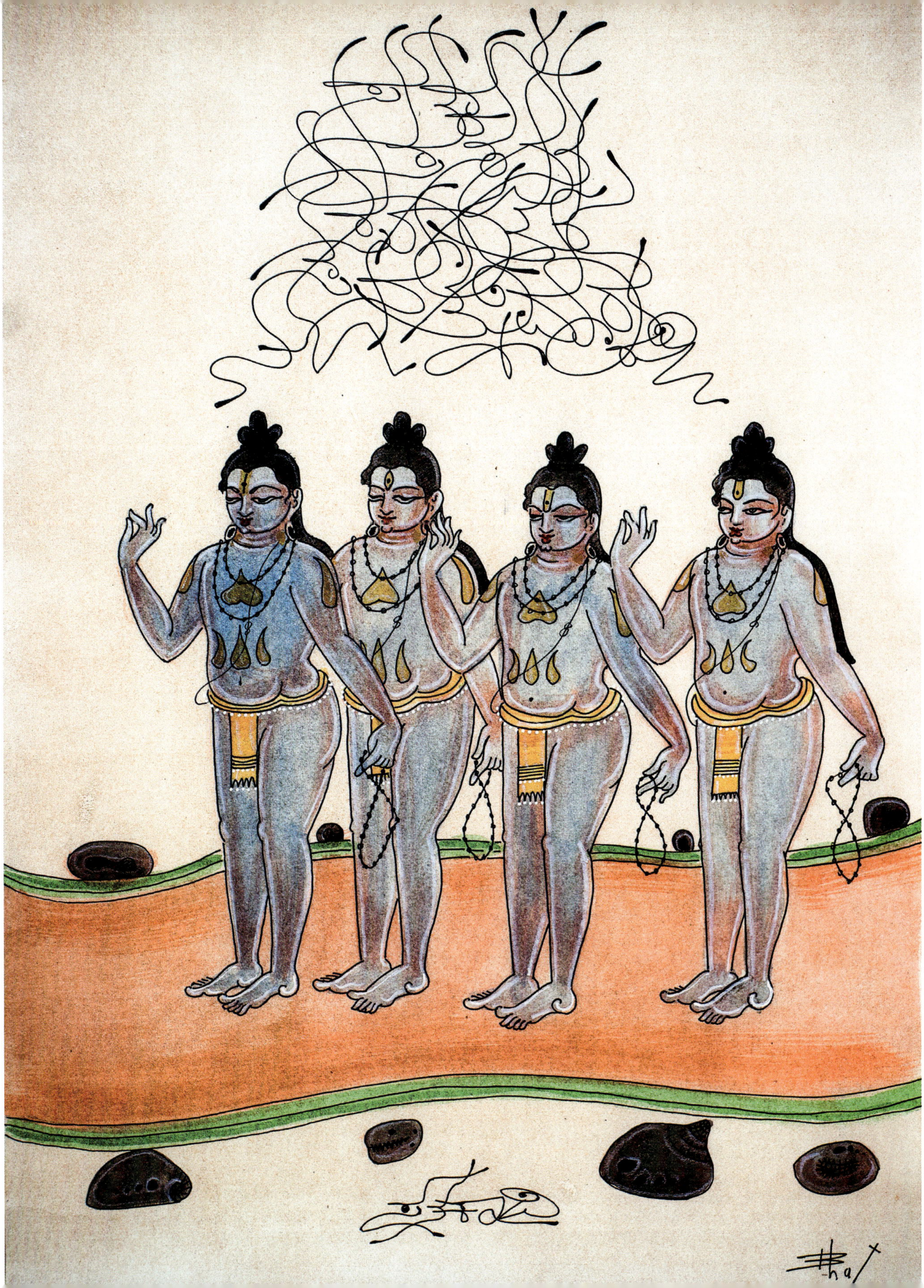

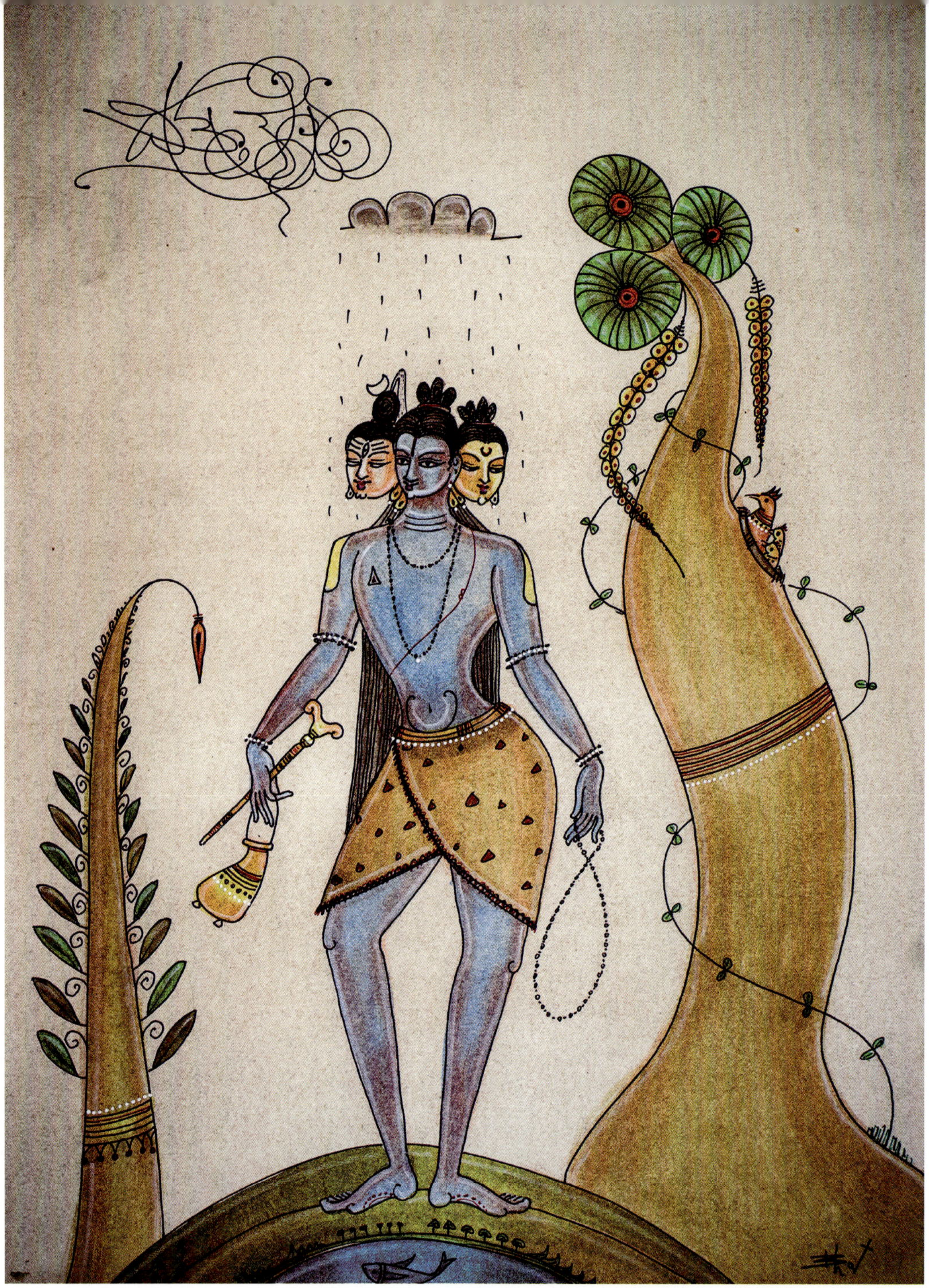

Dattatreya
Watercolor and pen on paper, 36 x 27 cm

Yajña couple >
Watercolour and pen on paper, 36 x 27 cm

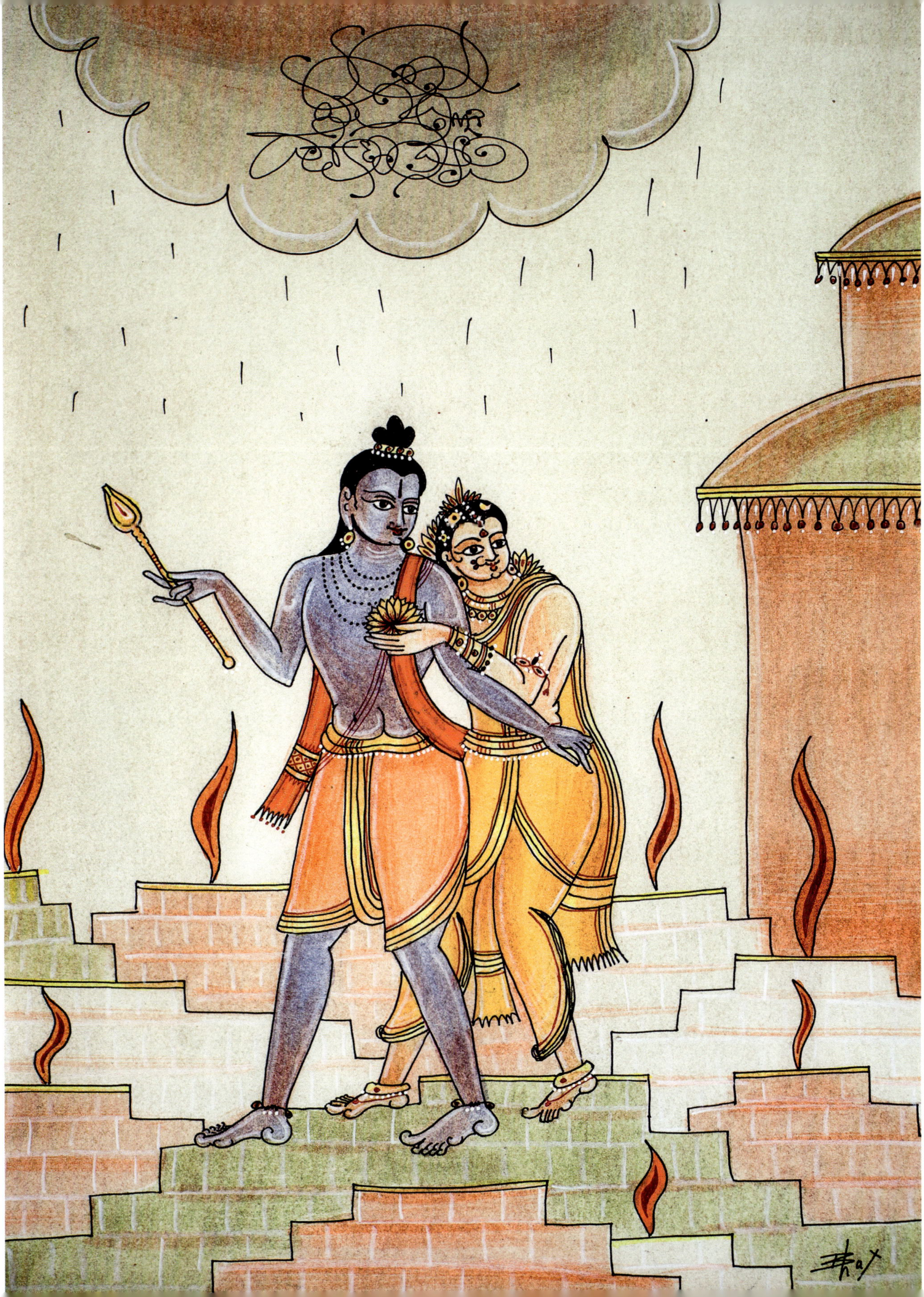

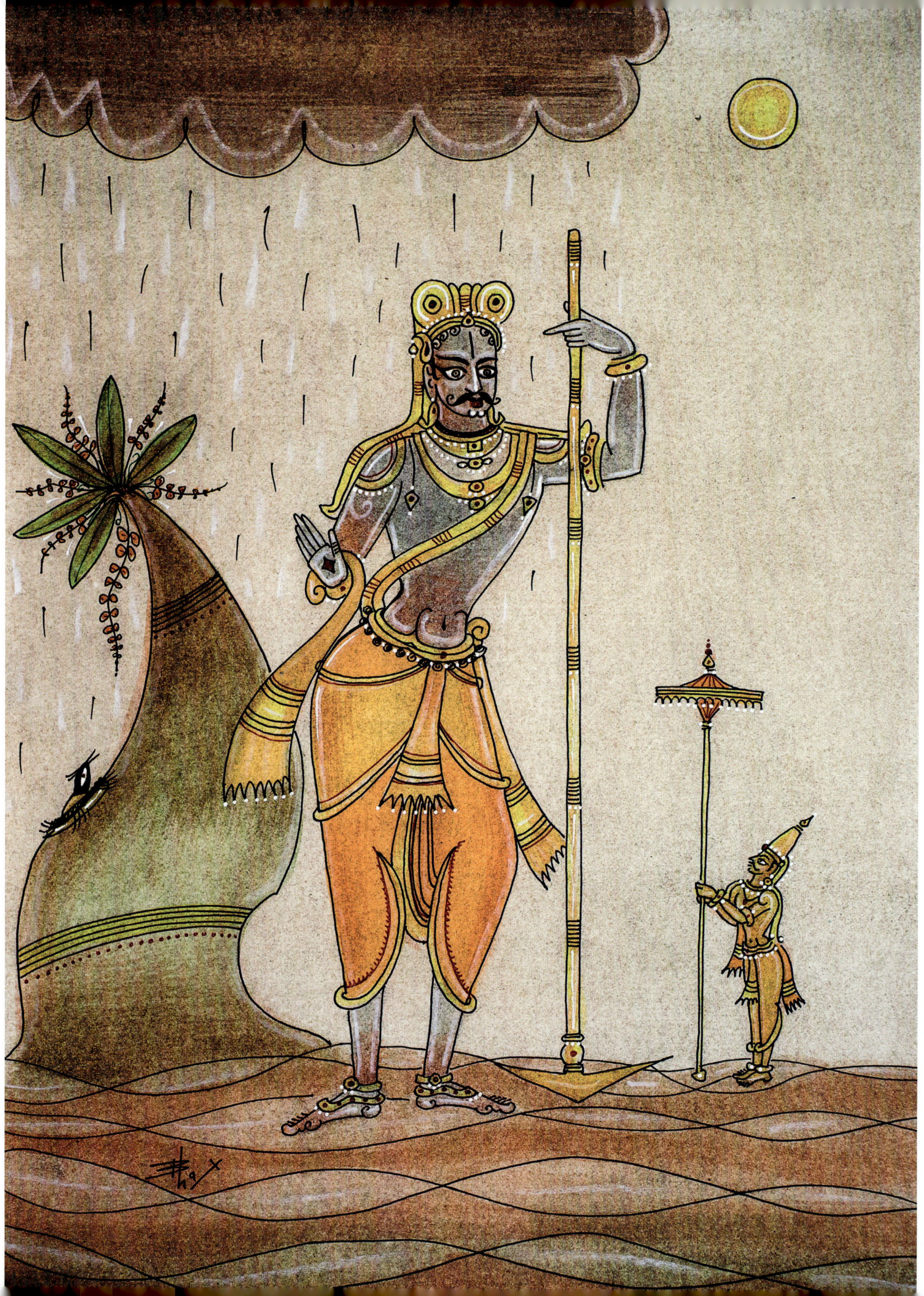

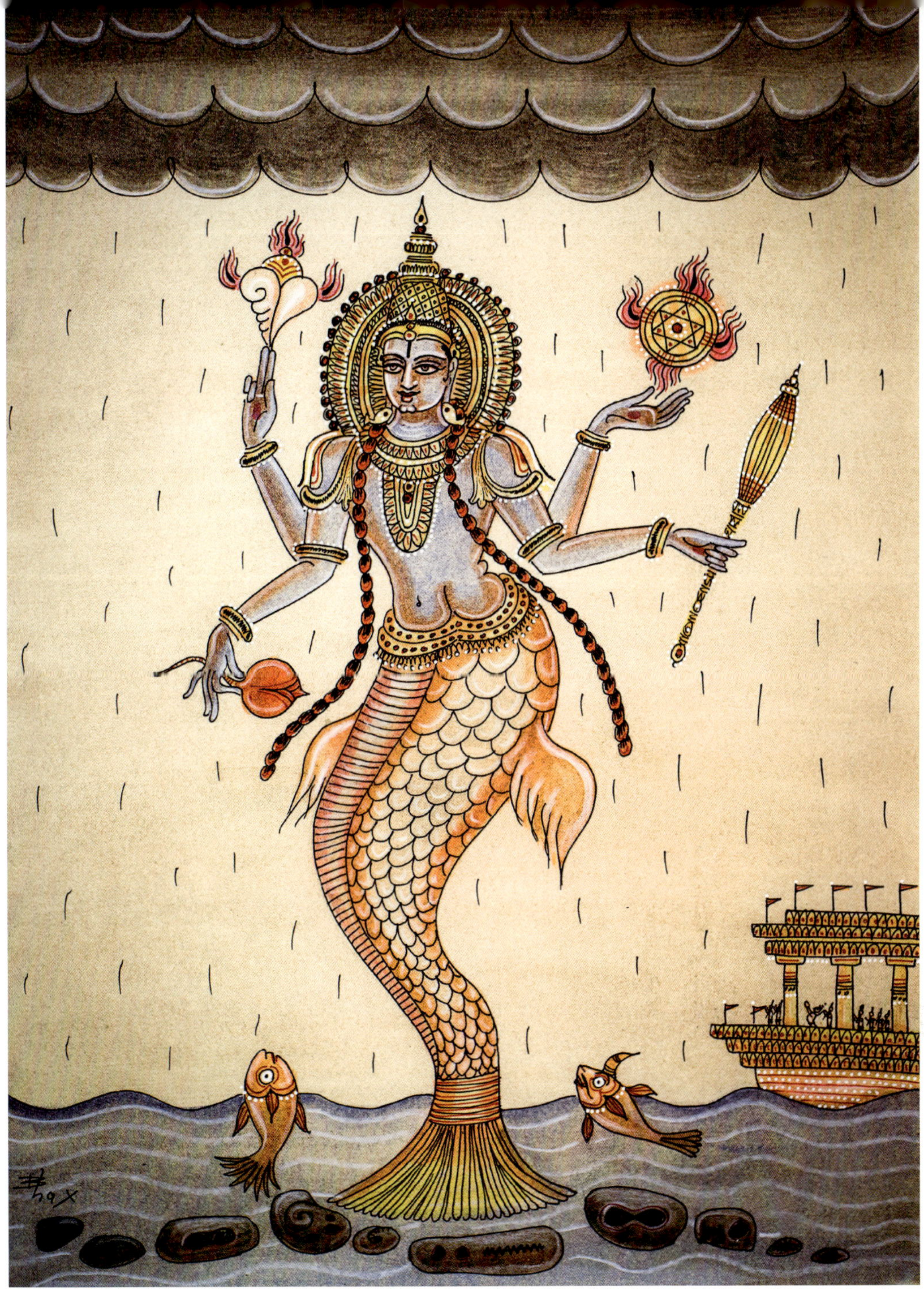

Matsya
Watercolor and pen on paper, 36 x 27 cm

< Pritu Maharaja
Watercolor and pen on paper, 36 x 27 cm

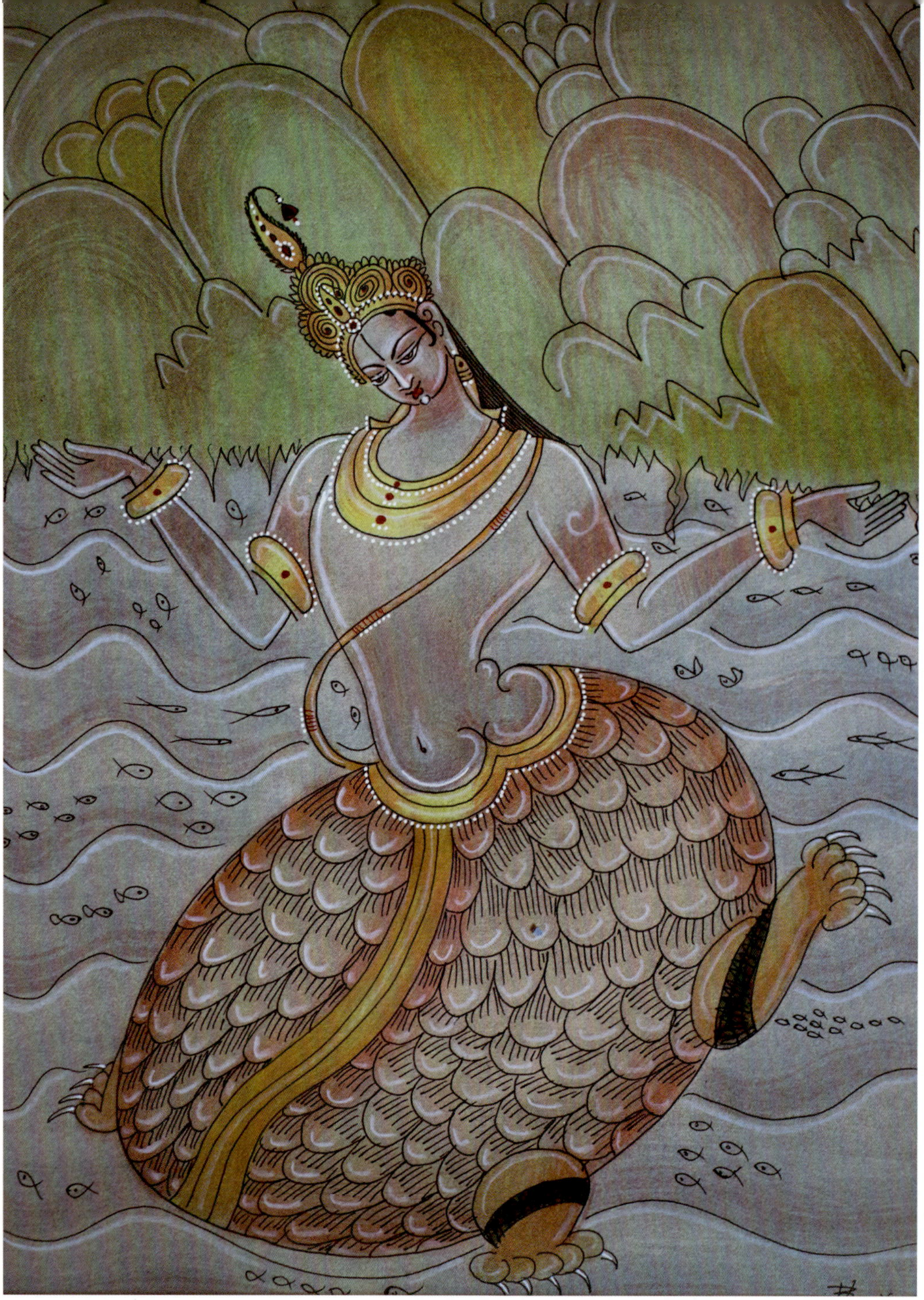

Kurma
Watercolor and pen on paper, 36 x 27 cm

Dhanvantari >
Watercolor and pen on paper, 36 x 27 cm

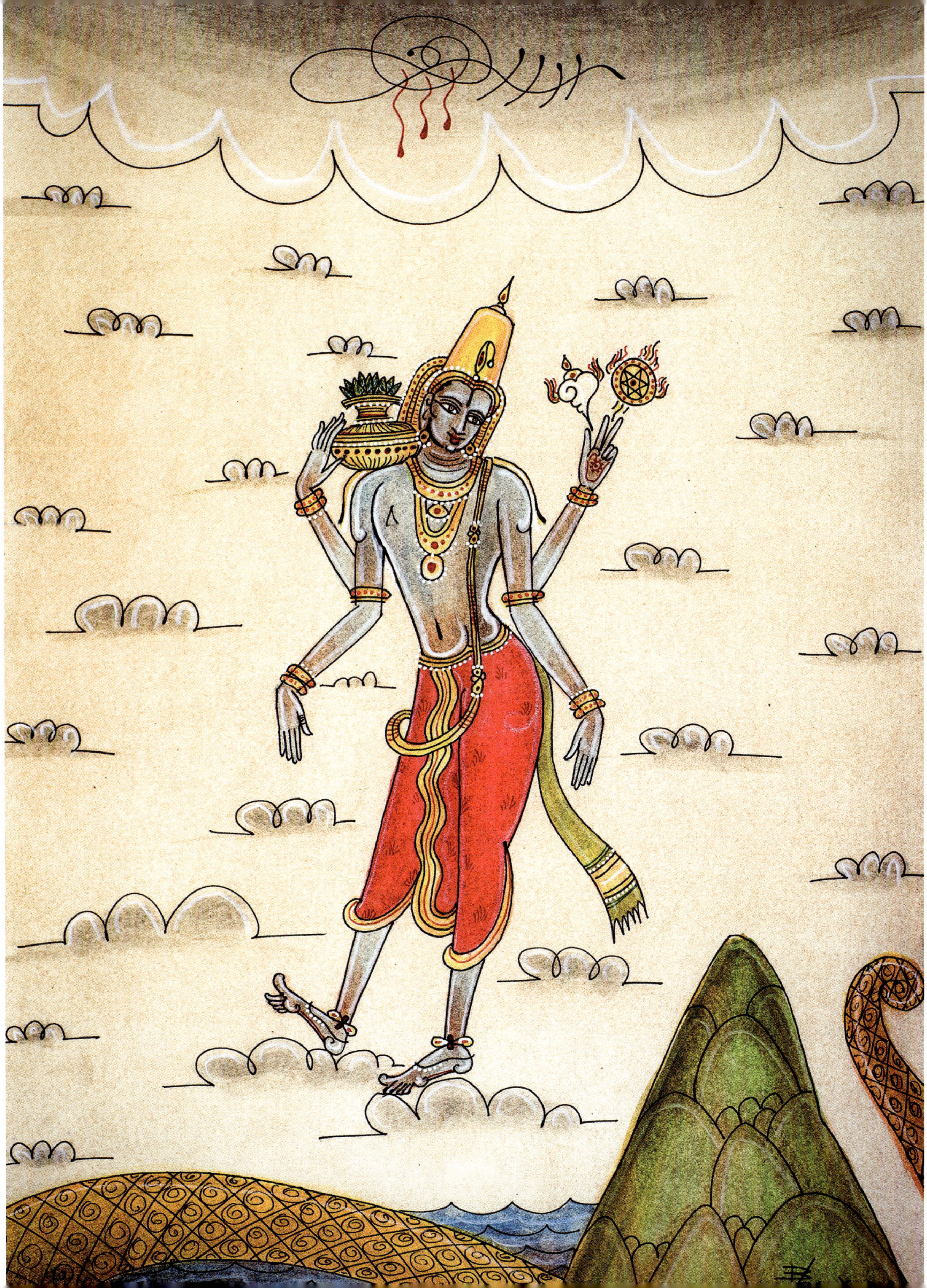

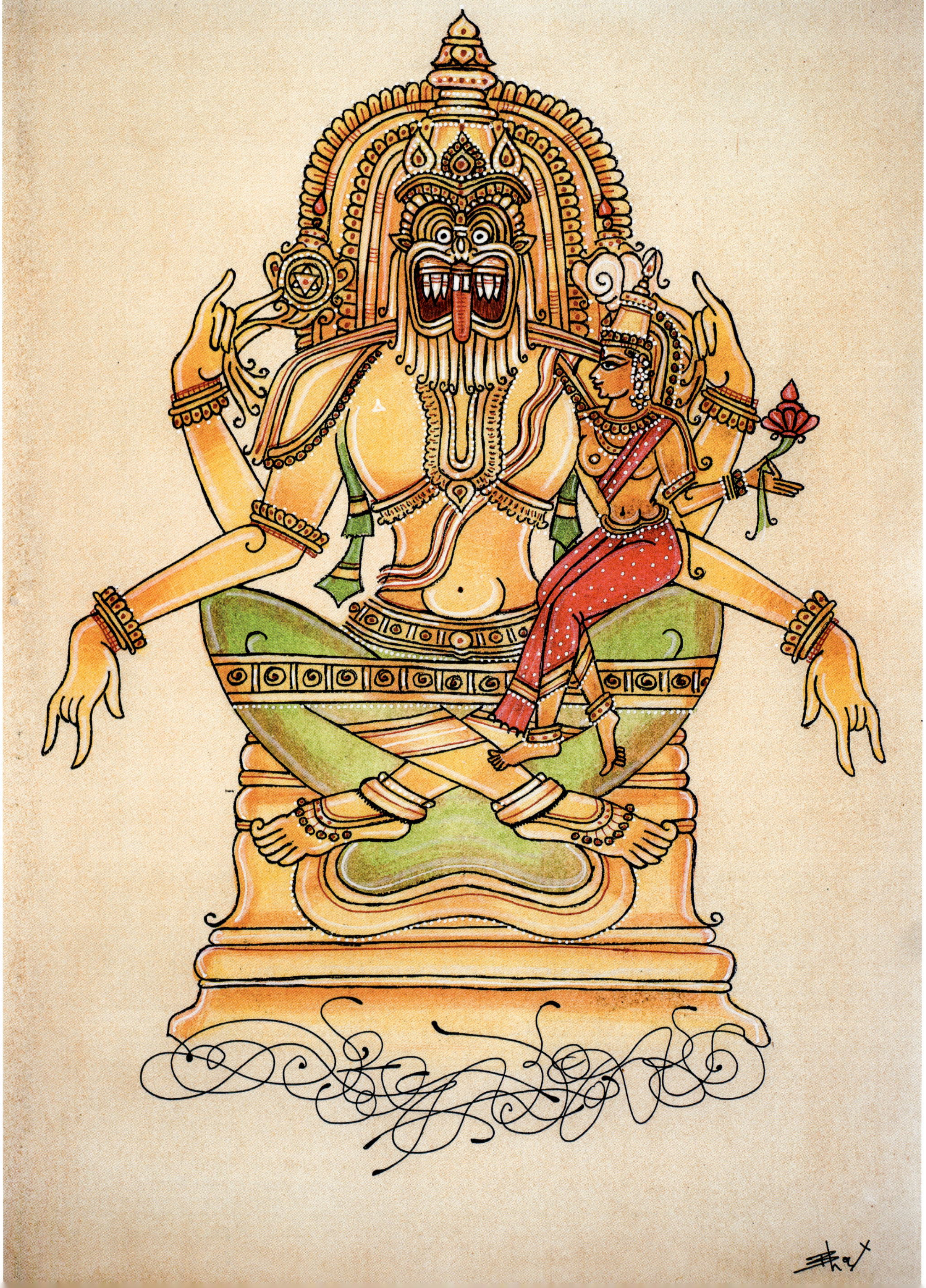

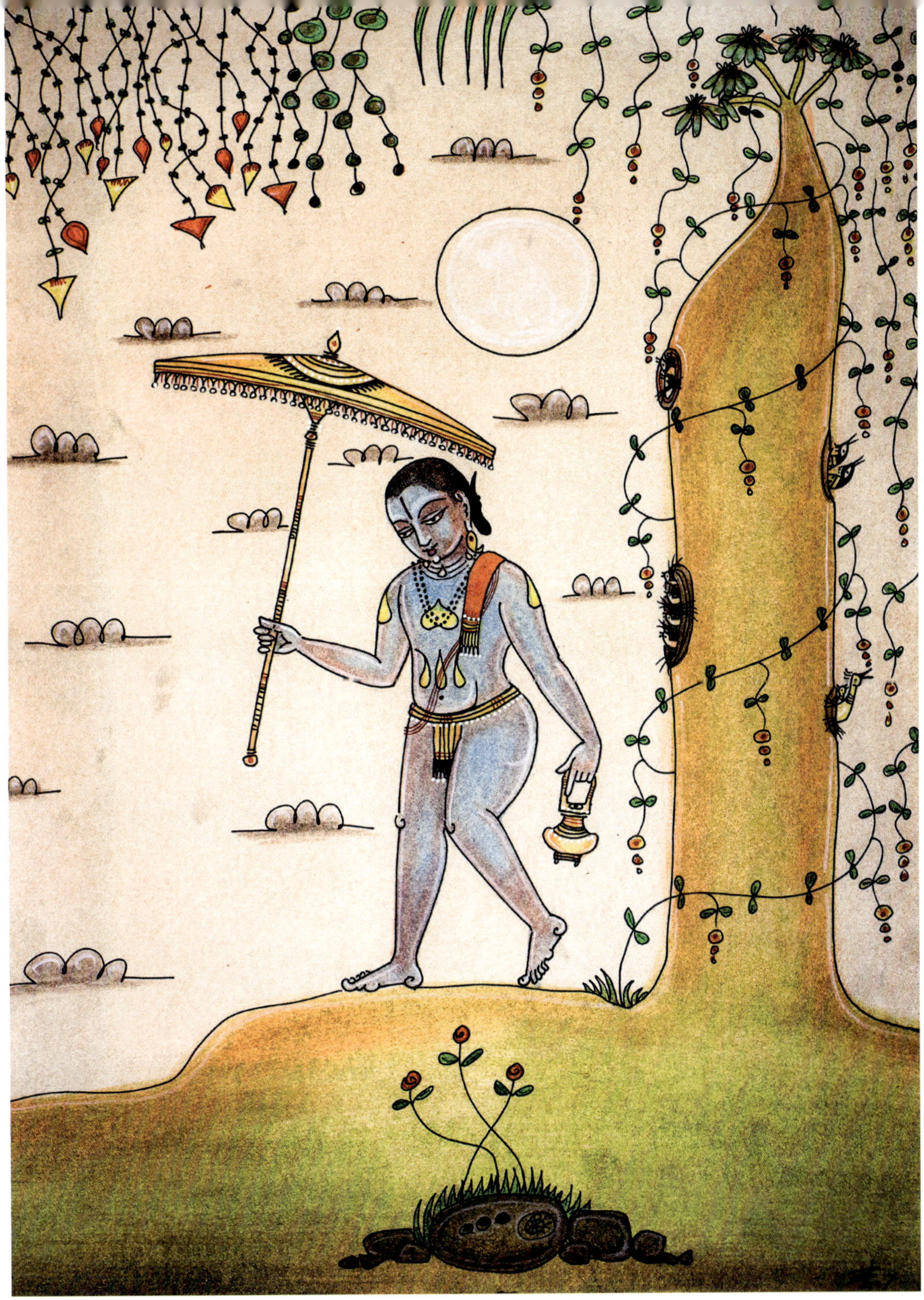

Vamana
Watercolor and pen on paper, 36 x 27 cm

< Lakshmi Narasimha
Watercolor and pen on paper, 36 x 27 cm

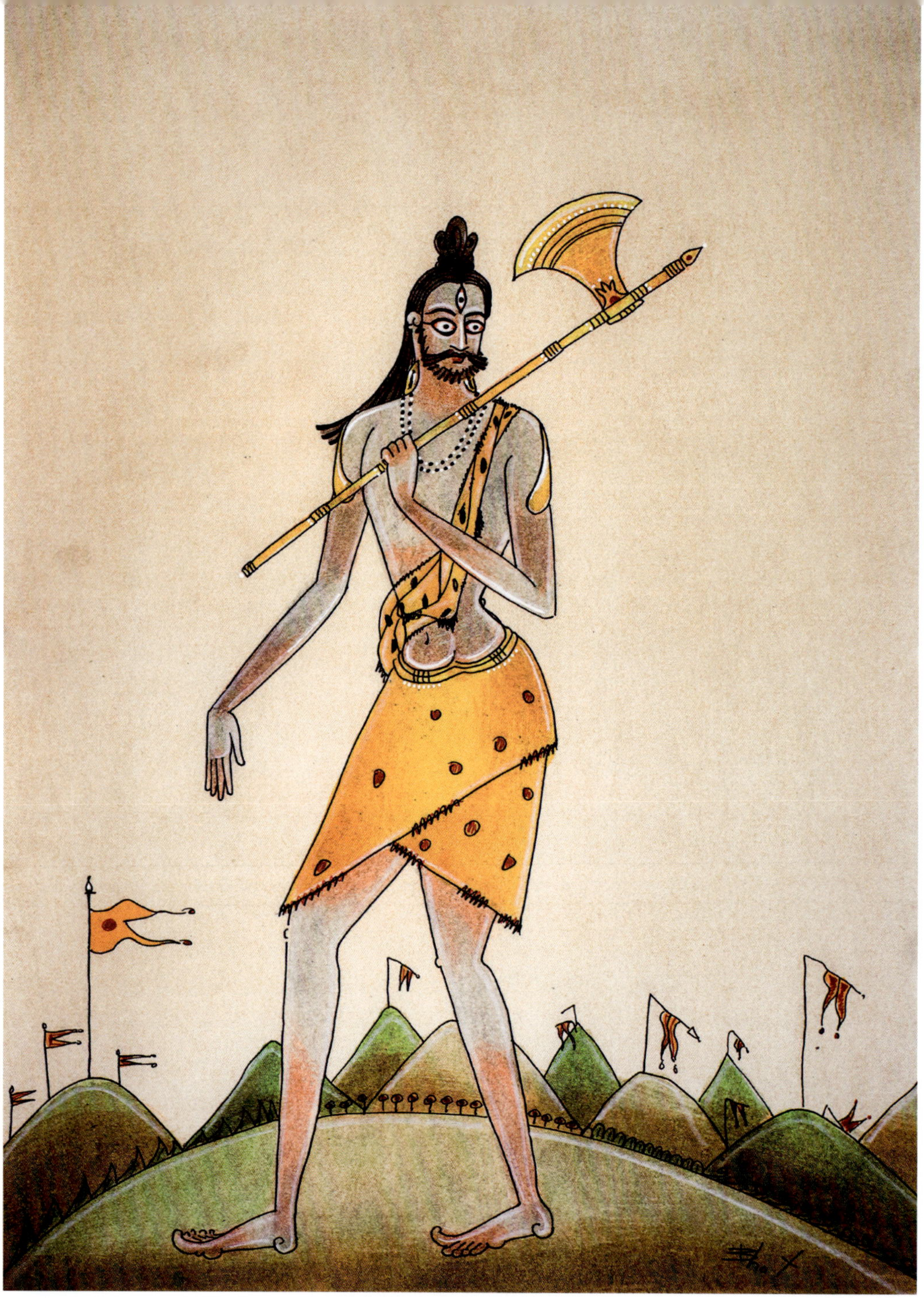

Parashurama
Watercolor and pen on paper, 36 x 27 cm

Veda-vyasa Maharishi >
Watercolor and pen on paper, 36 x 27 cm

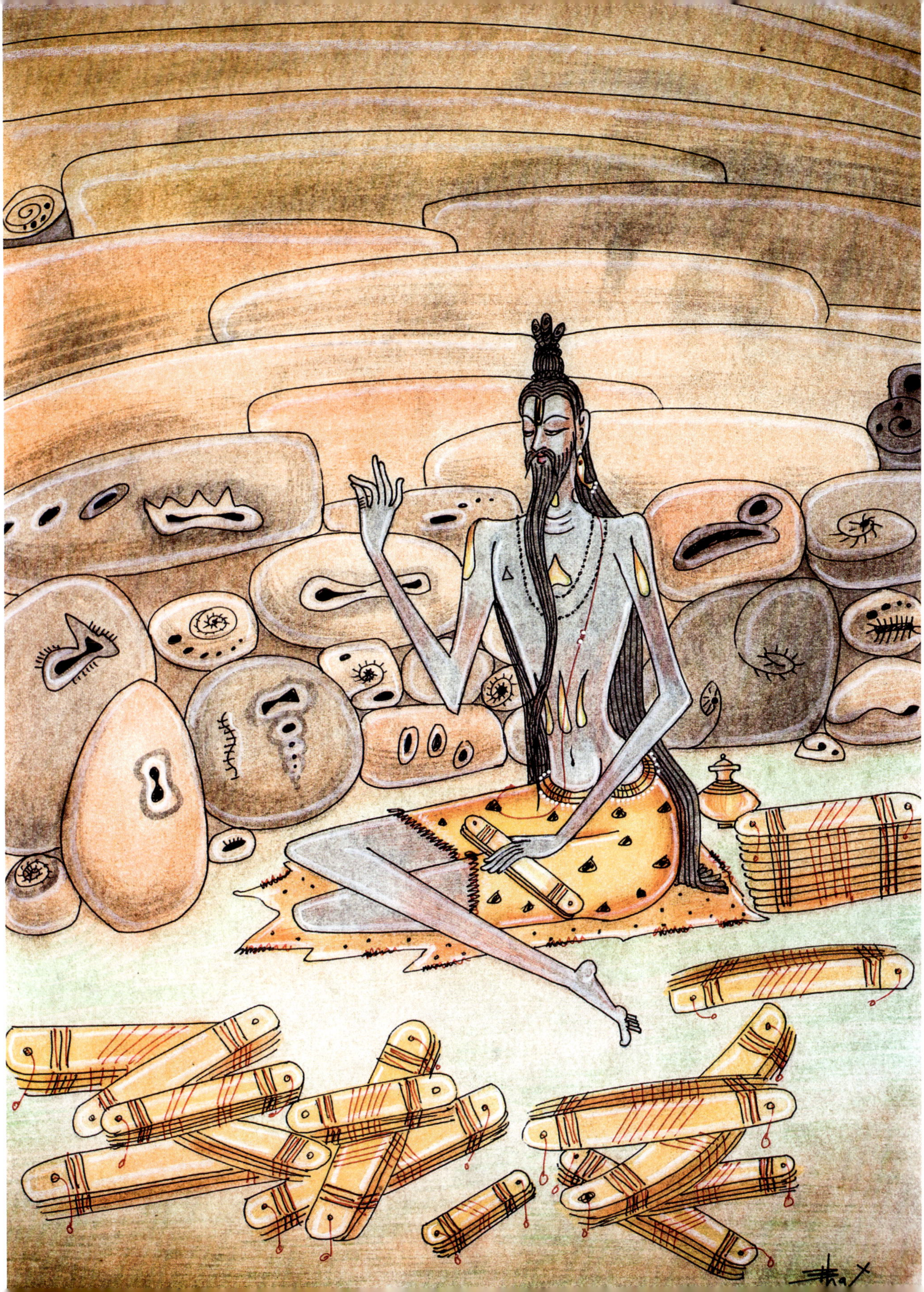

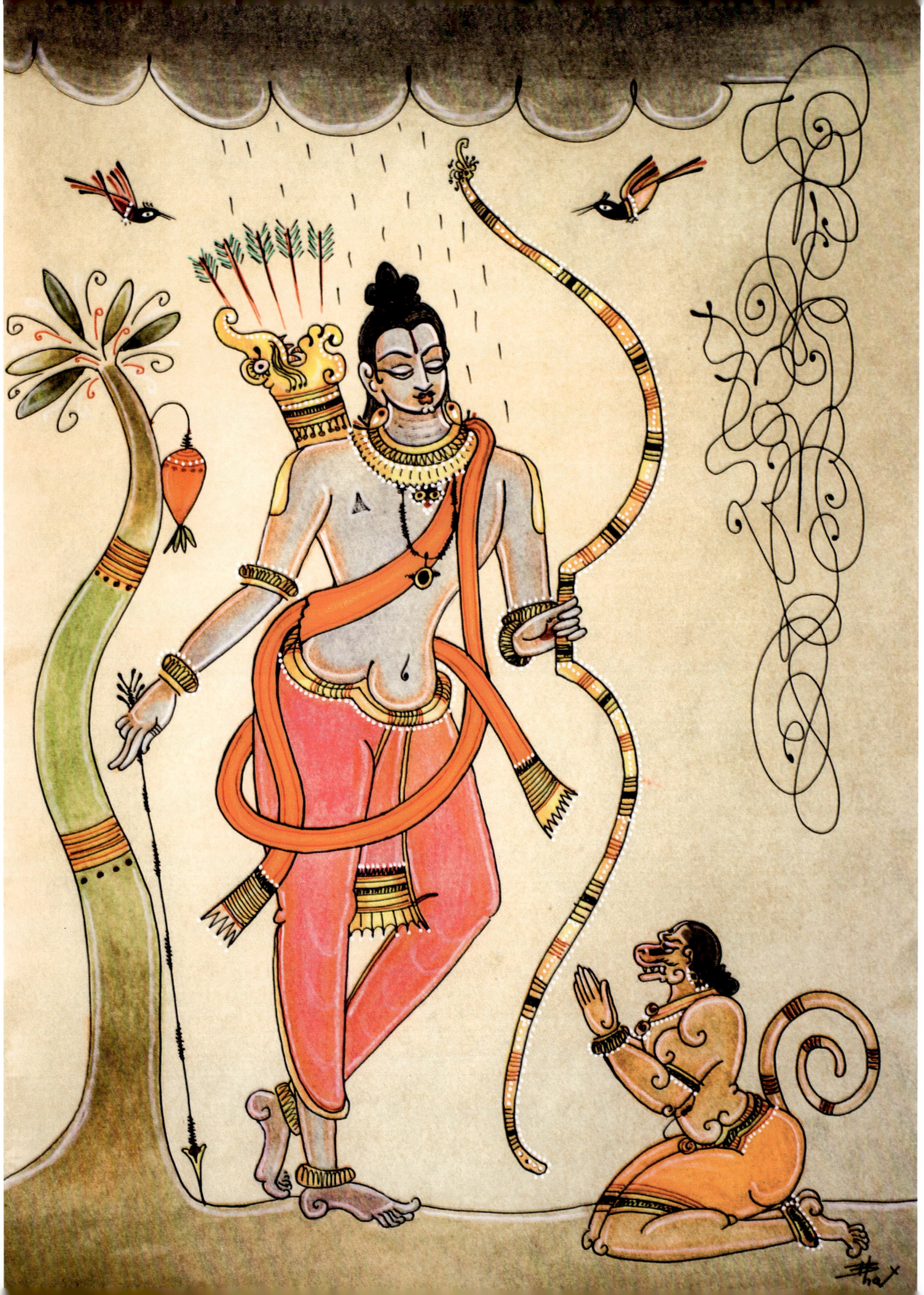

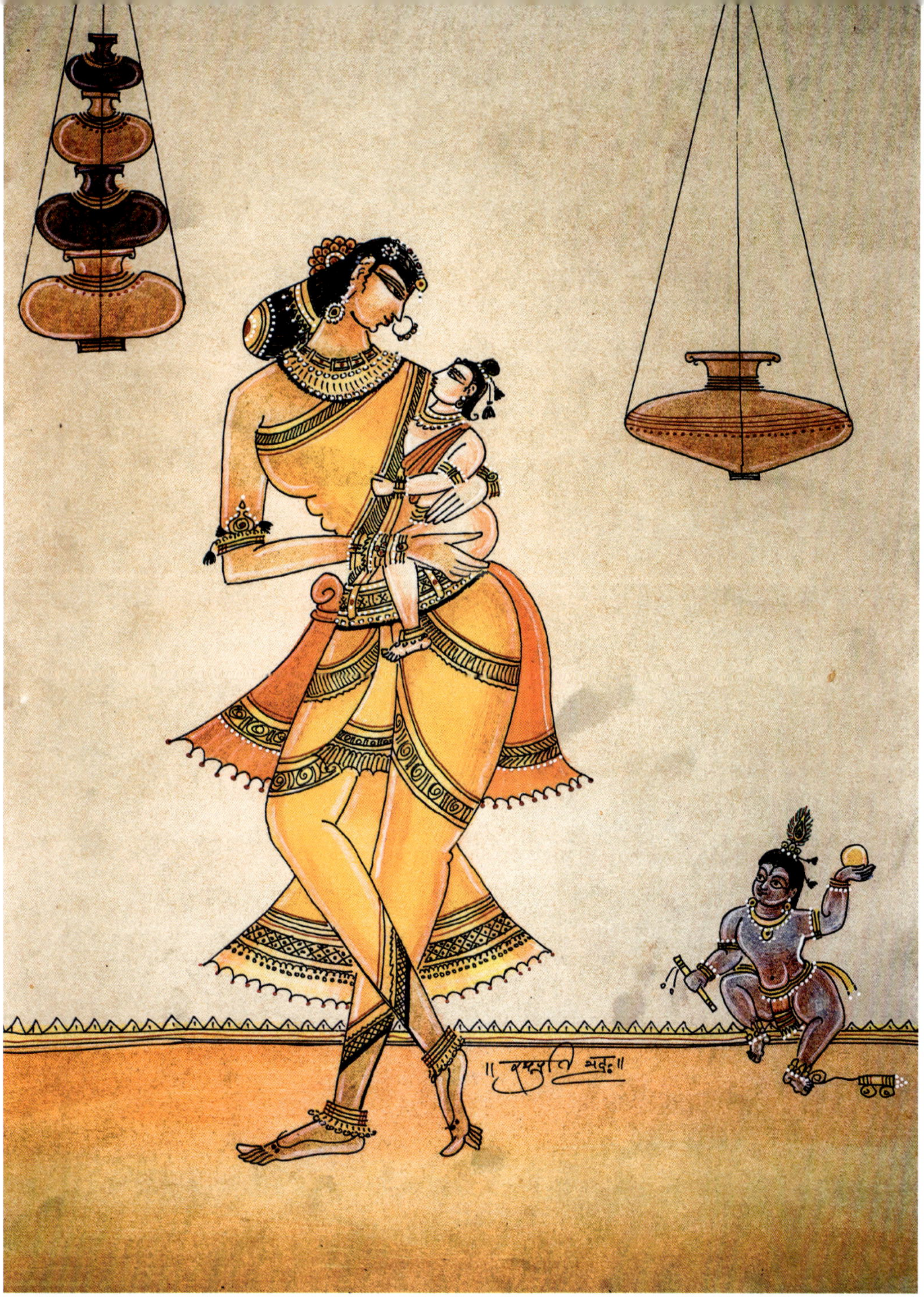

Balarama
Watercolor and pen on paper, 36 x 27 cm

< Rama
Watercolor and pen on paper, 36 x 27 cm

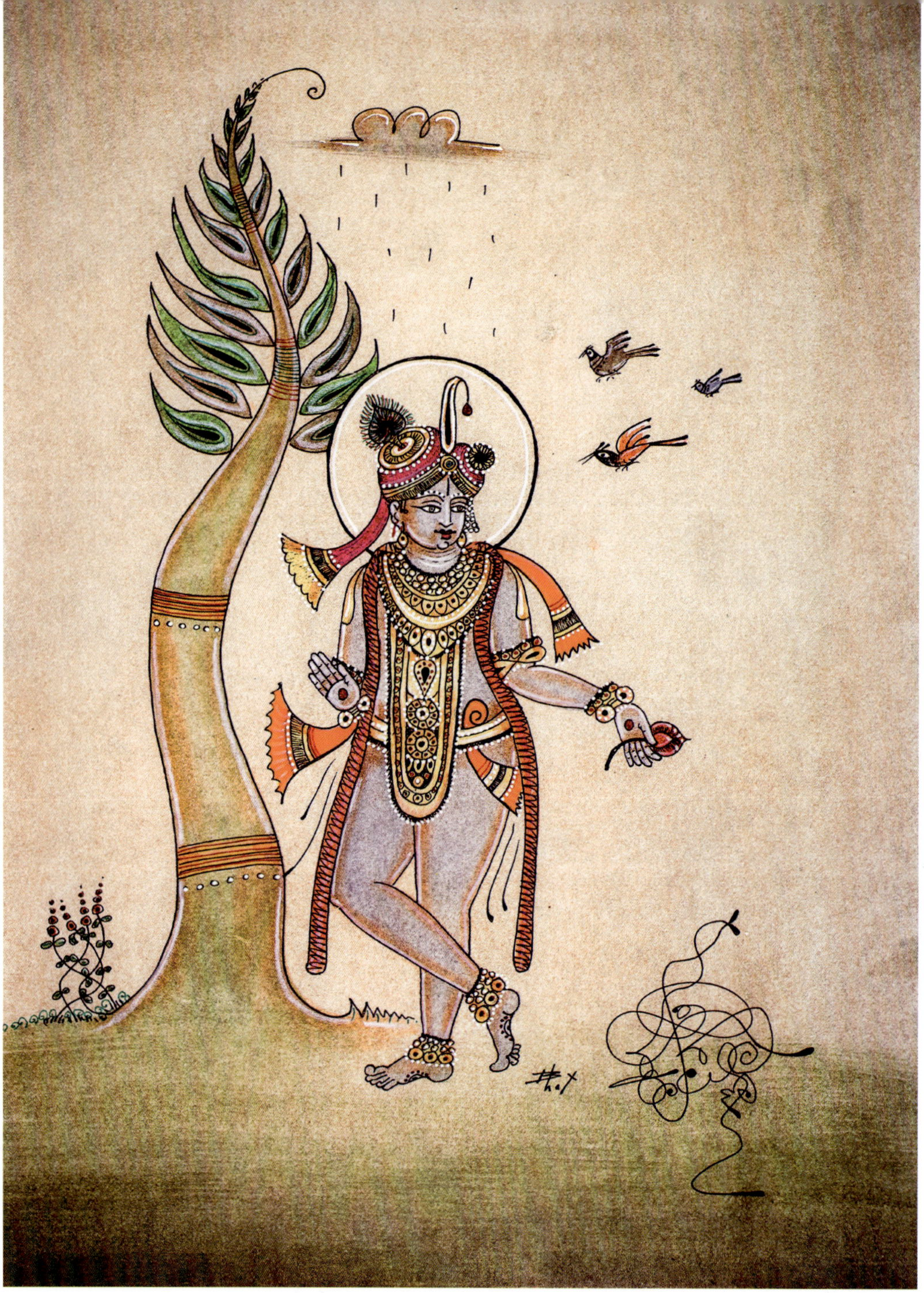

Krishna
Watercolor and pen on paper, 36 x 27 cm

Buddha >
Watercolor and pen on paper, 36 x 27 cm

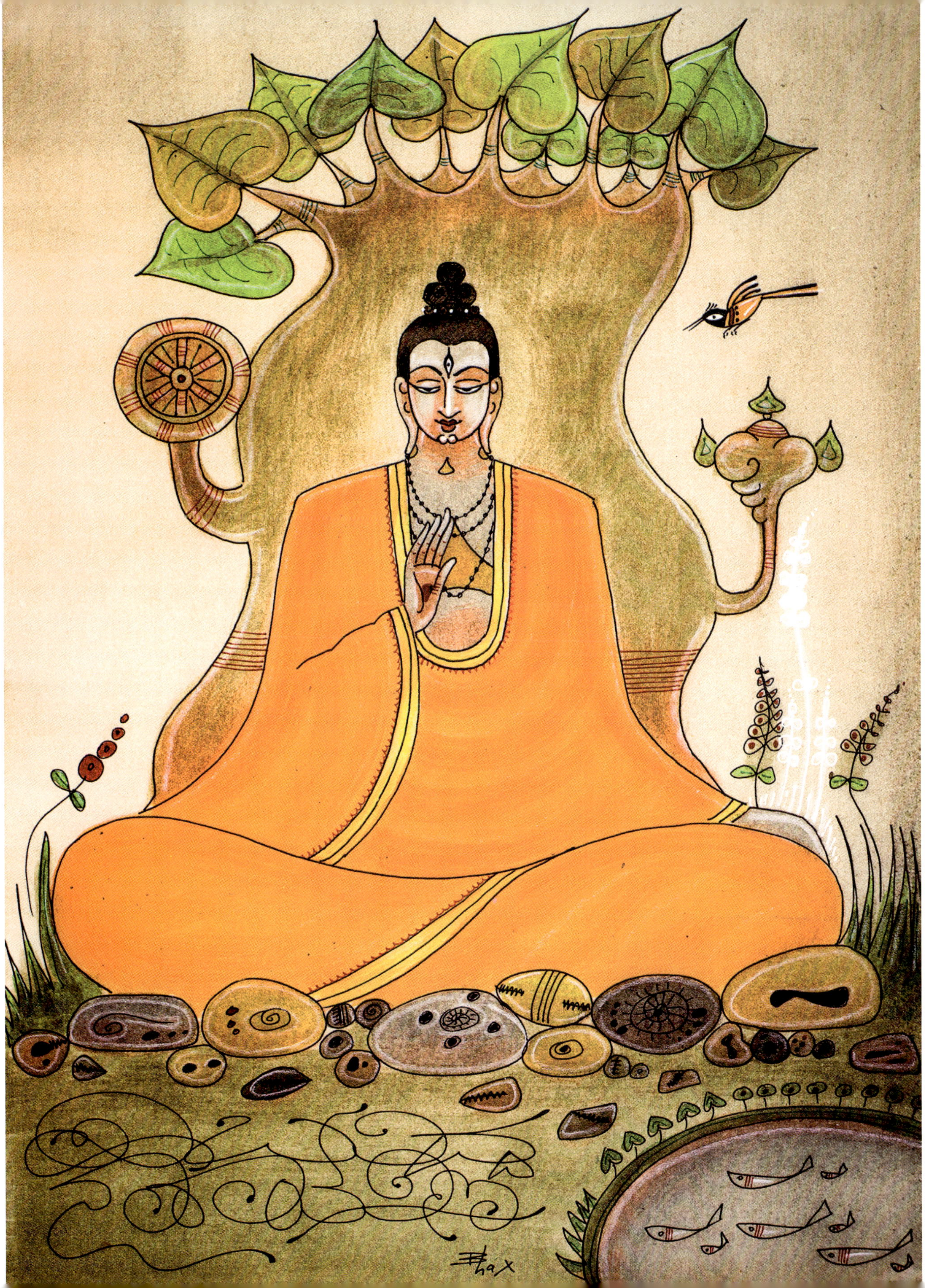

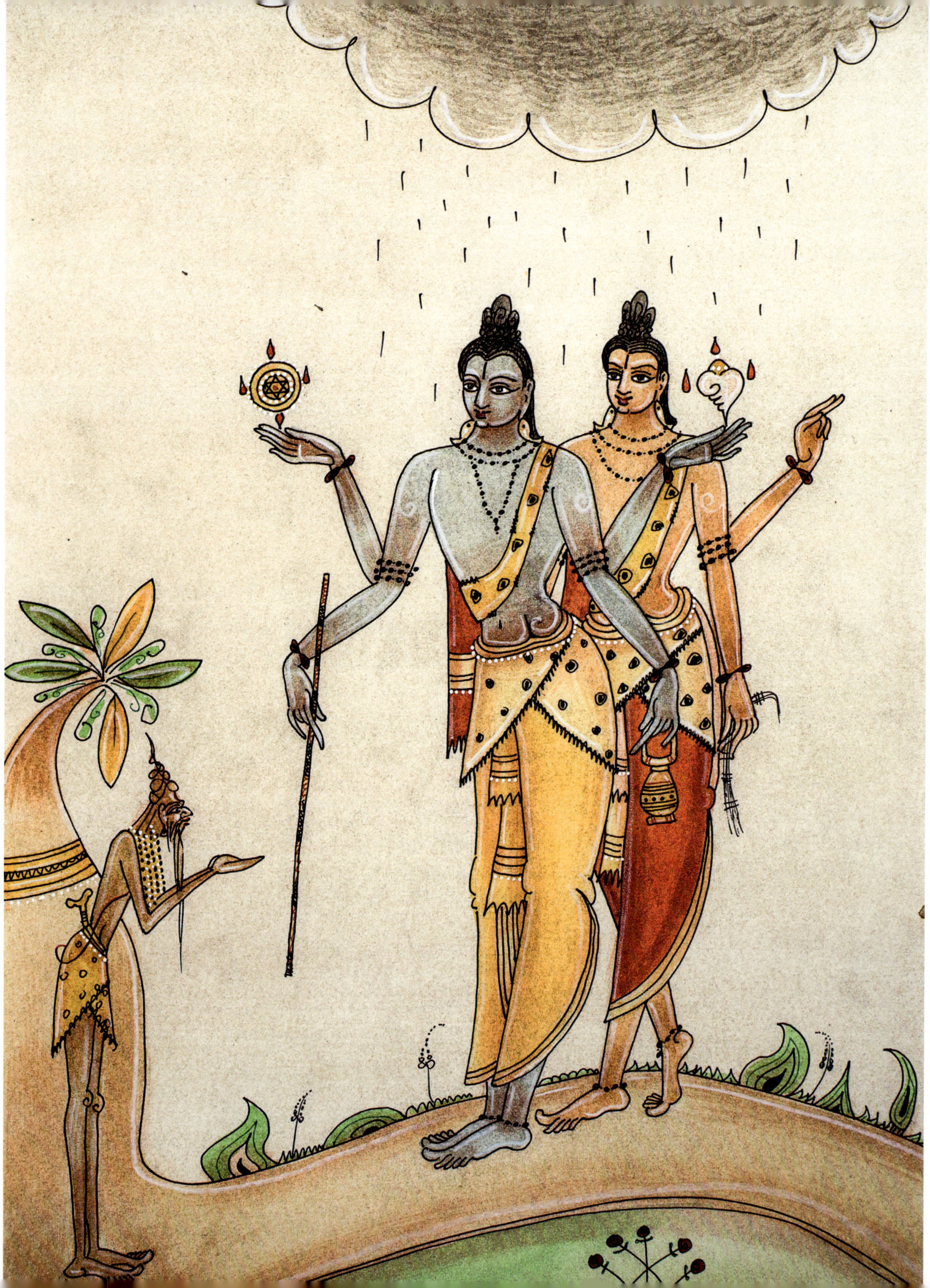

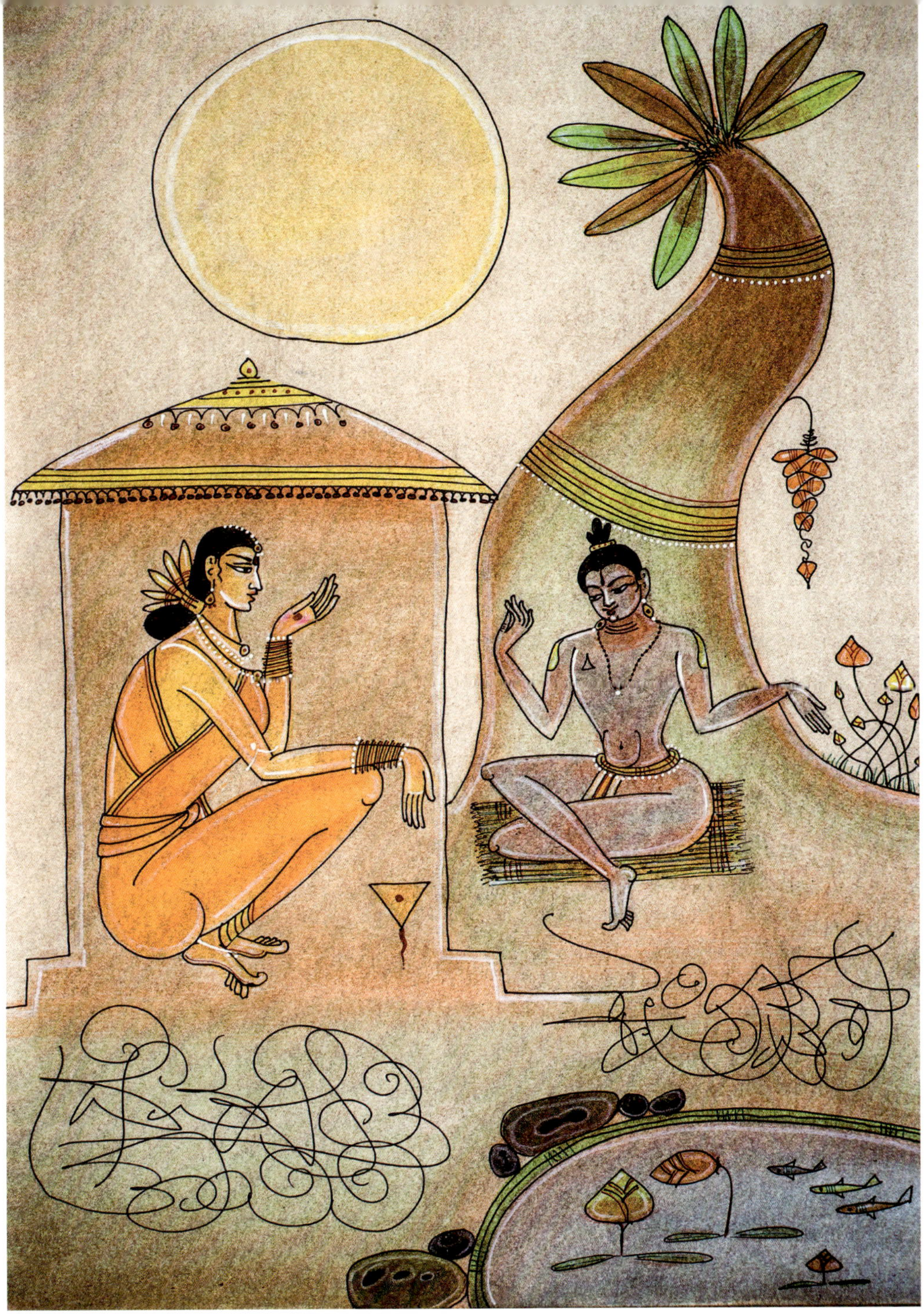

Kapila with his mother Devahuti
Watercolor and pen on paper, 36 x 27 cm

< Nara and Narayana
Watercolor and pen on paper, 36 x 27 cm

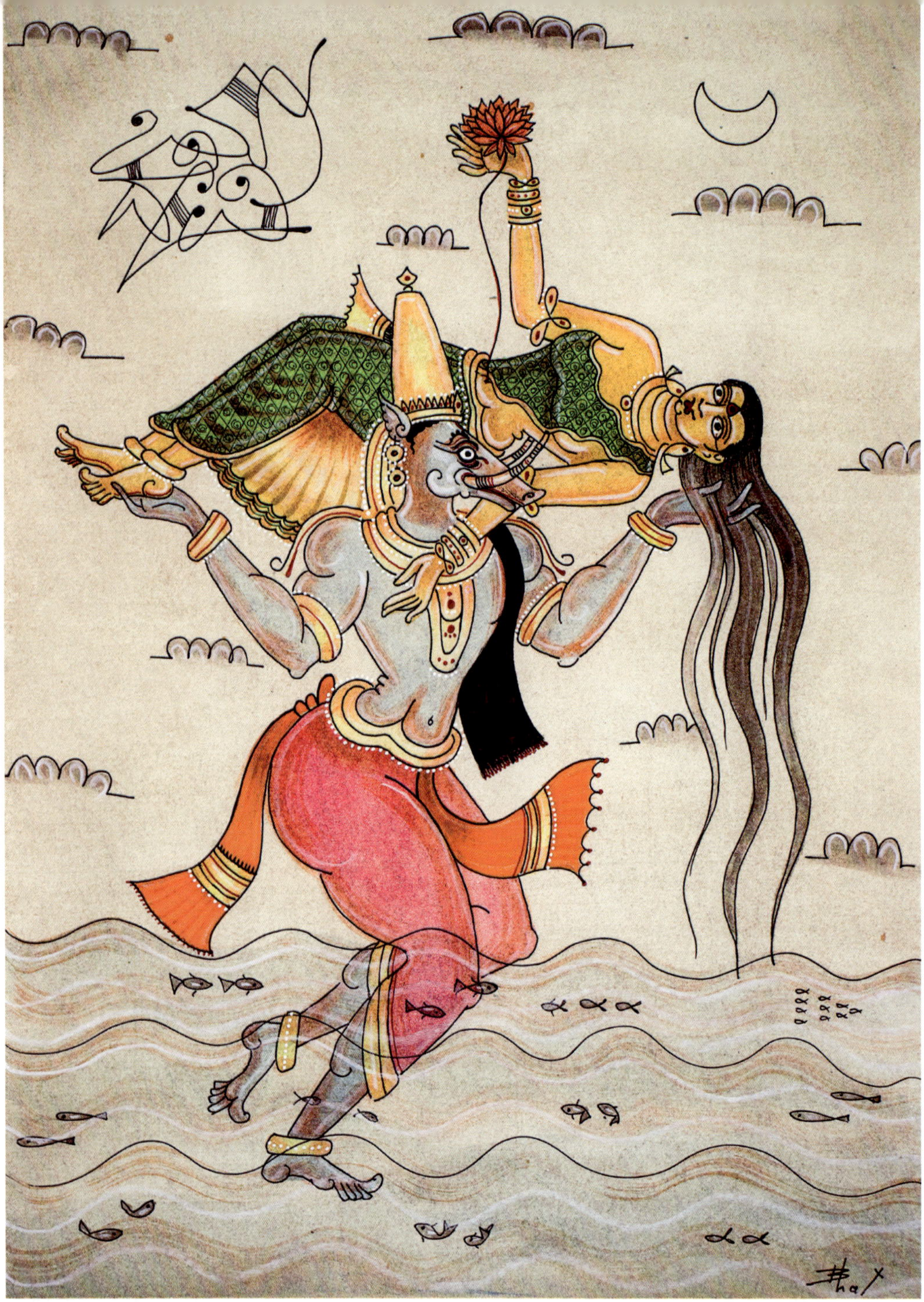

Varaha
Watercolor and pen on paper, 36 x 27 cm

Dhruva >
Watercolor and pen on paper, 36 x 27 cm

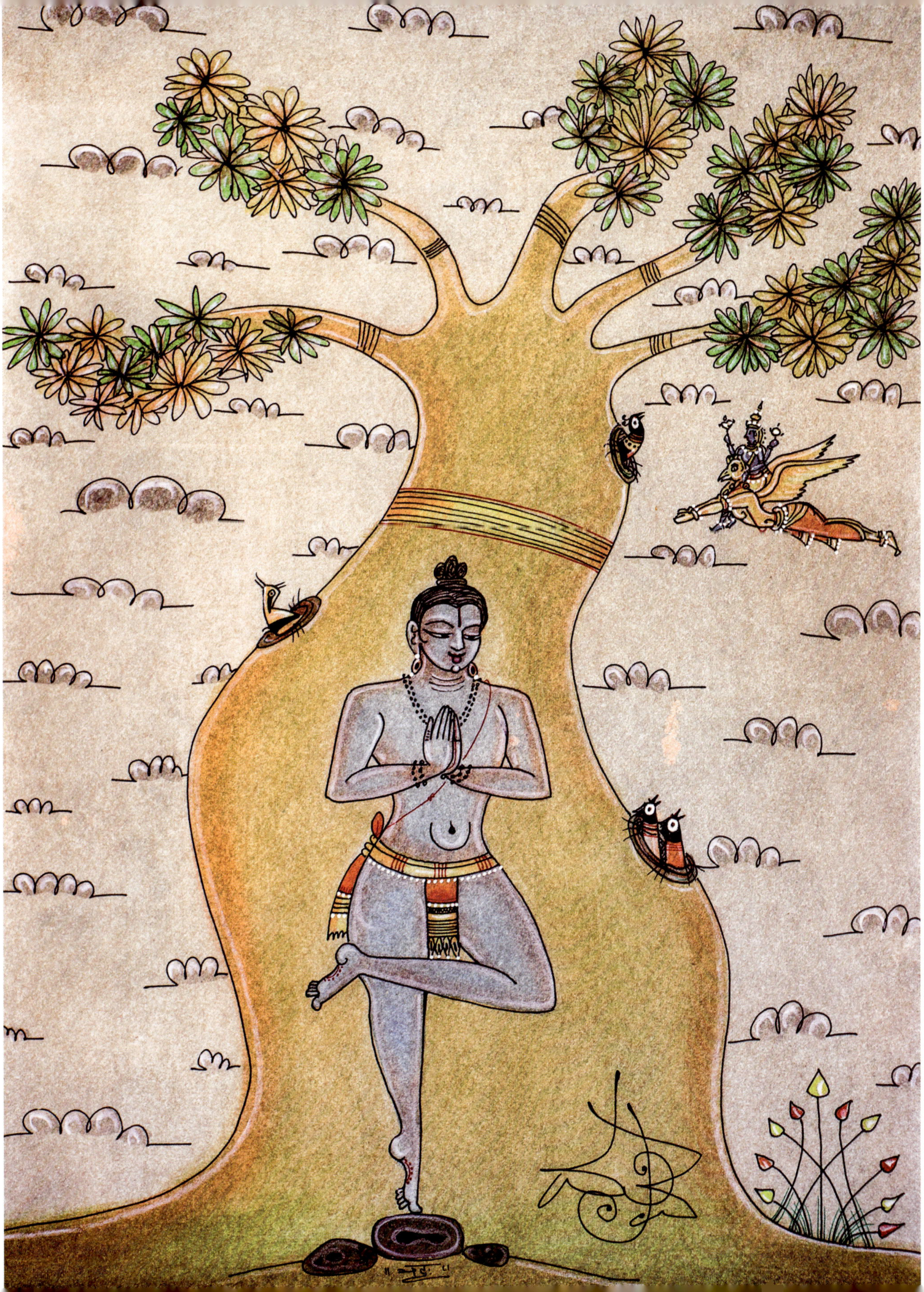

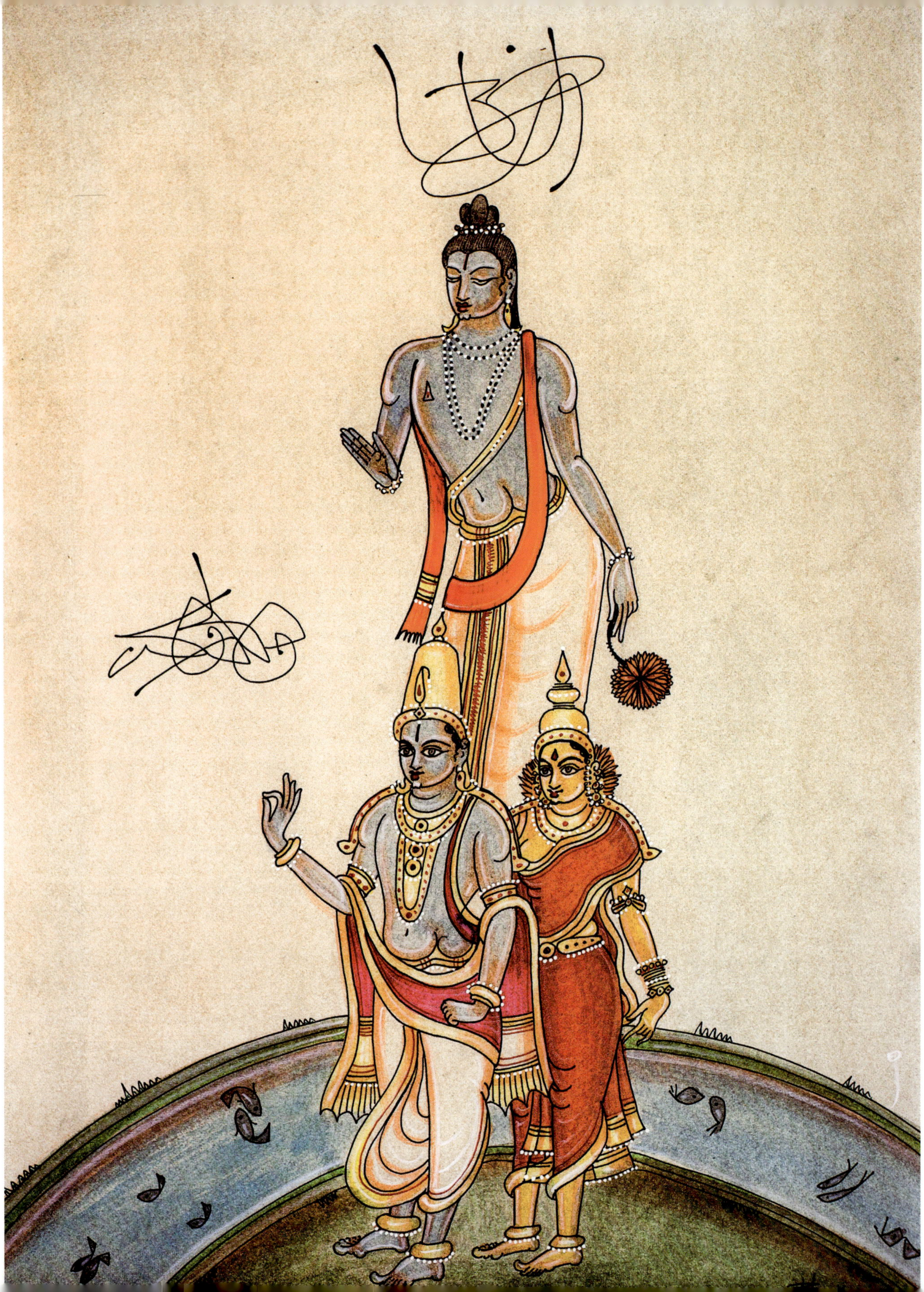

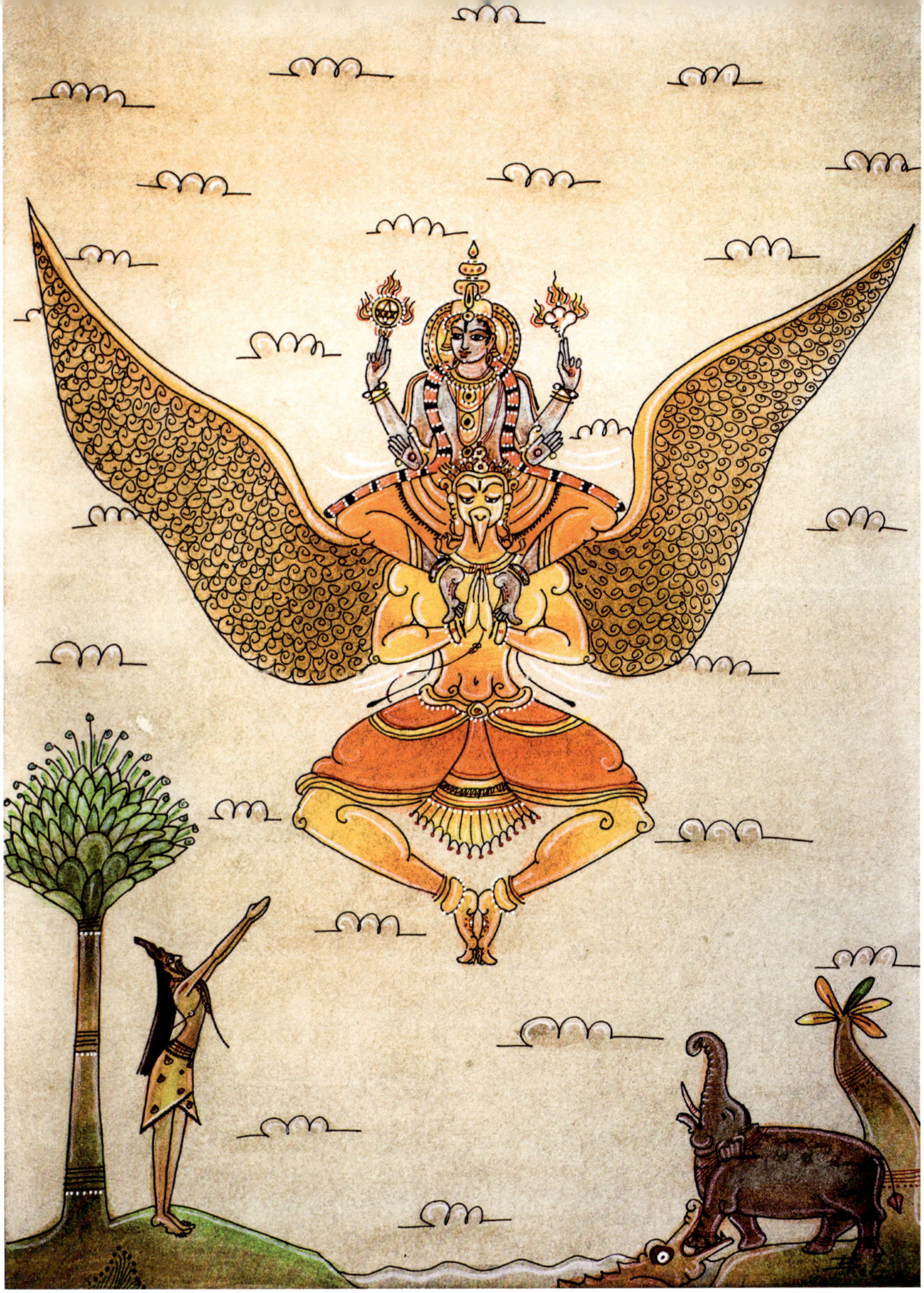

Gajendra Moksha
Watercolor and pen on paper, 36 x 27 cm

< Svayambhuva Manu
Watercolor and pen on paper, 36 x 27 cm

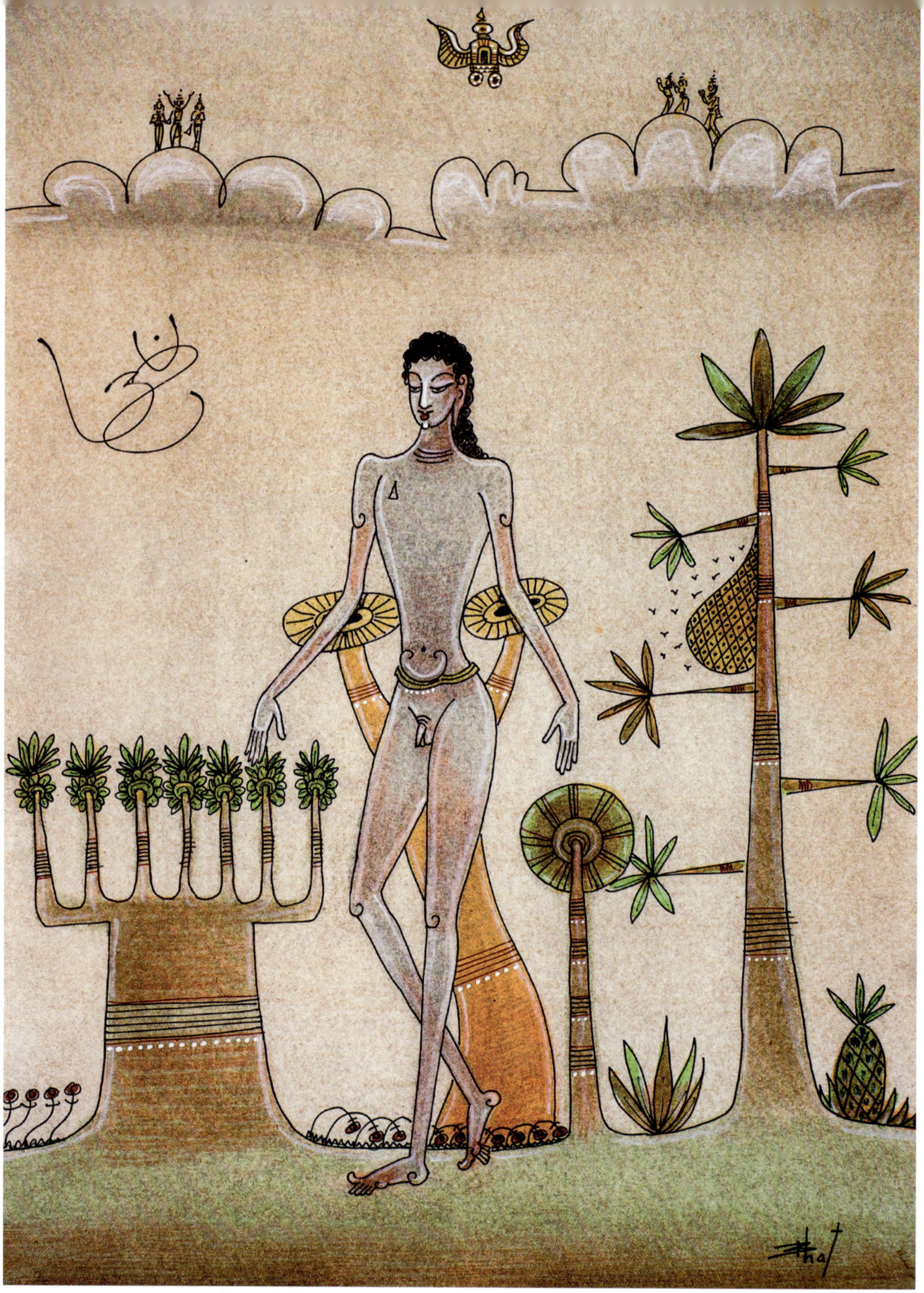

Rishabhadeva
Watercolor and pen on paper, 36 x 27 cm

Hamsa revealed to Sanakadis >
Watercolor and pen on paper, 36 x 27 cm

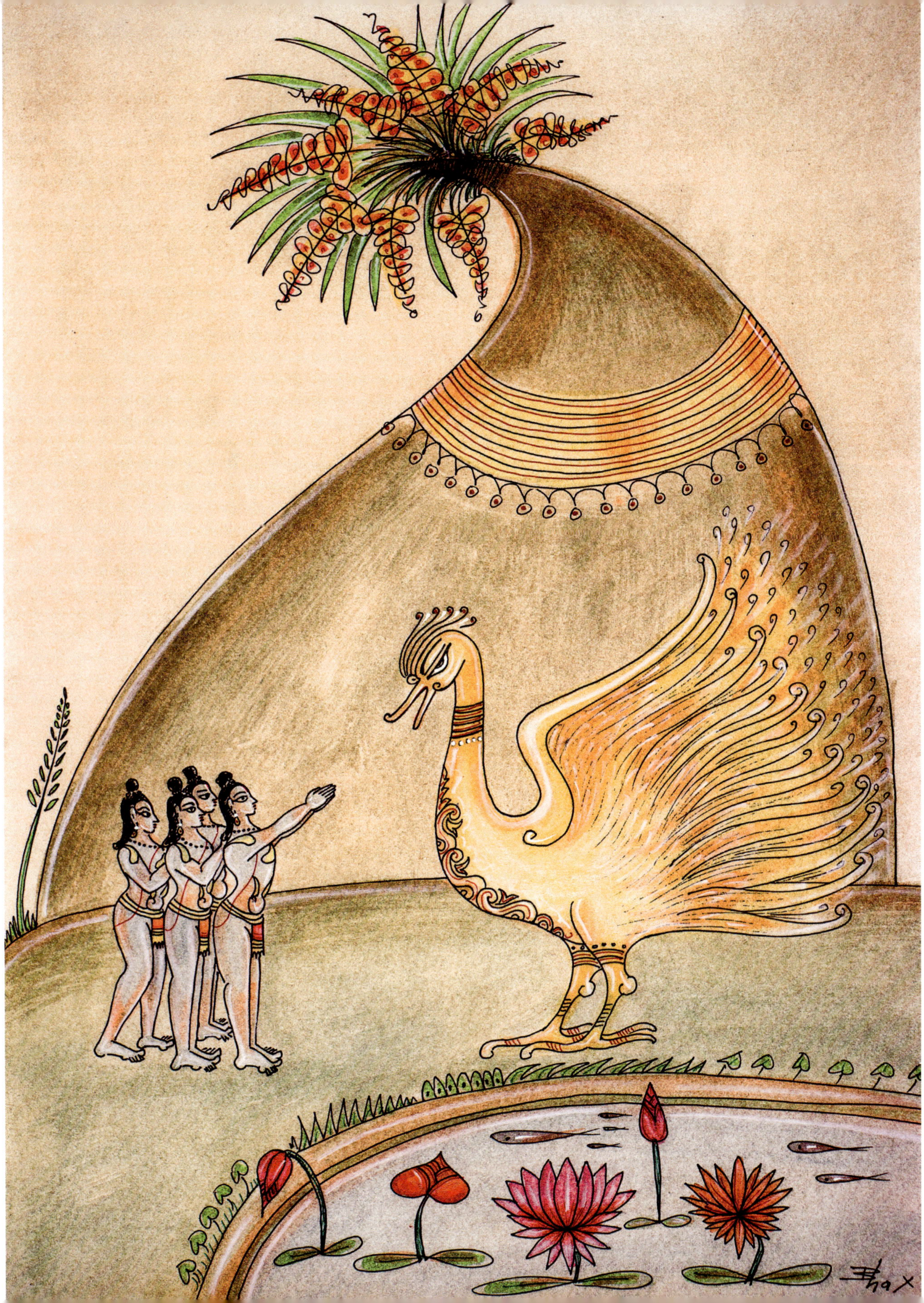

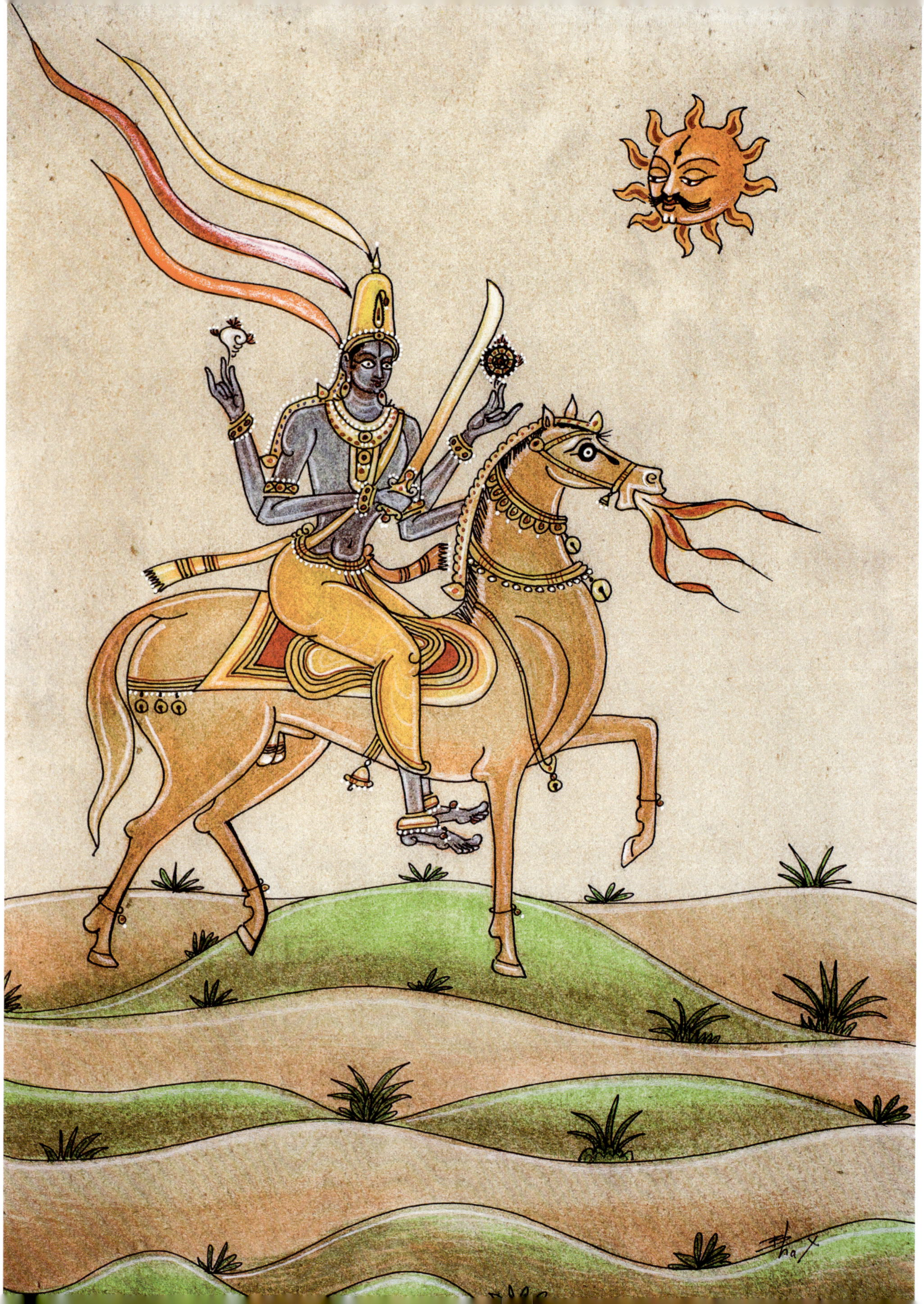

< Kalki
Watercolor and pen on paper, 36 x 27 cm

RAMAYANA

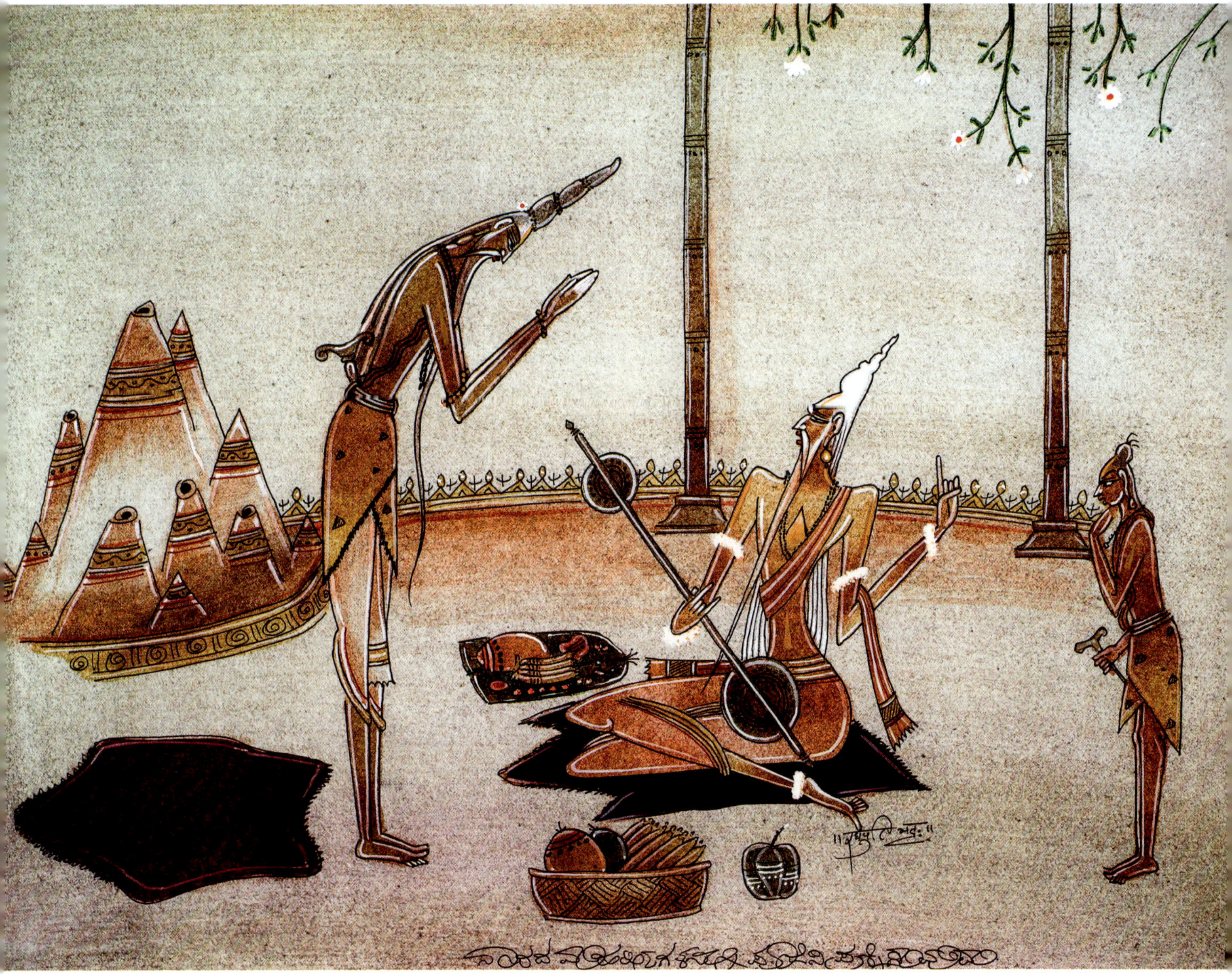

Narada Muni tells Valmiki Maharishi to write the Ramayana
Watercolor and pen on paper, 36 x 27 cm

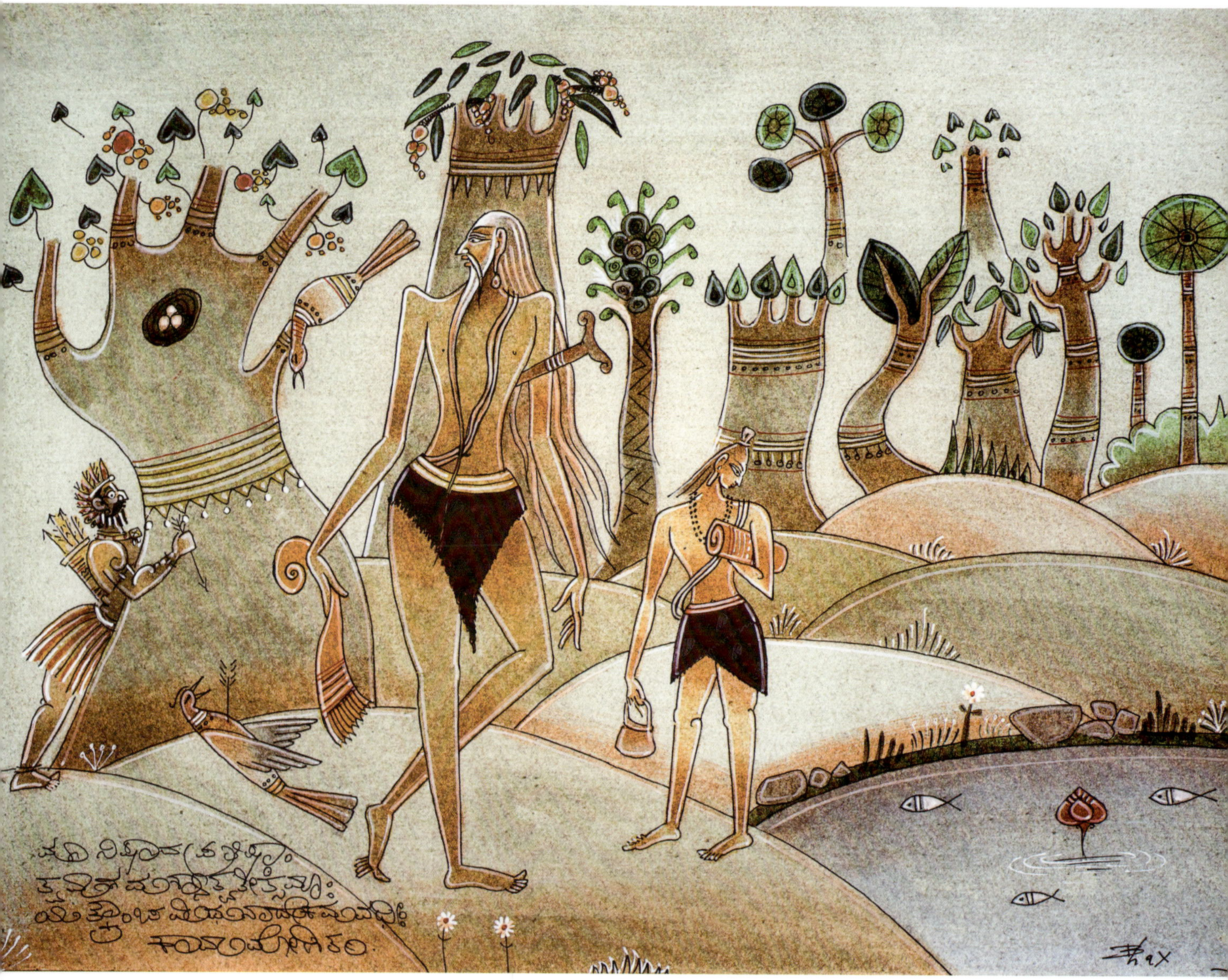

Valmiki Maharishi
Watercolor and pen on paper, 36 x 27 cm

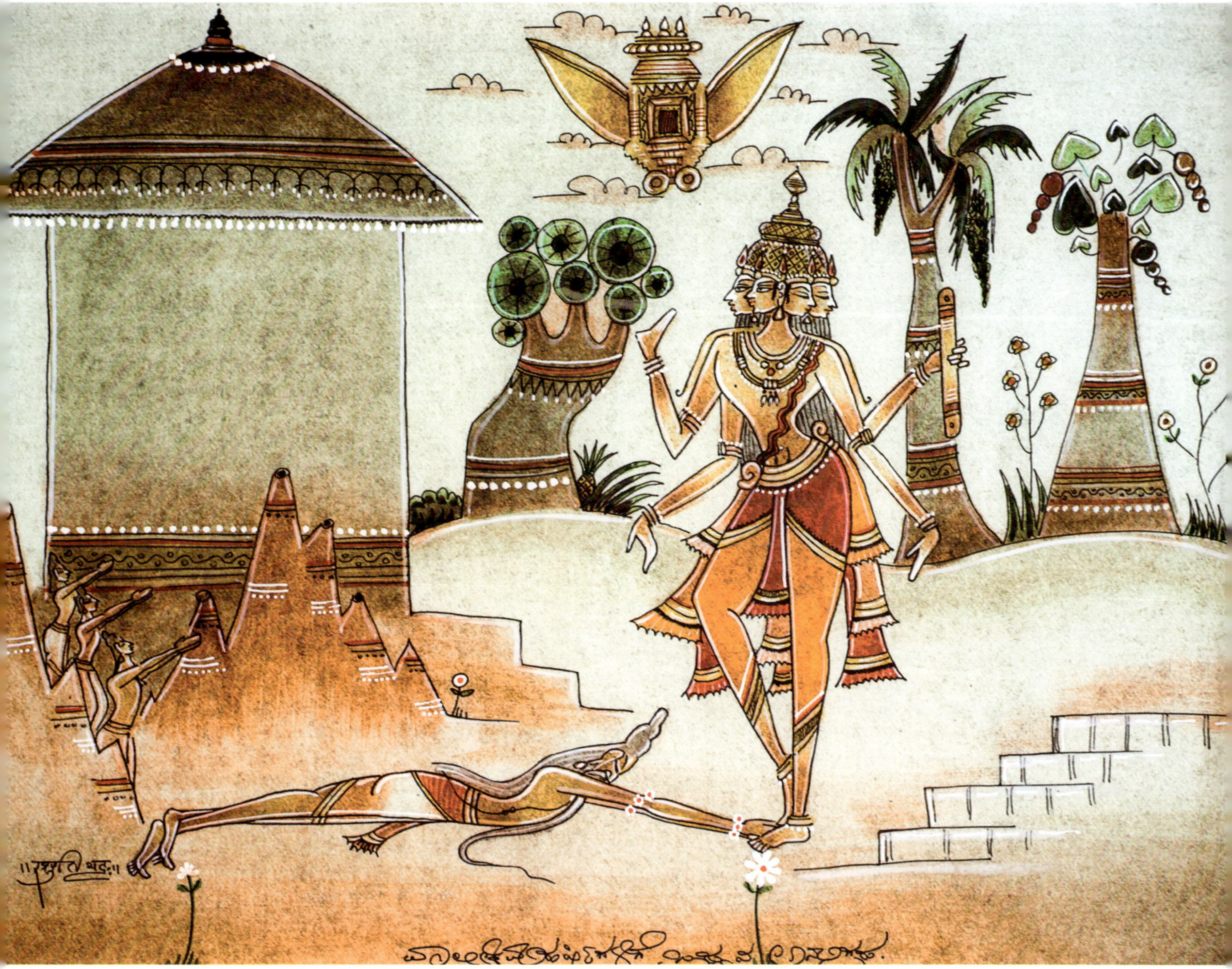

Valmiki and Brahma
Watercolor and pen on paper, 36 x 27 cm

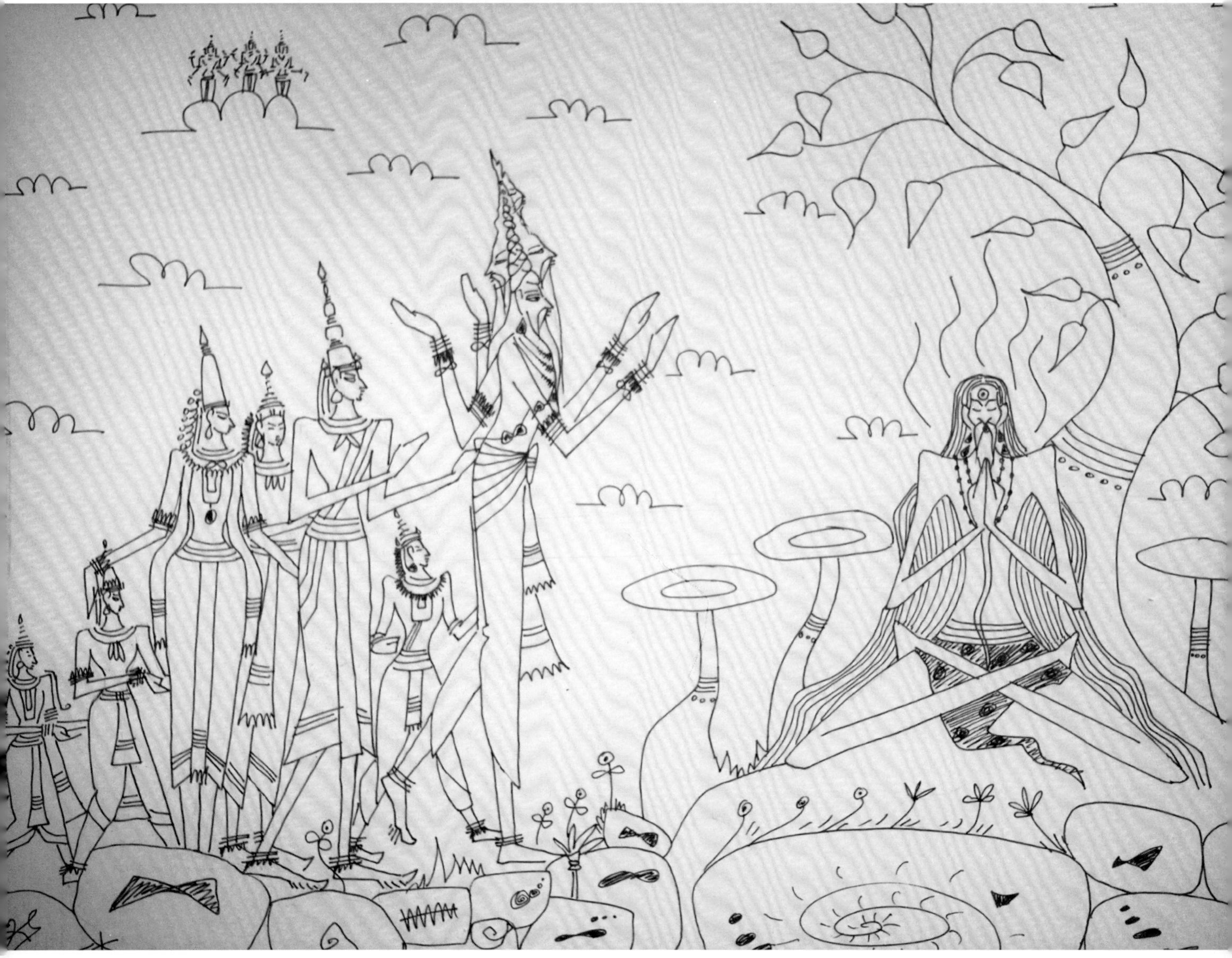

Vishwamitra comes to bramha rushi (bramha sage)
Pen on paper, 36 x 27 cm

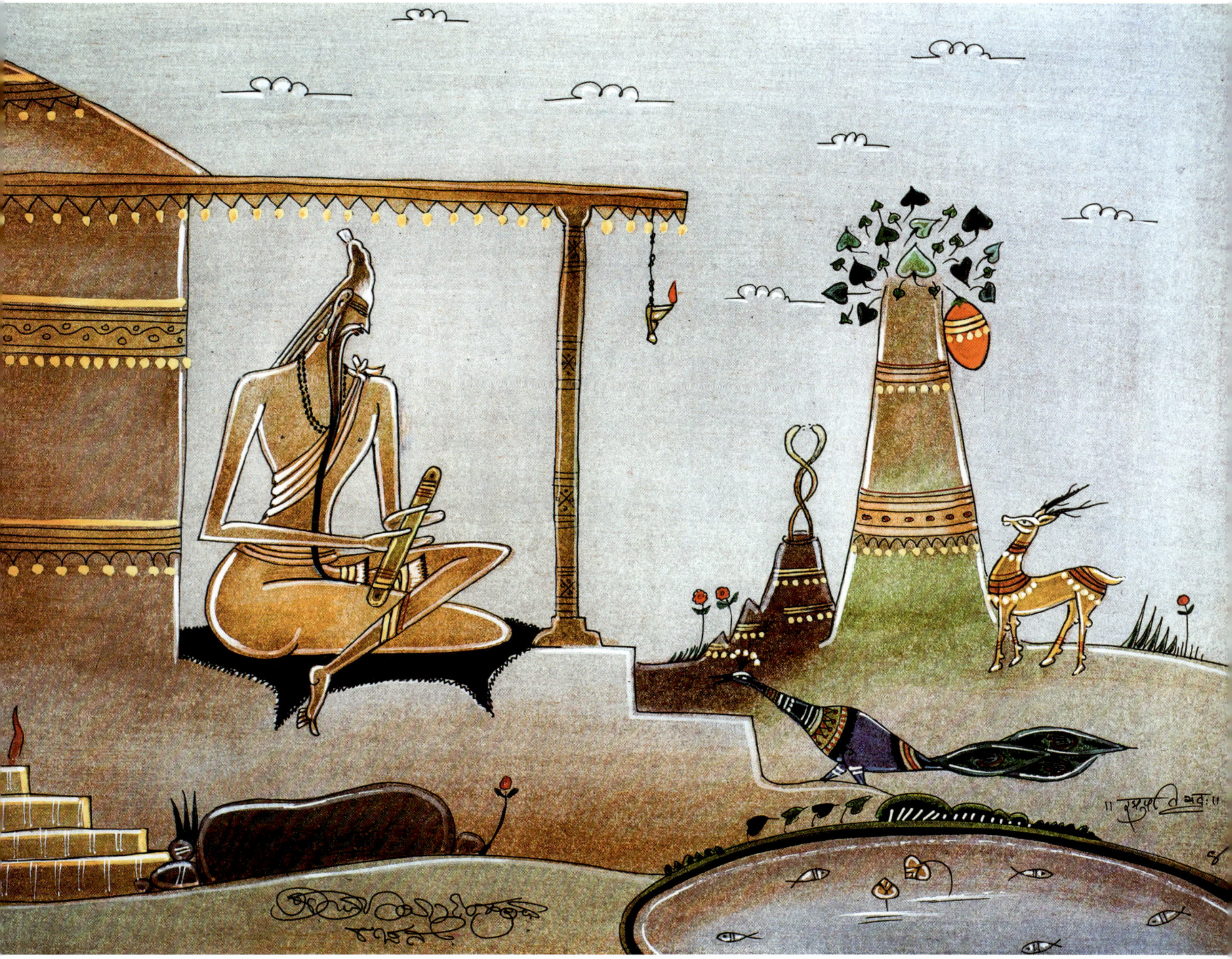

Valmiki Maharishi
Watercolor and pen on paper, 36 x 27 cm

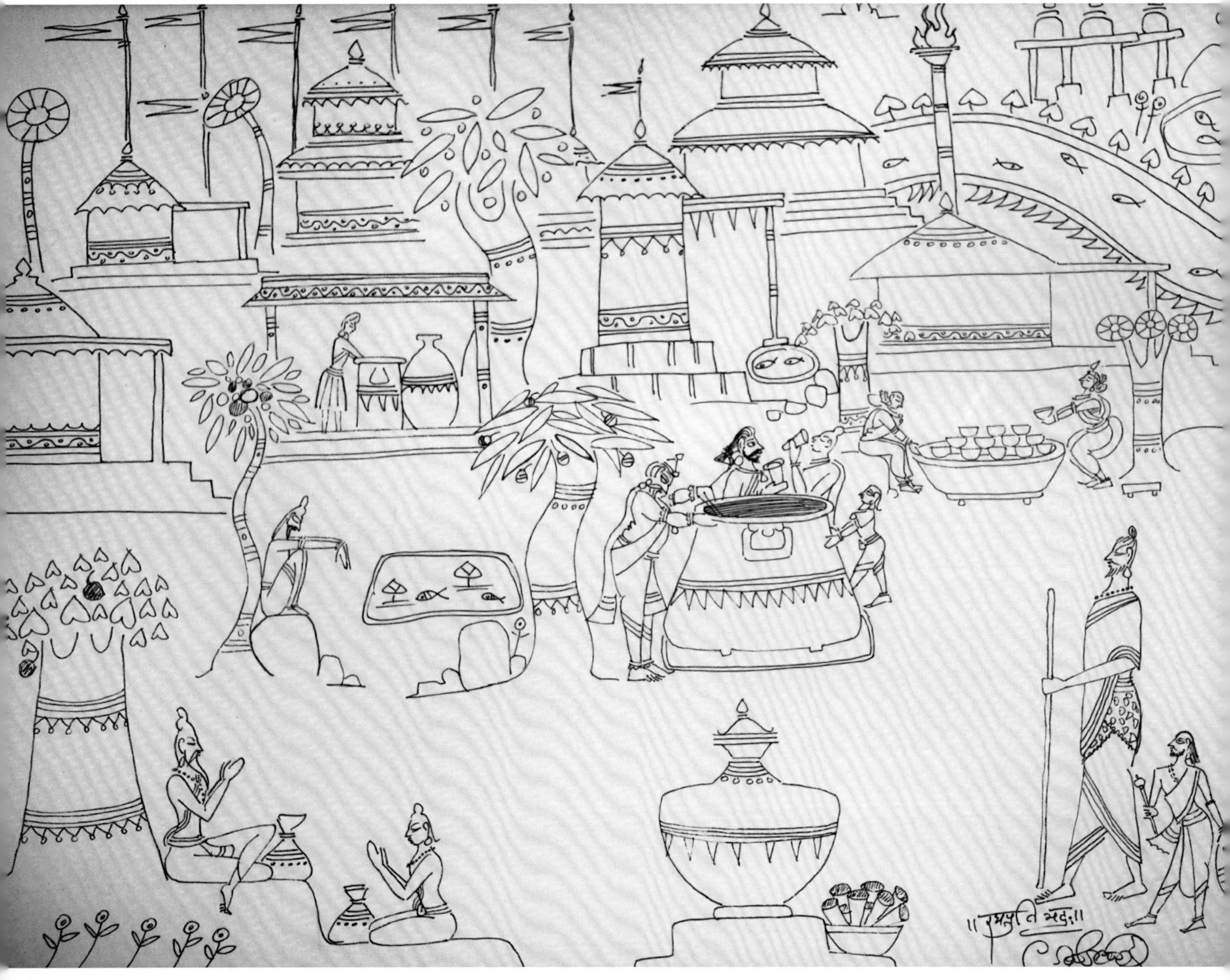

Preparing for the yajña
Pen on paper, 36 x 27 cm

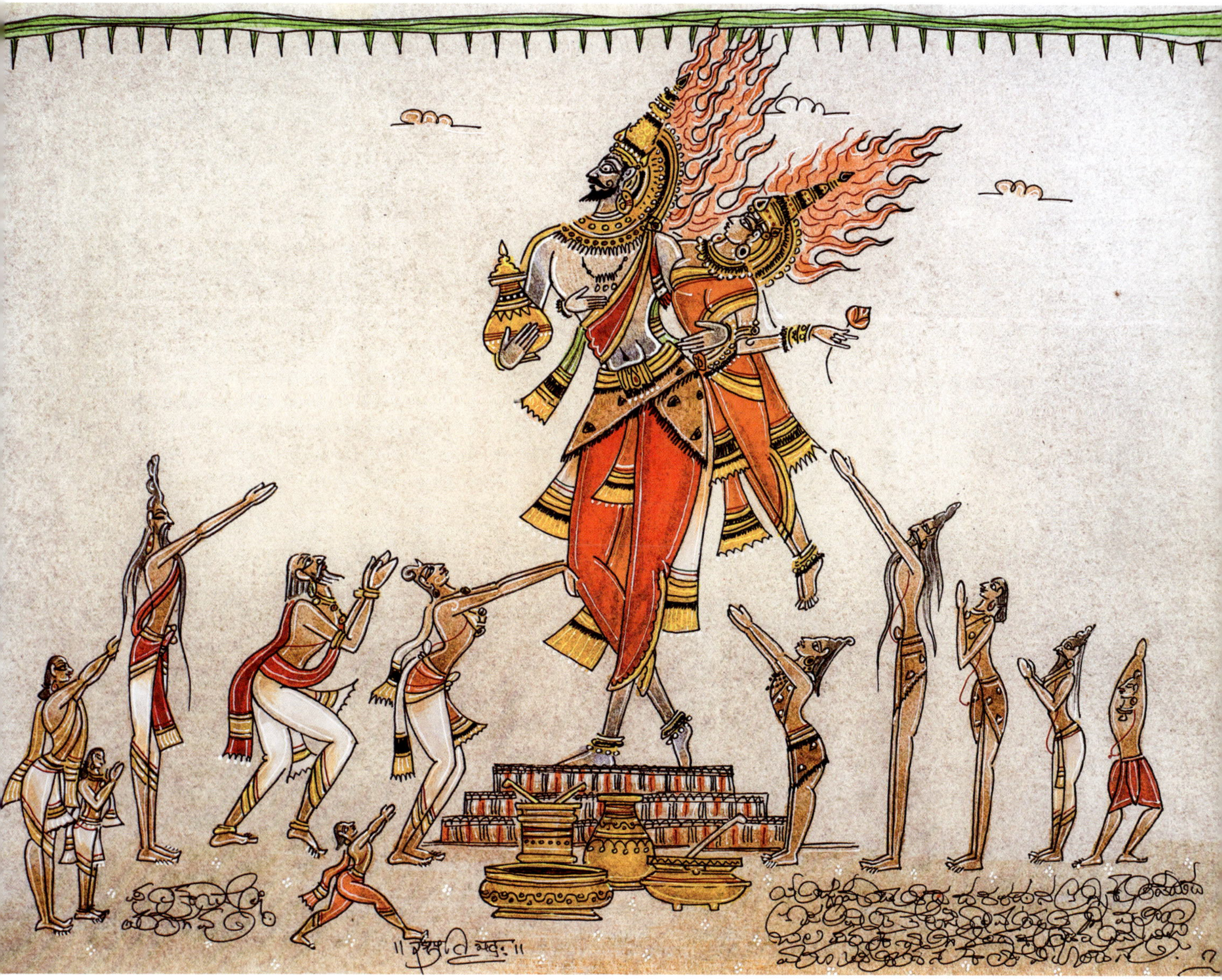

Putra Kameshti yajña
Watercolor and pen on paper, 36 x 27 cm

Birth of Rama, Lakshmana, Bharata and Shatrugna >
Watercolor and pen on paper, 36 x 27 cm

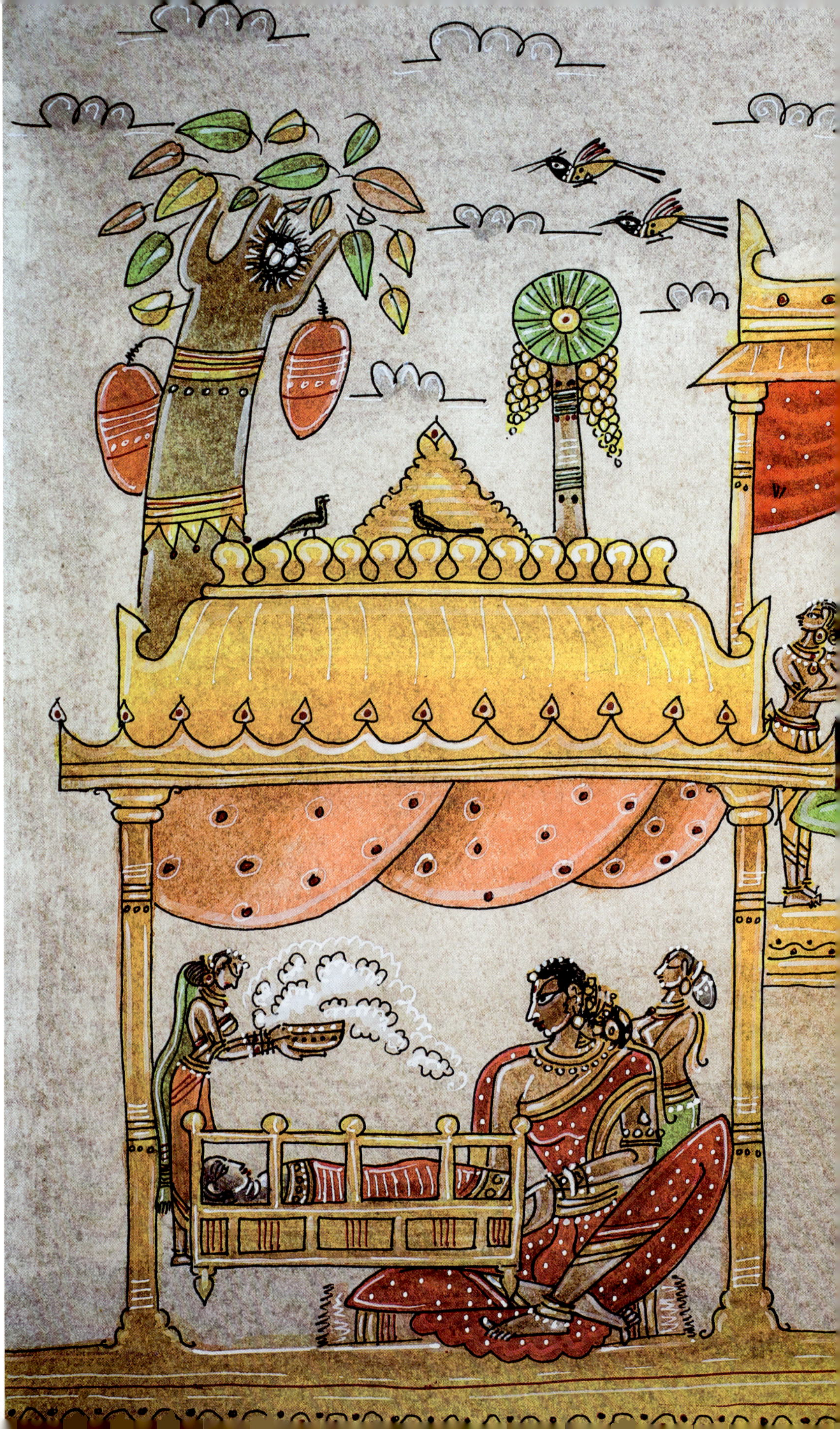

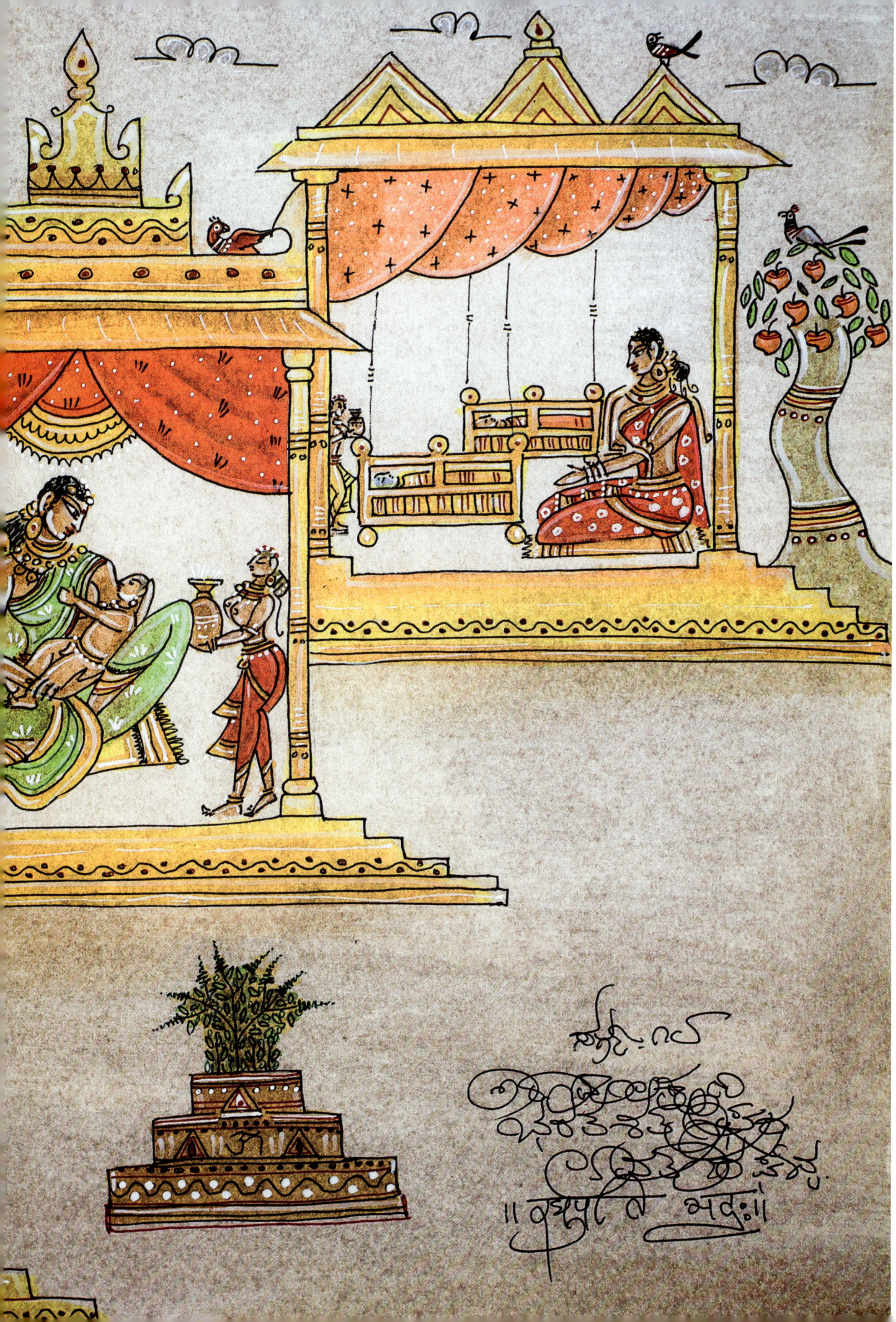

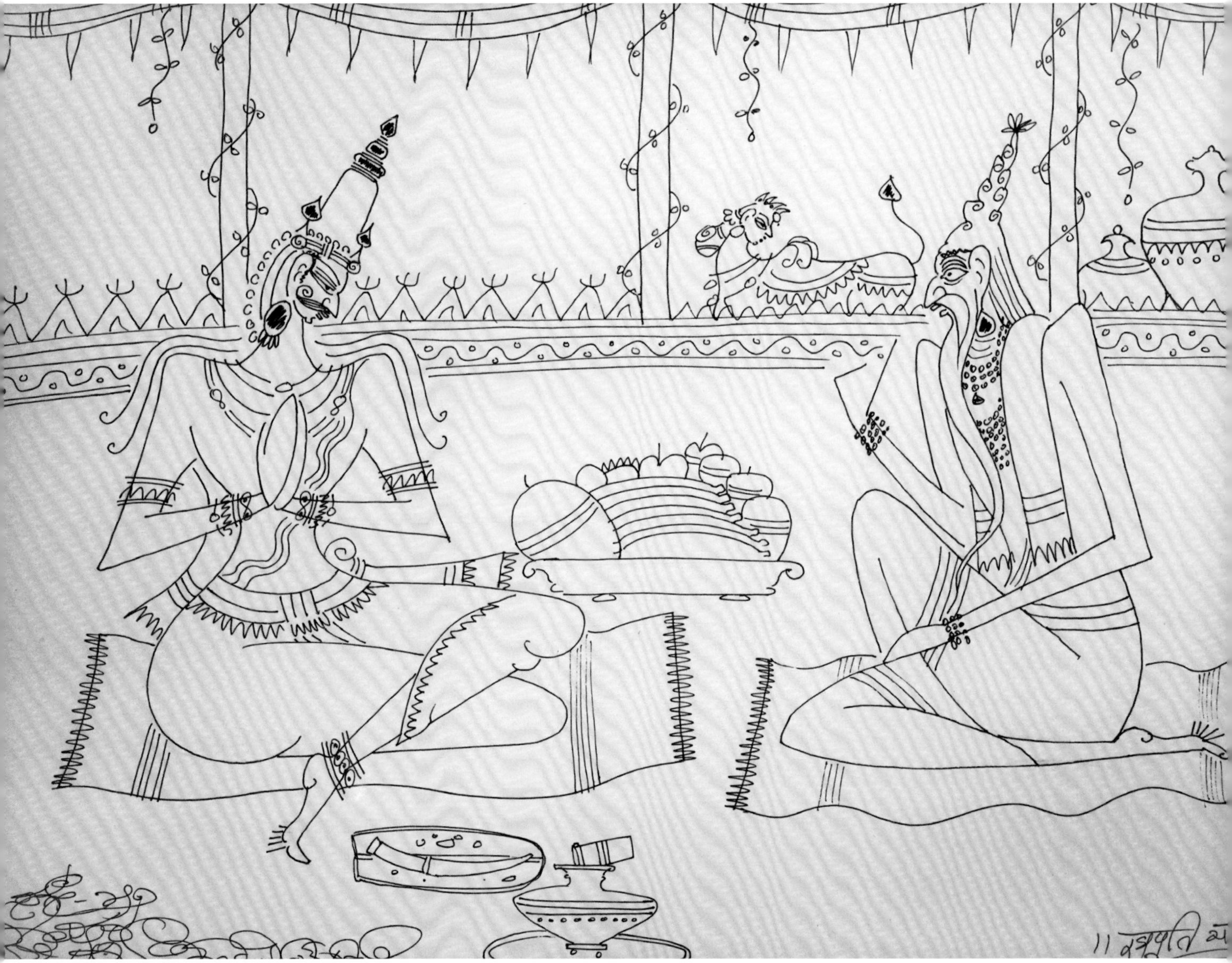

Vasishta and Vishwamitra
Pen on paper, 36 x 27 cm

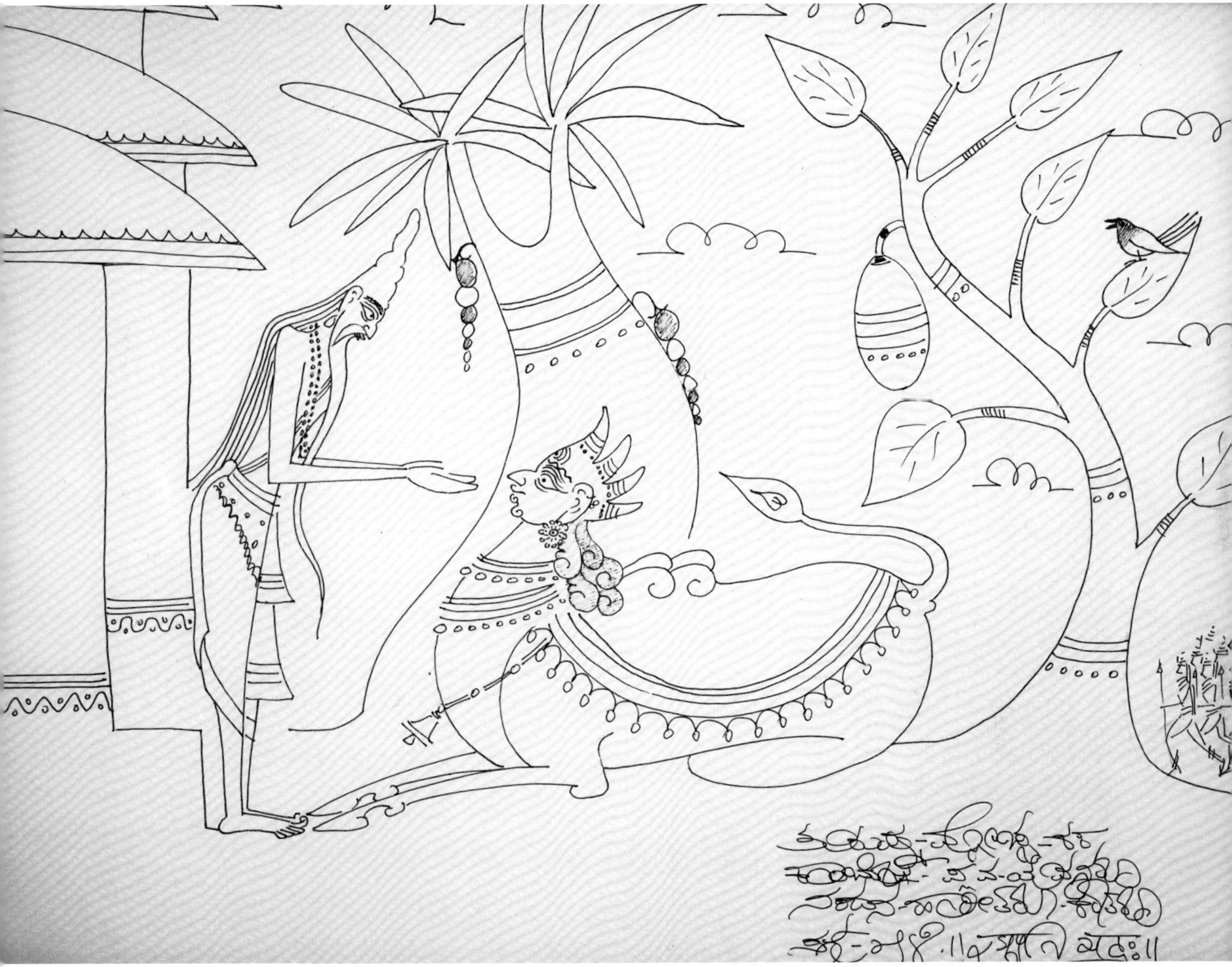

Kamadhenu and Vasishta
Pen on paper, 36 x 27 cm

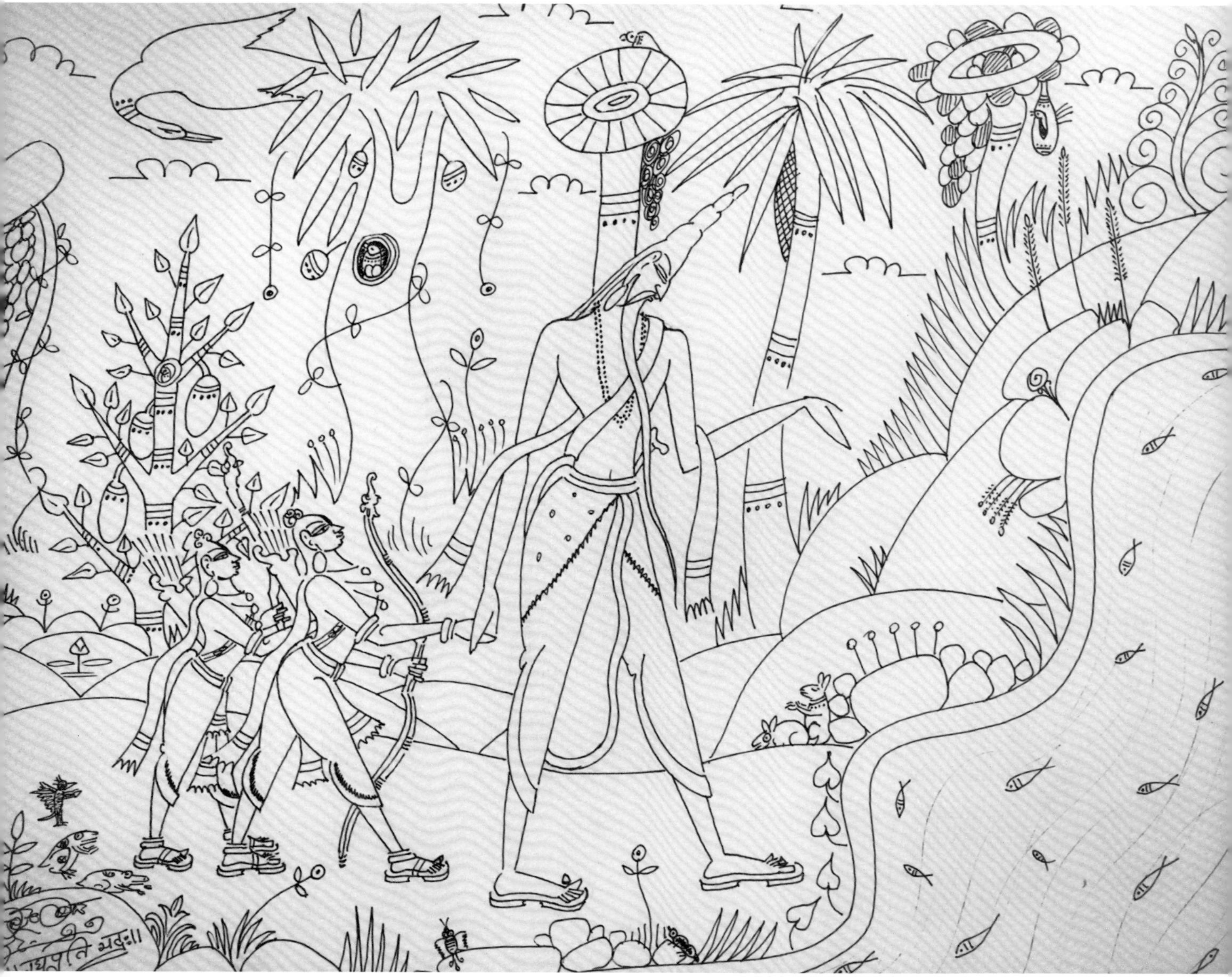

Vishwamitra, Rama and Lakshaman leave Ayodha
Pen on paper, 36 x 27 cm

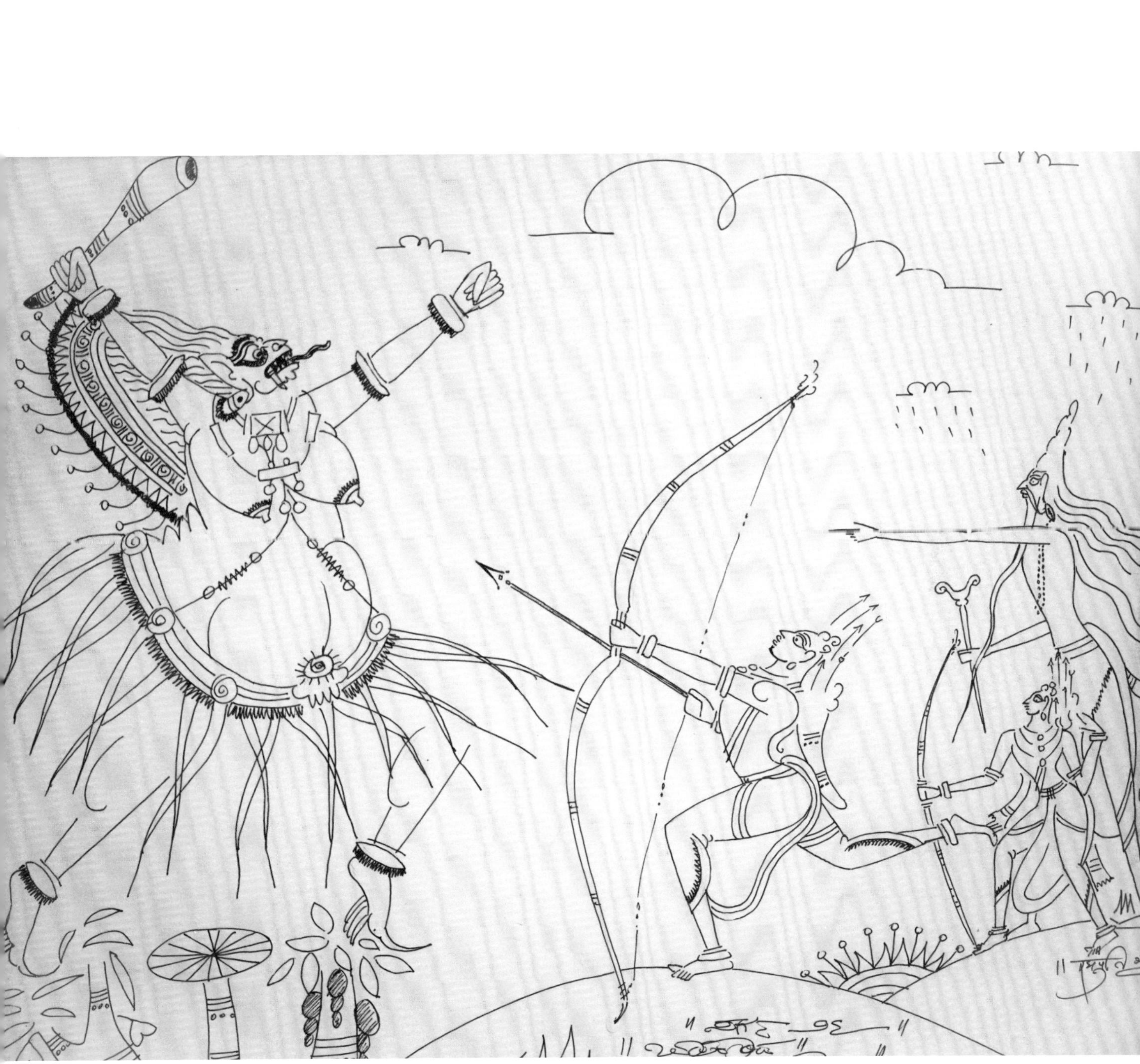

Rama kills a demon
Pen on paper, 36 x 27 cm

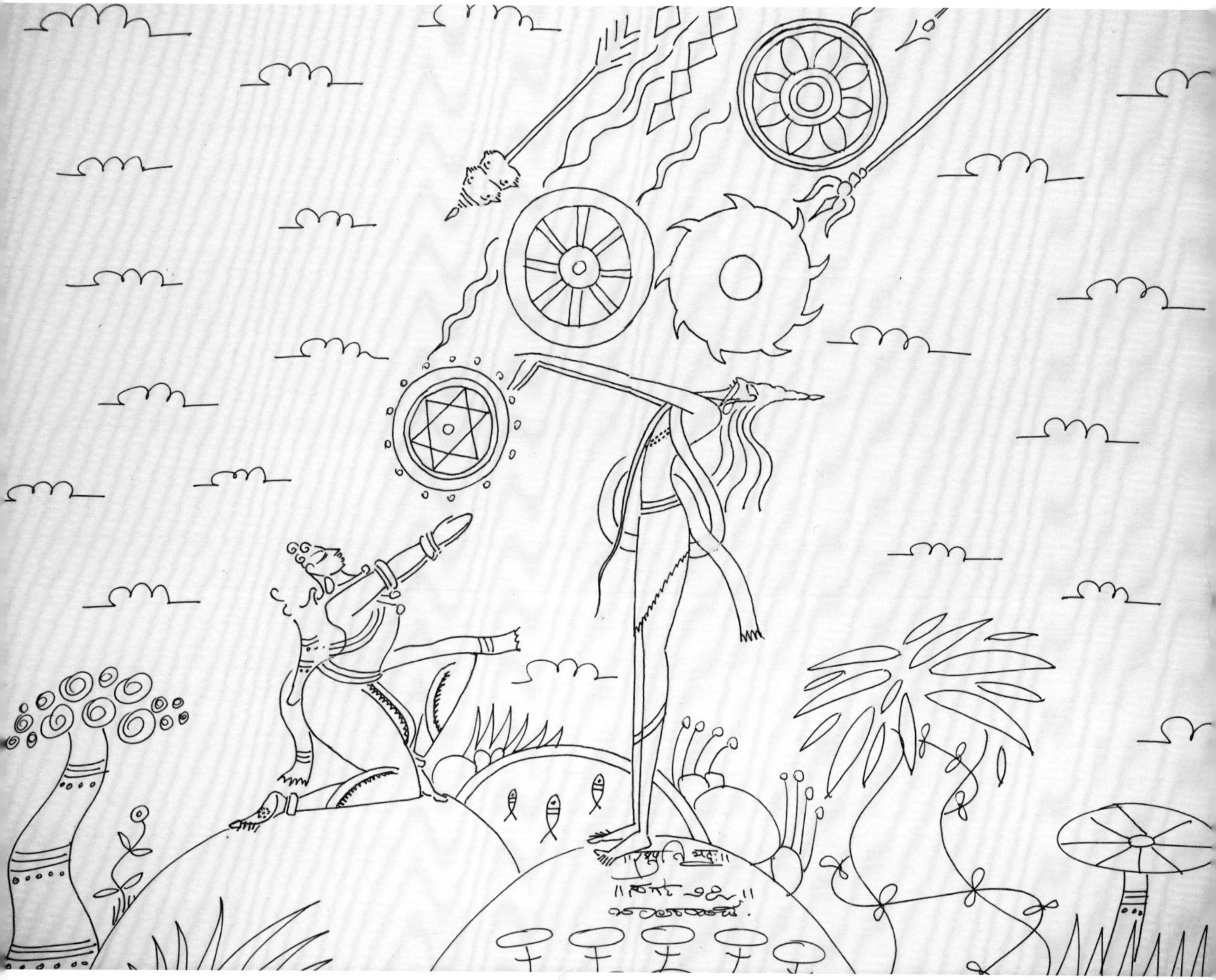

Vishwamitra presents astras to Rama
Pen on paper, 36 x 27 cm

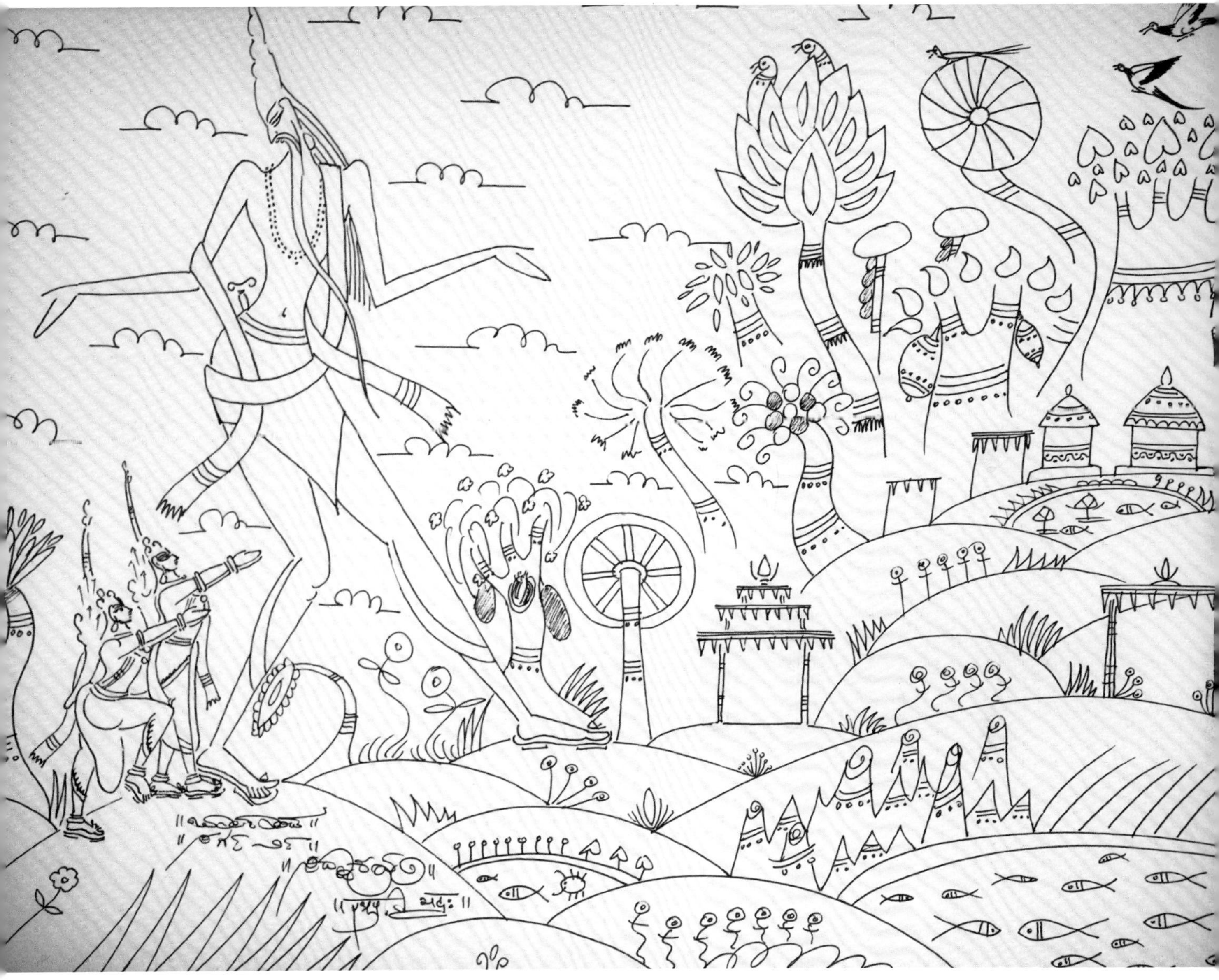

Vishwamitra, Rama and Lakshamana approaching the hermitage of the sages
Pen on paper, 36 x 27 cm

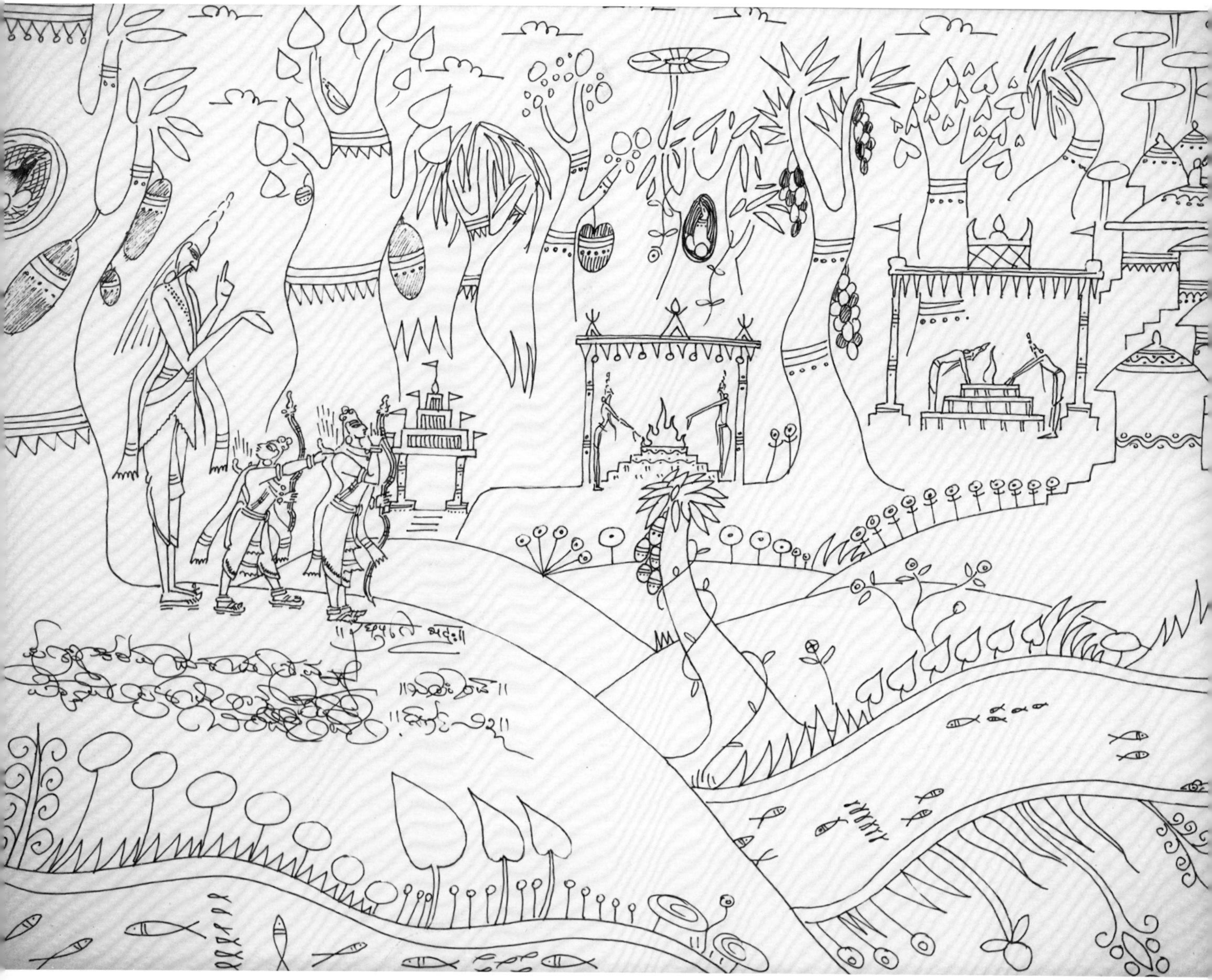

Arrival at the hermitage of the sages
Pen on paper, 36 x 27 cm

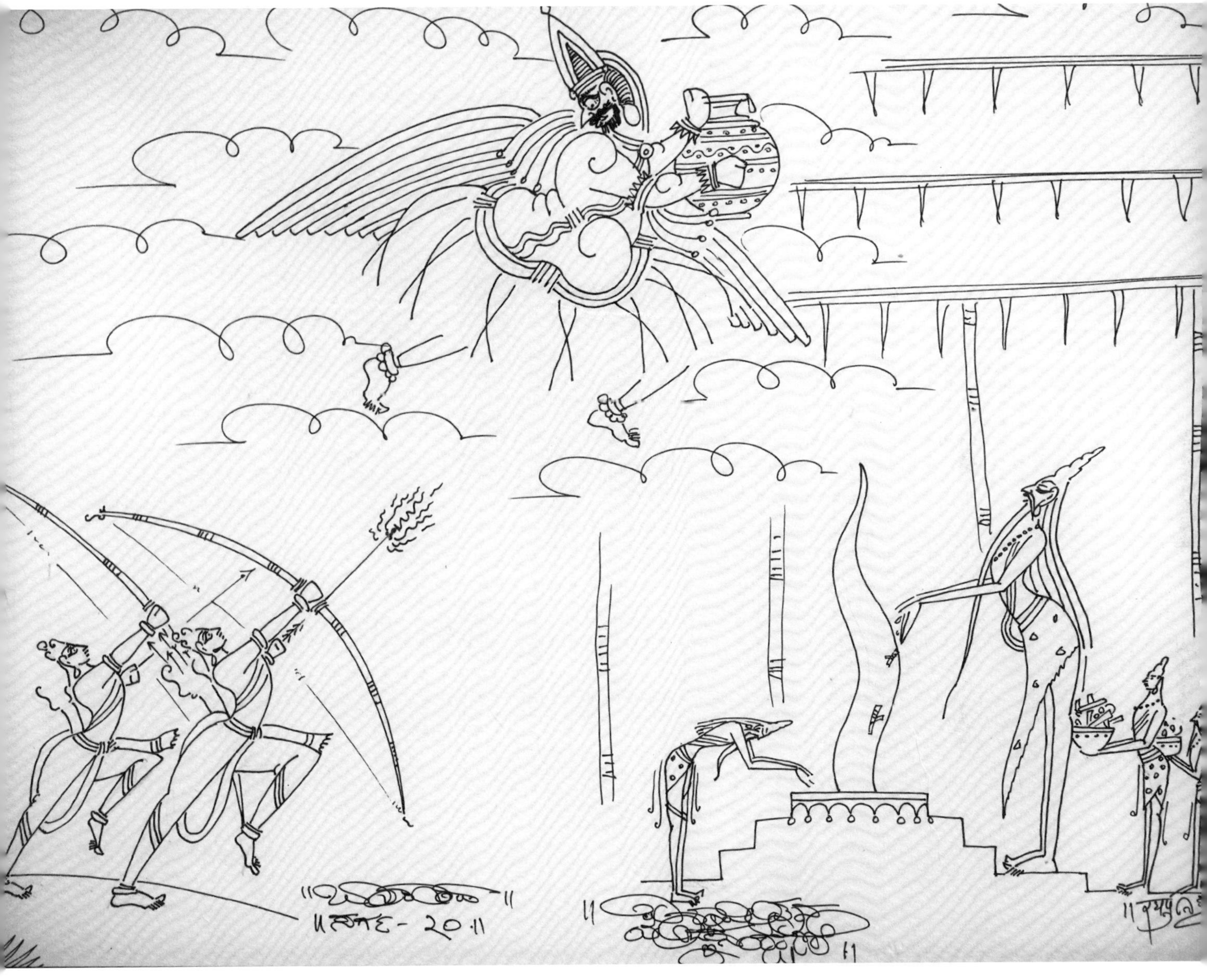

Rama and Lakshmana protect yajña from the demons (1)
Pen on paper, 36 x 27 cm

Rama and Lakshmana protect yajña from the demons (2) >
Watercolor and pen on paper, 36 x 27 cm

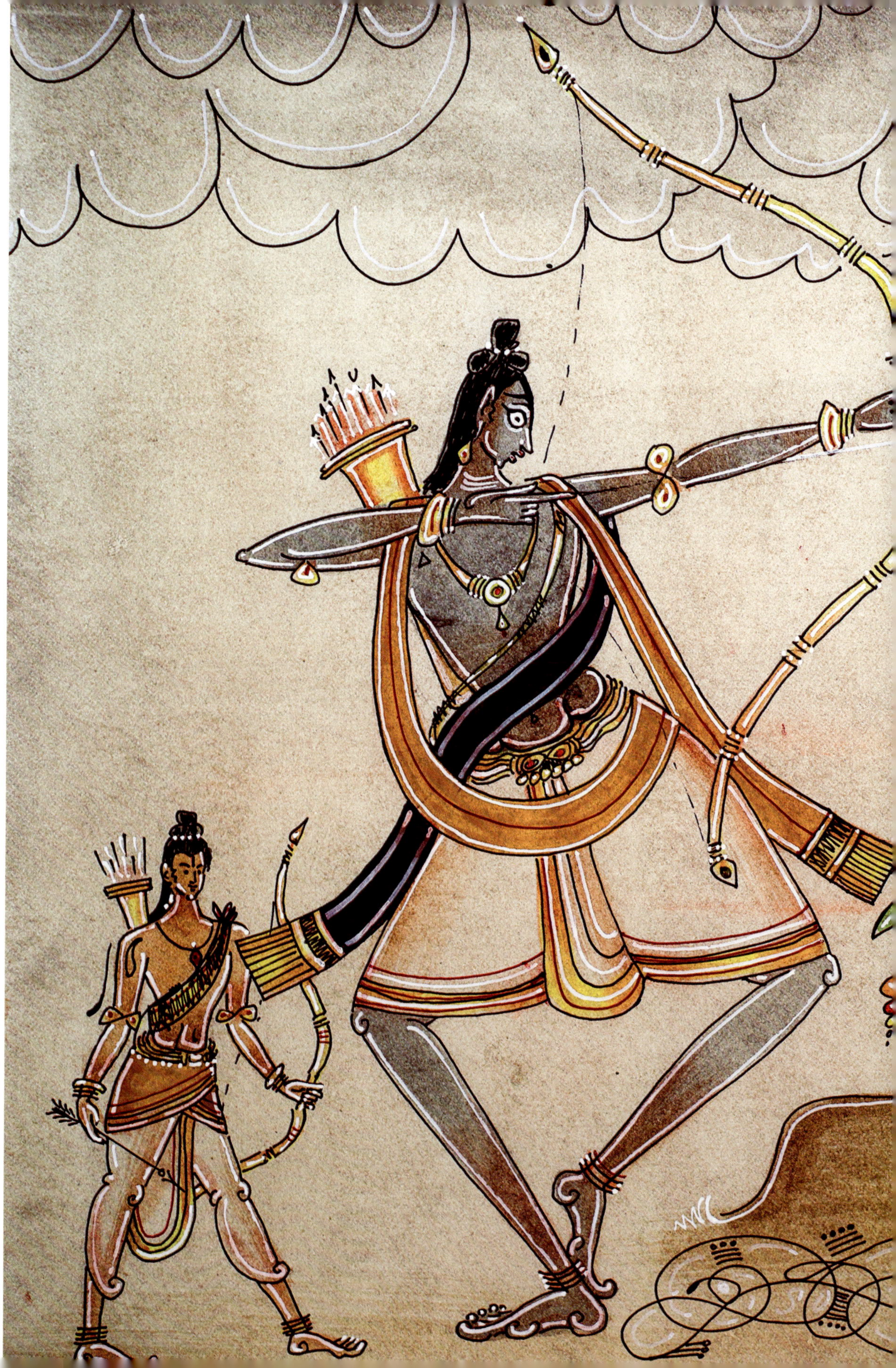

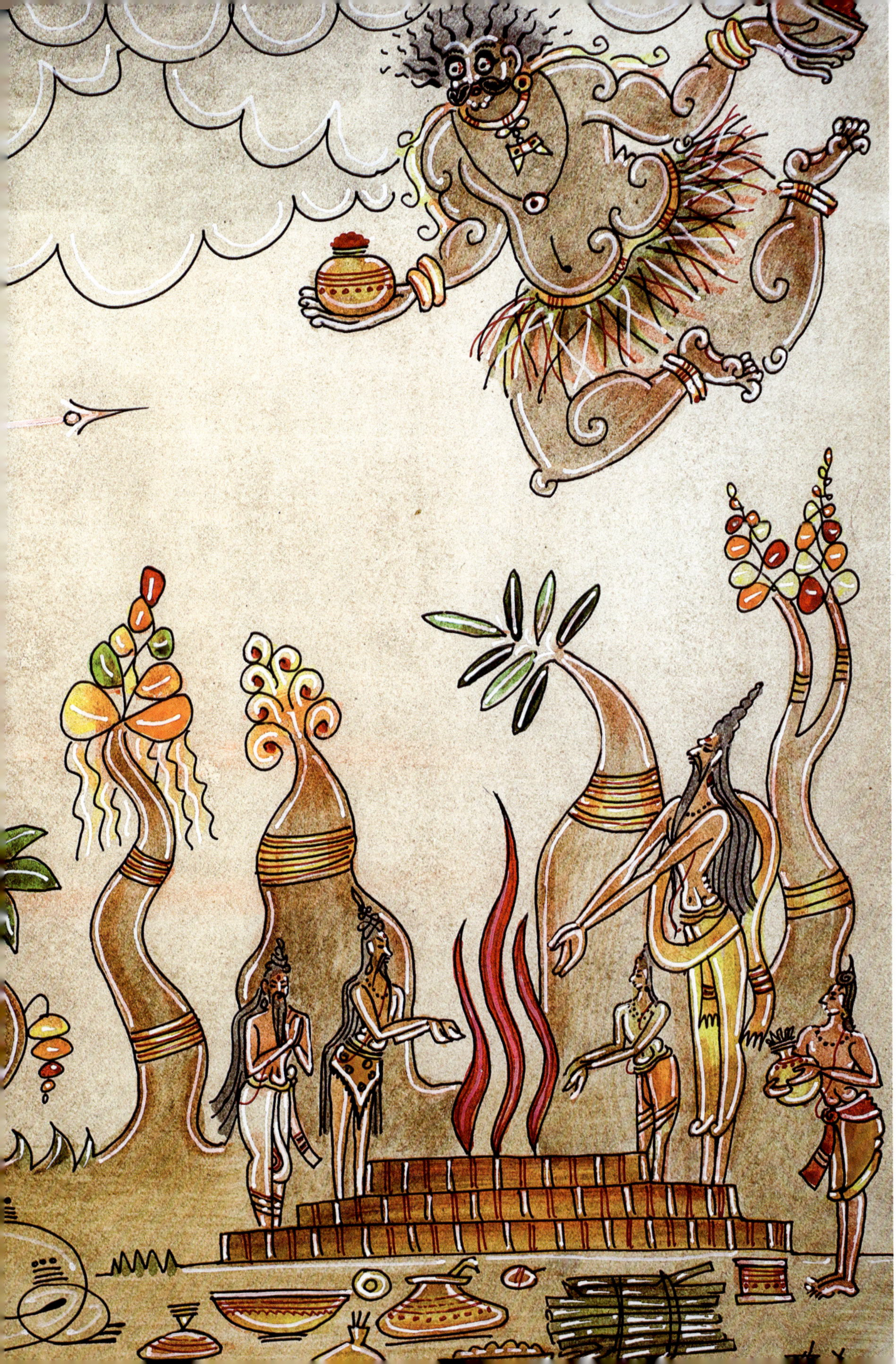

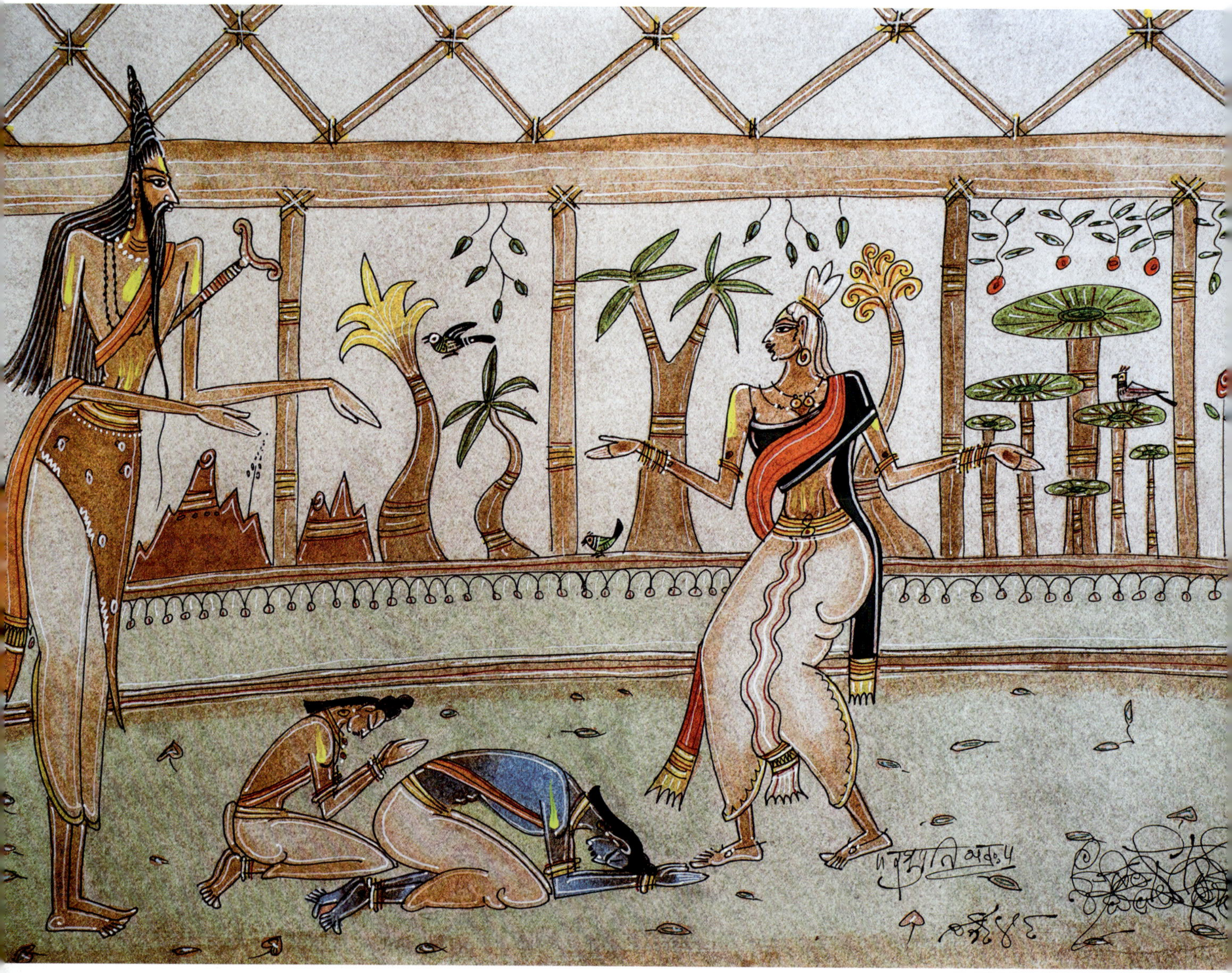

Ahalya Shapavimochana released from a curse
Watercolor and pen on paper, 36 x 27 cm

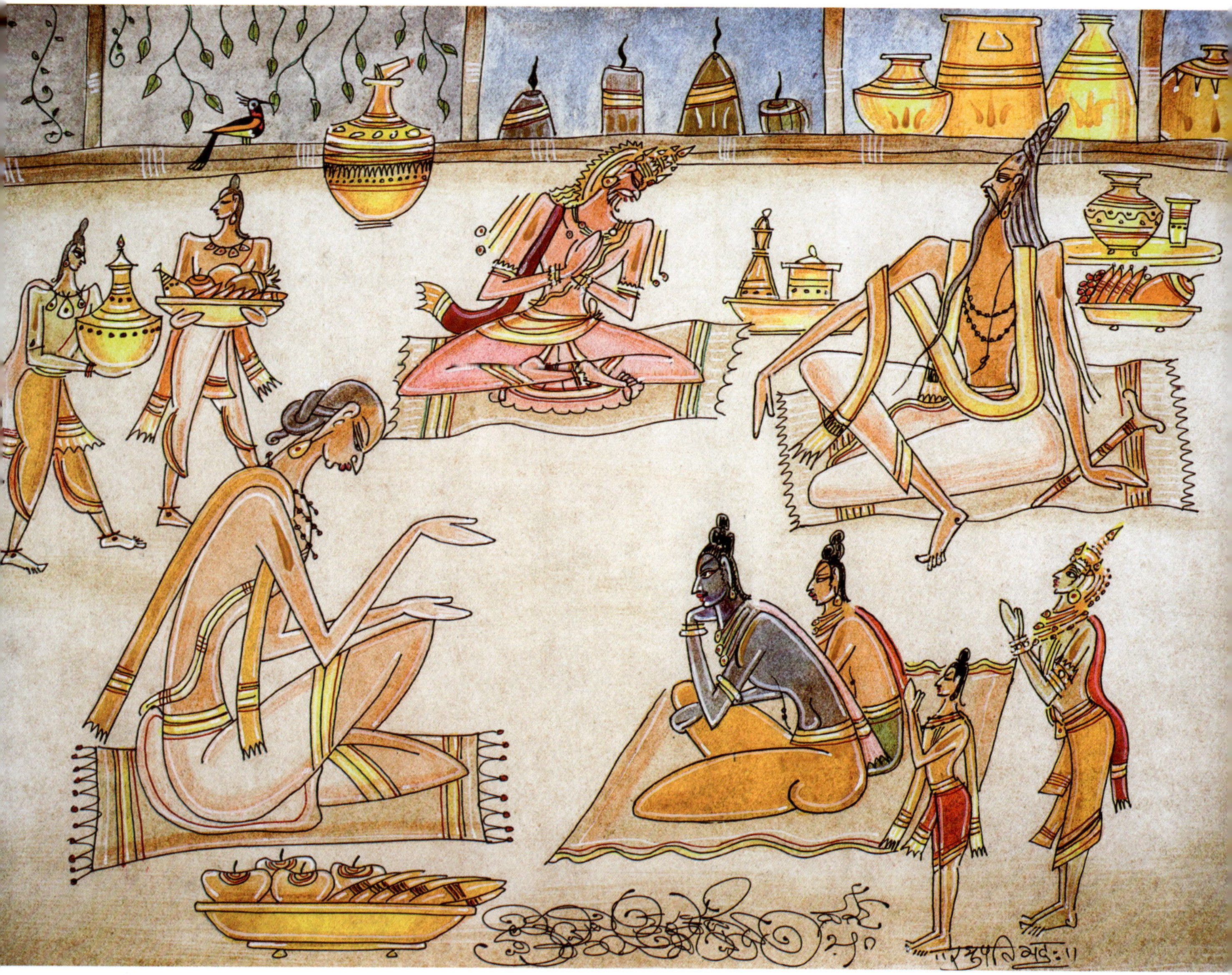

Shatananda recites Vishwamitra's story to Rama
Watercolor and pen on paper, 36 x 27 cm

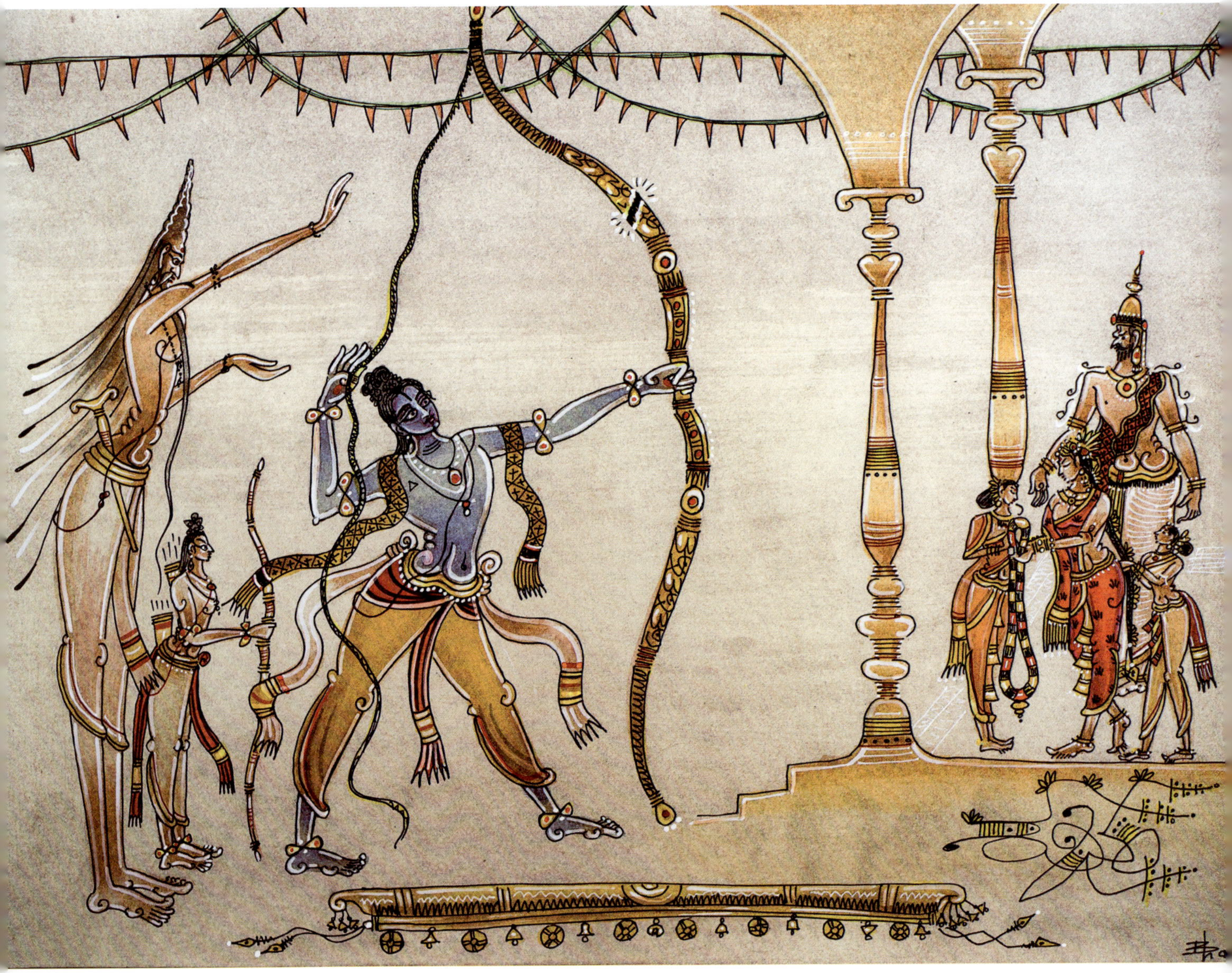

Sita Swayamvara
Watercolor and pen on paper, 36 x 27 cm

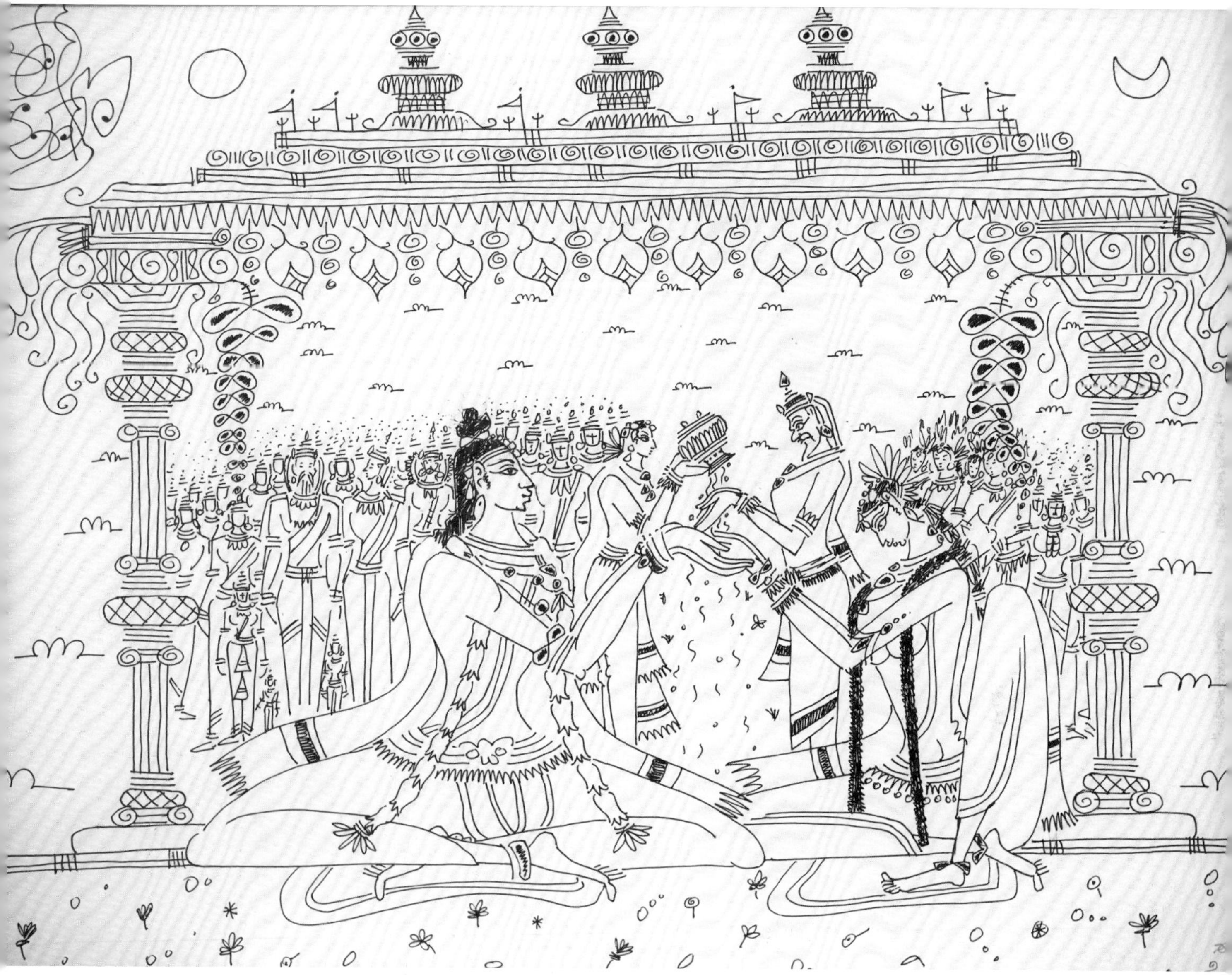

Kalyana
Pen on paper, 36 x 27 cm

Crossing the river Ganga >
Watercolor and pen on paper, 36 x 27 cm

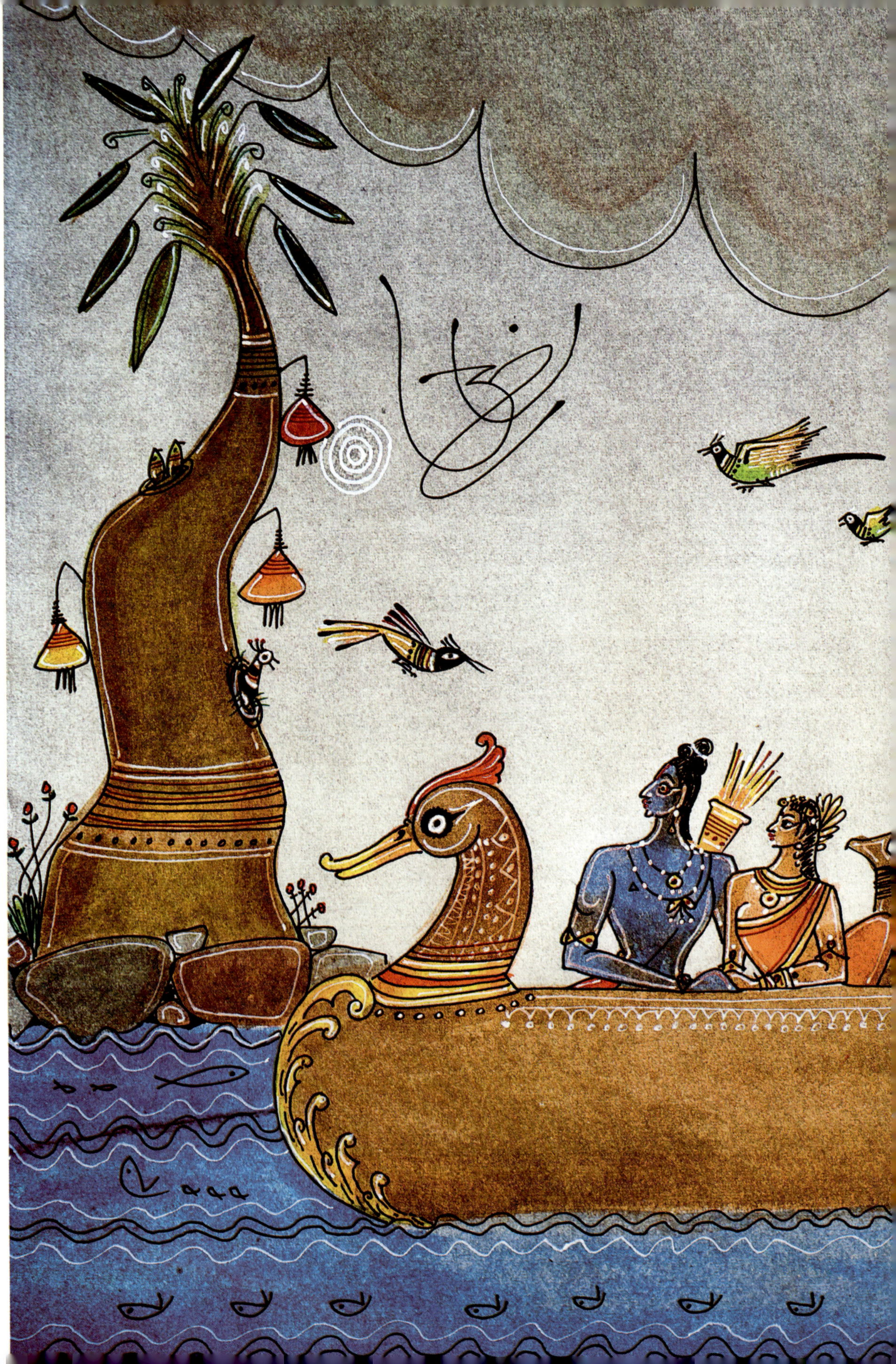

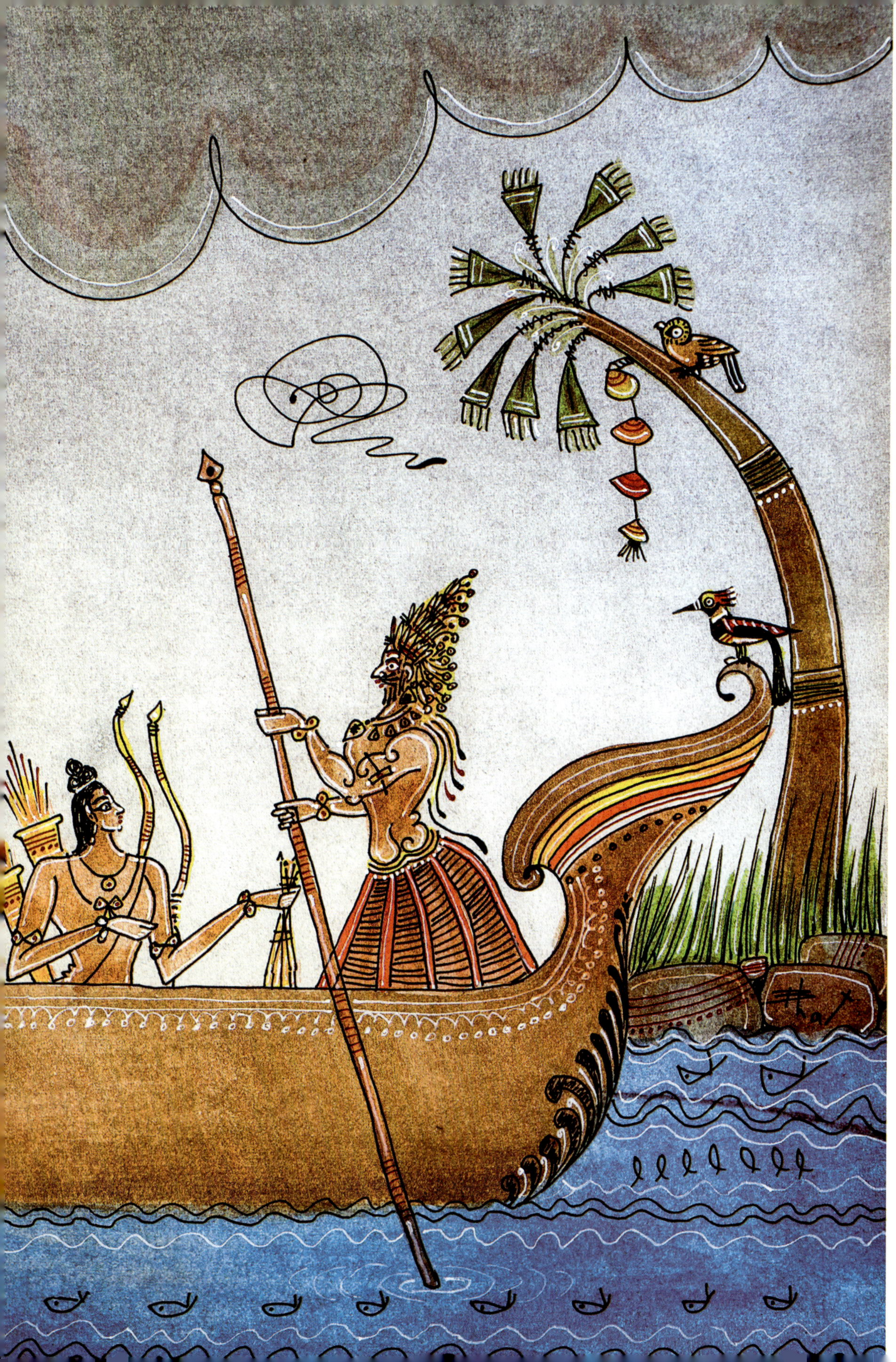

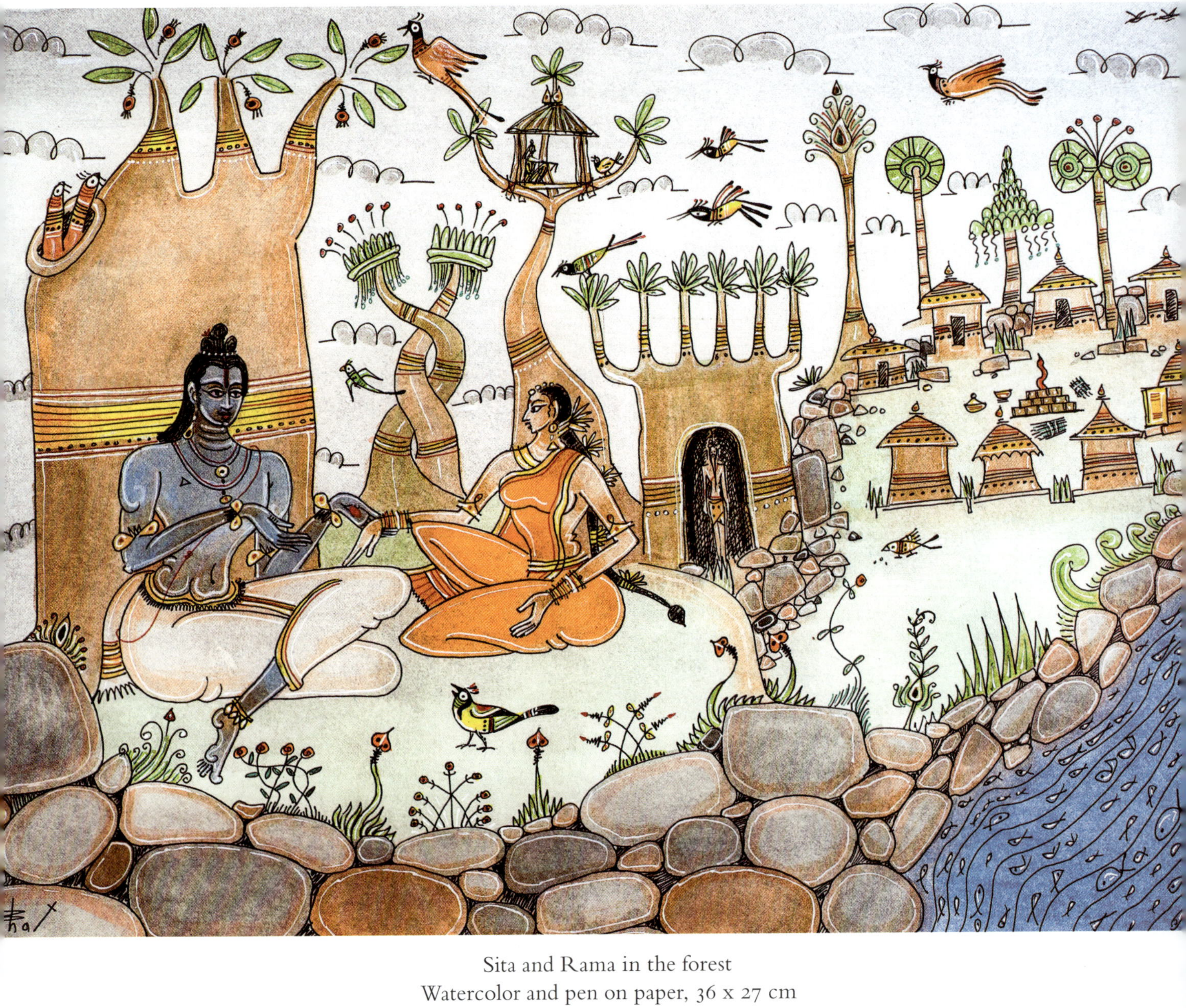

Sita and Rama in the forest
Watercolor and pen on paper, 36 x 27 cm

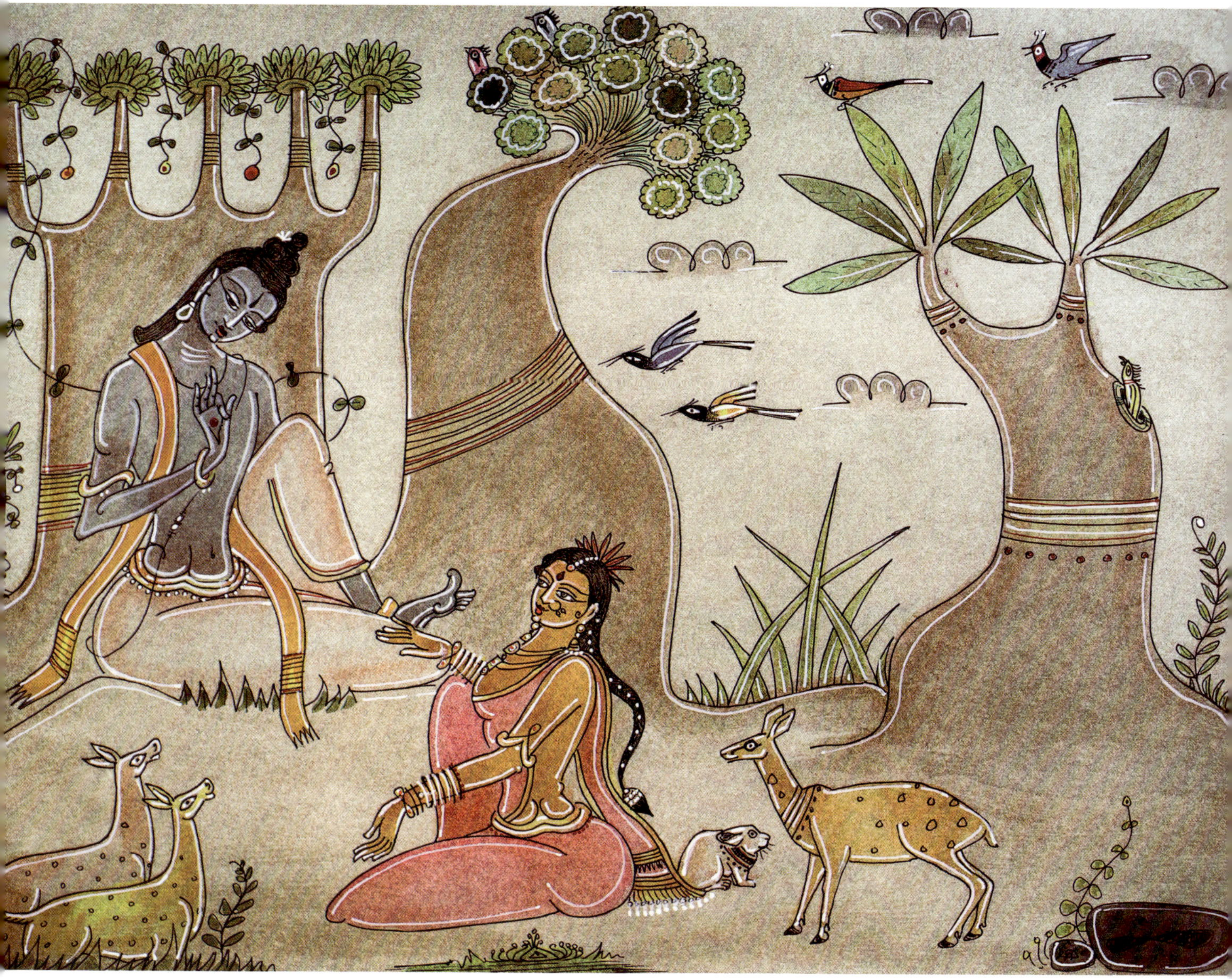

Sita and Rama in Chitrakuta forest
Watercolor and pen on paper, 36 x 27 cm

Jatayu >
Watercolor and pen on paper, 36 x 27 cm

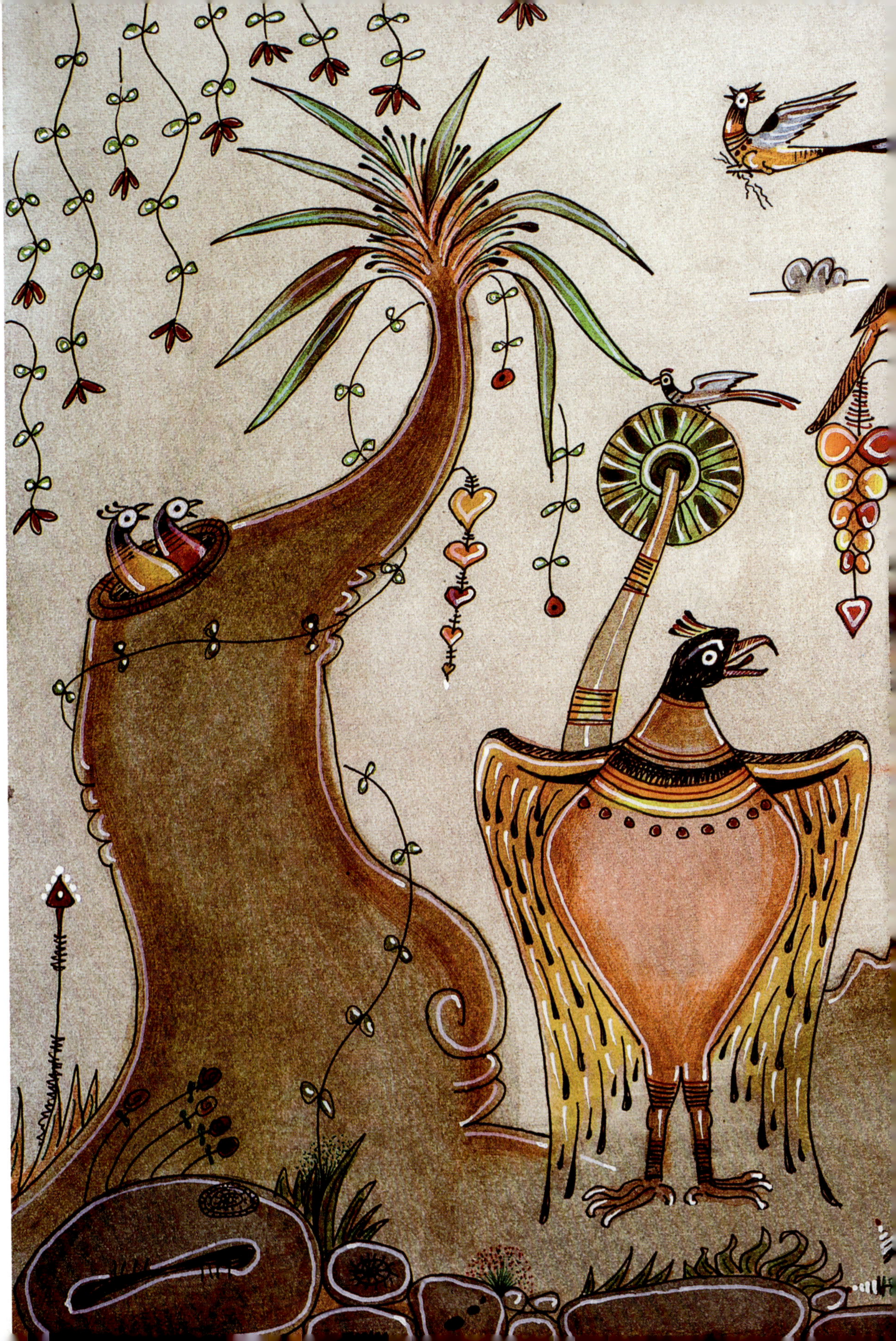

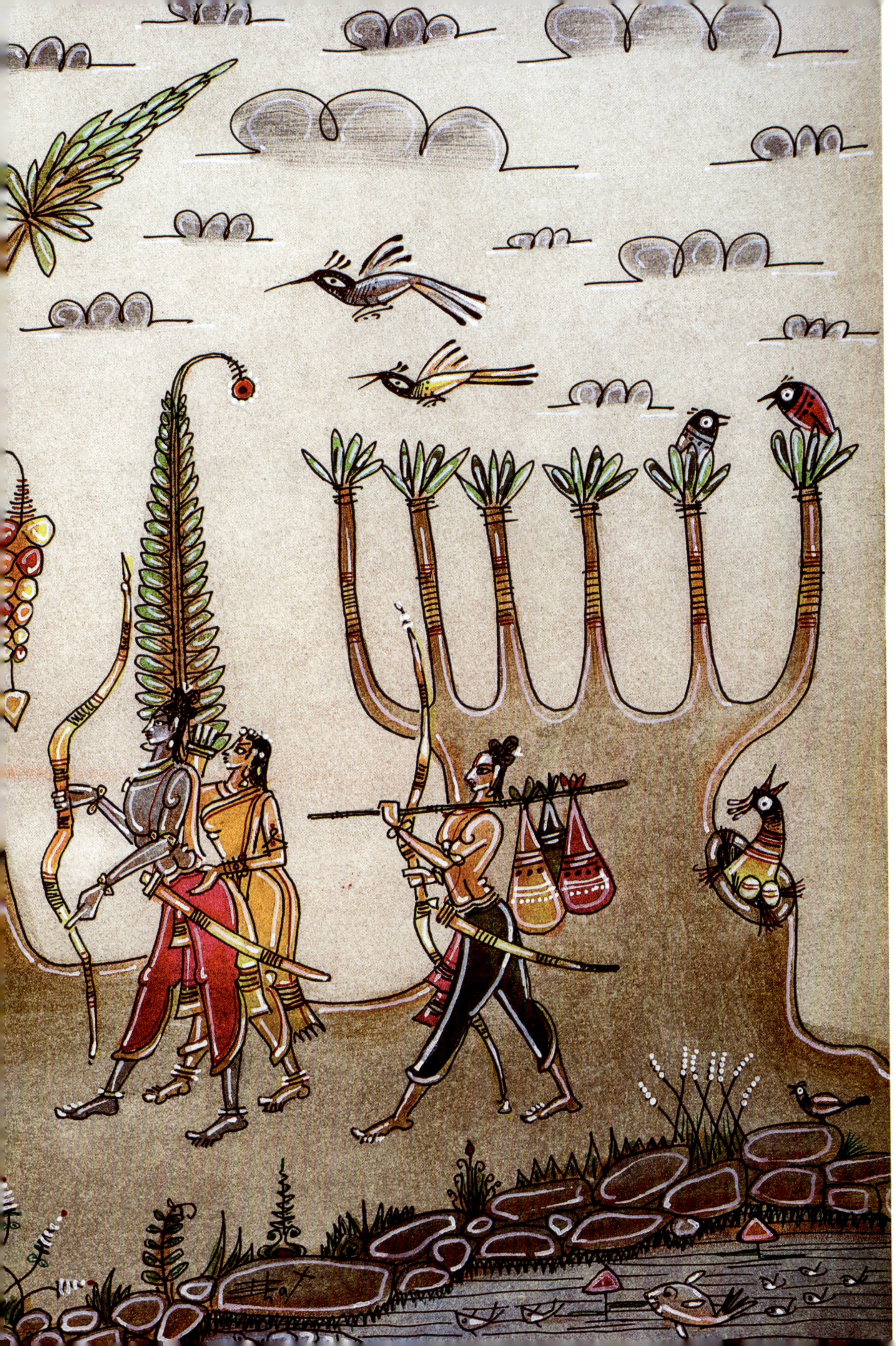

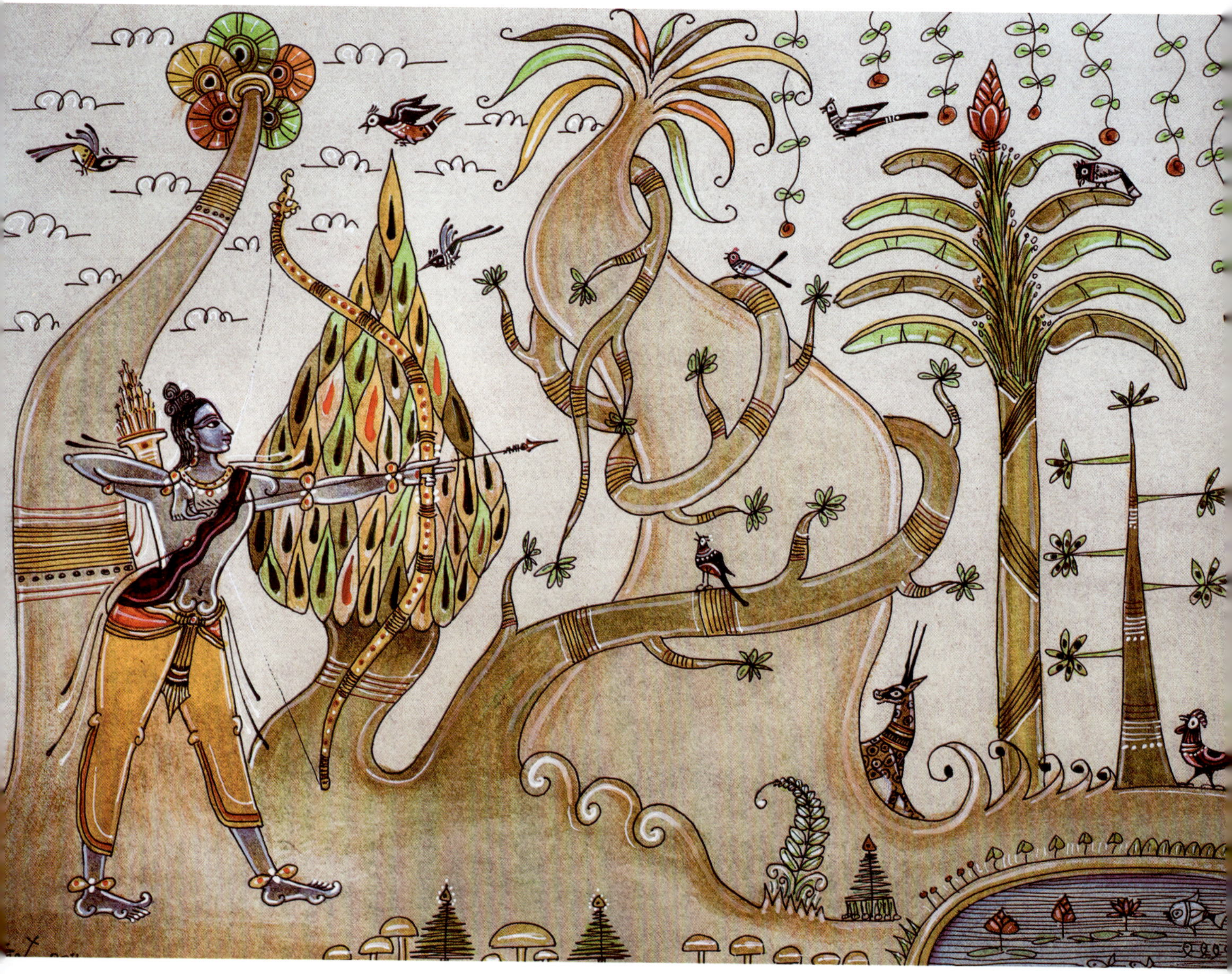

Mayajinke disguised as a deer
Watercolor and pen on paper, 36 x 27 cm

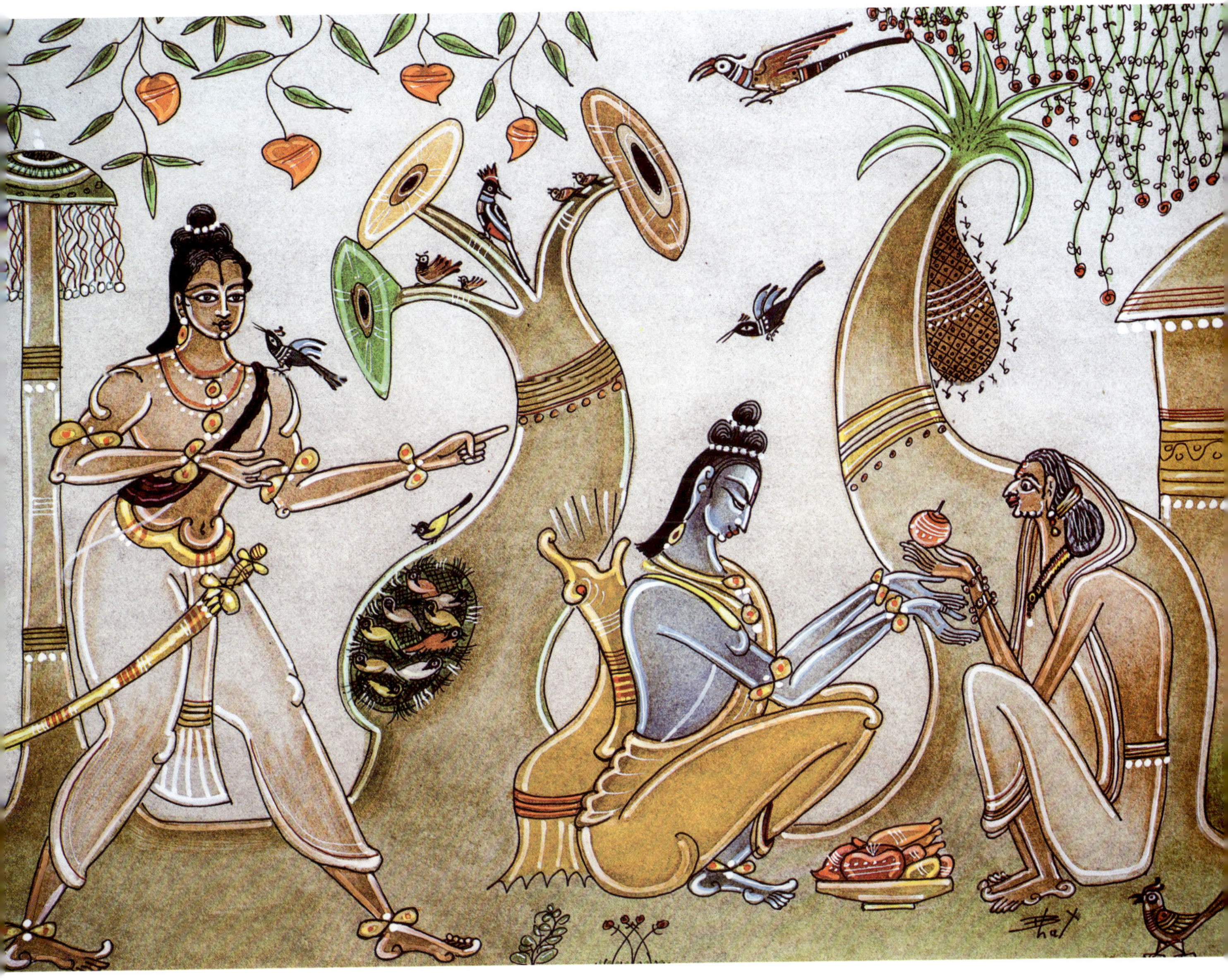

Rama and Lakshmana visiting Shabari
Watercolor and pen on paper, 36 x 27 cm

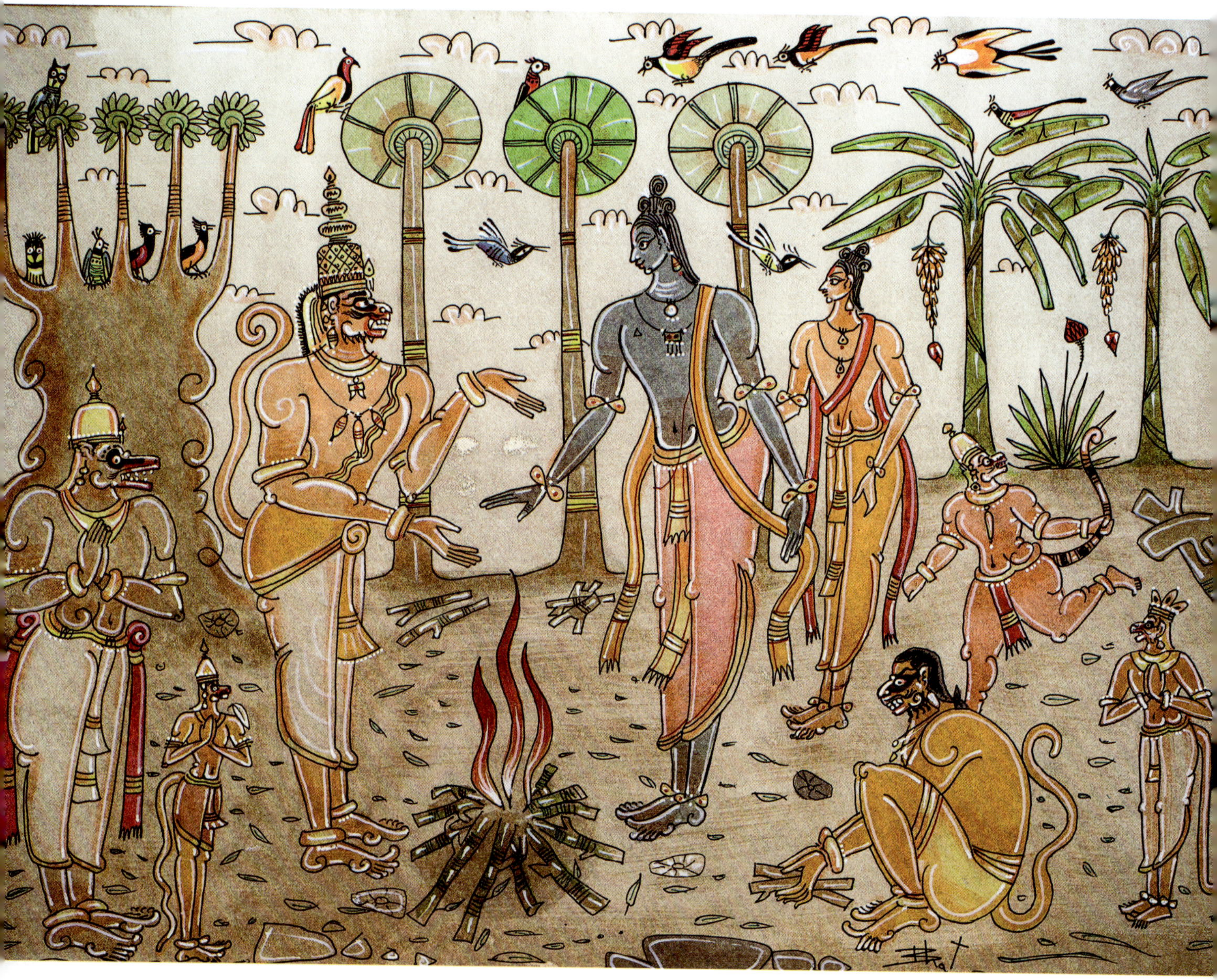

Rama and Lakshmana meet Sugreeva Sakhya
Watercolor and pen on paper, 36 x 27 cm

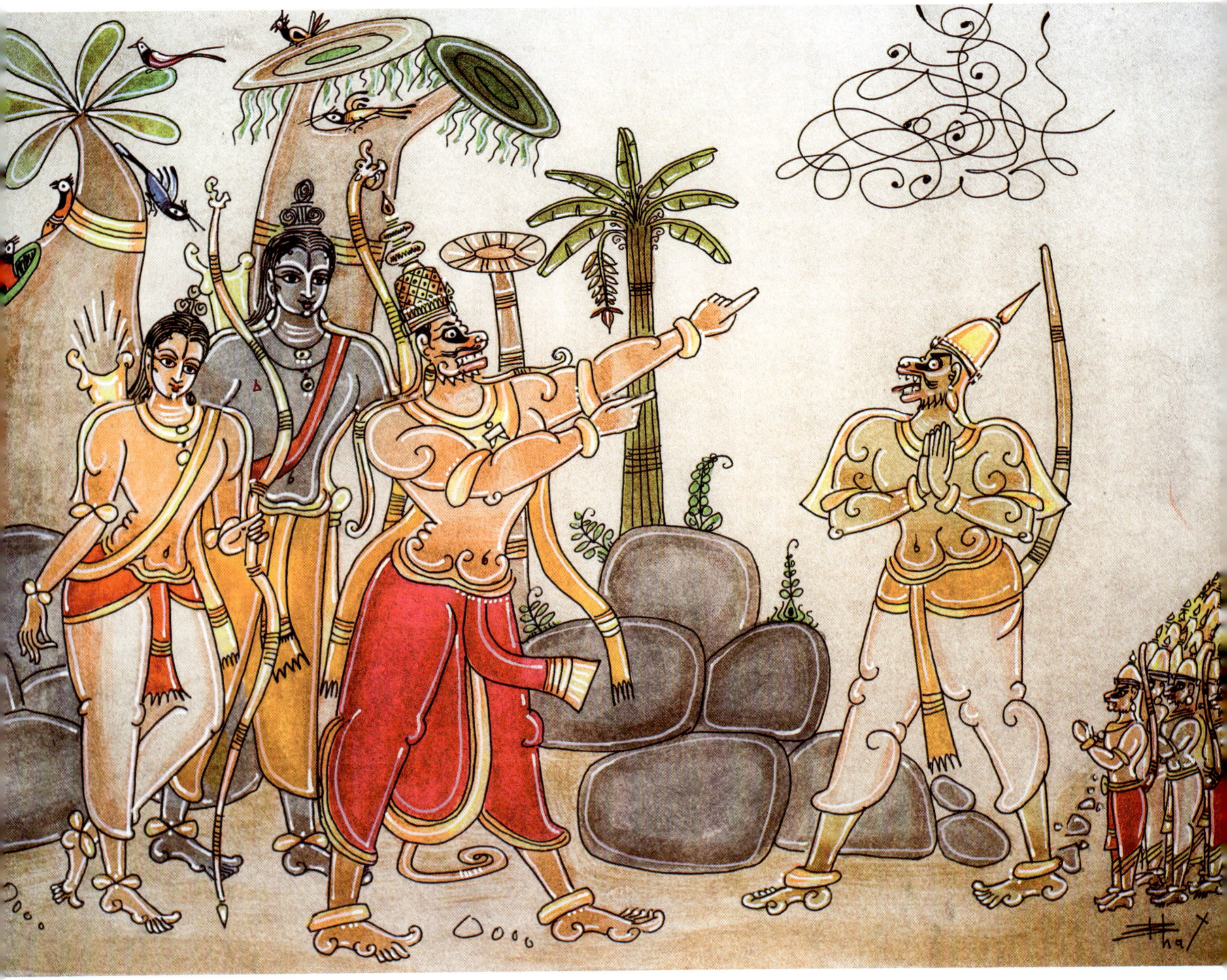

Rama and Lakshmana visiting Shabari
Watercolor and pen on paper, 36 x 27 cm

Hanuman crossing ocean to reach Lanka >
Watercolor and pen on paper, 36 x 27 cm

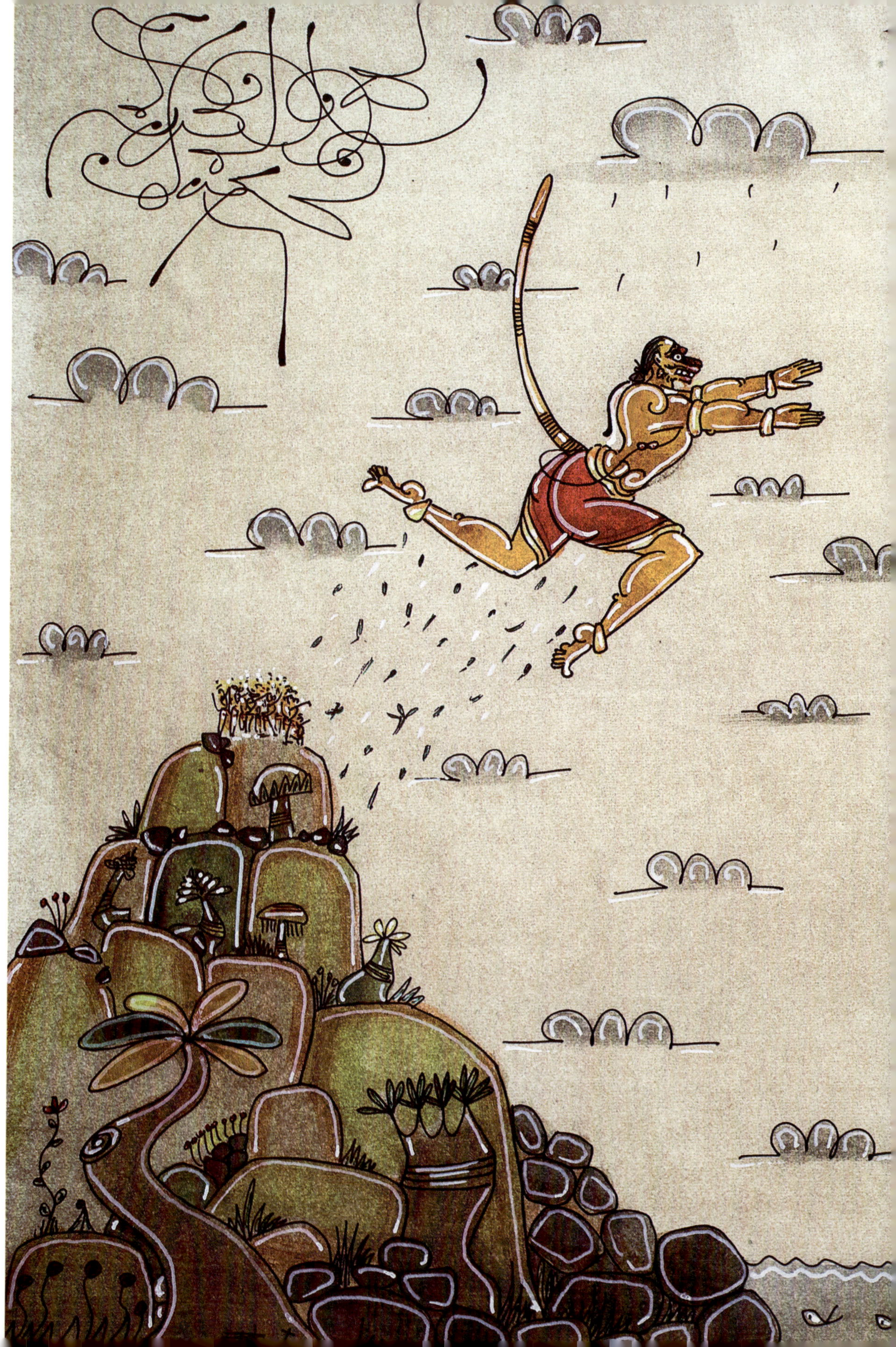

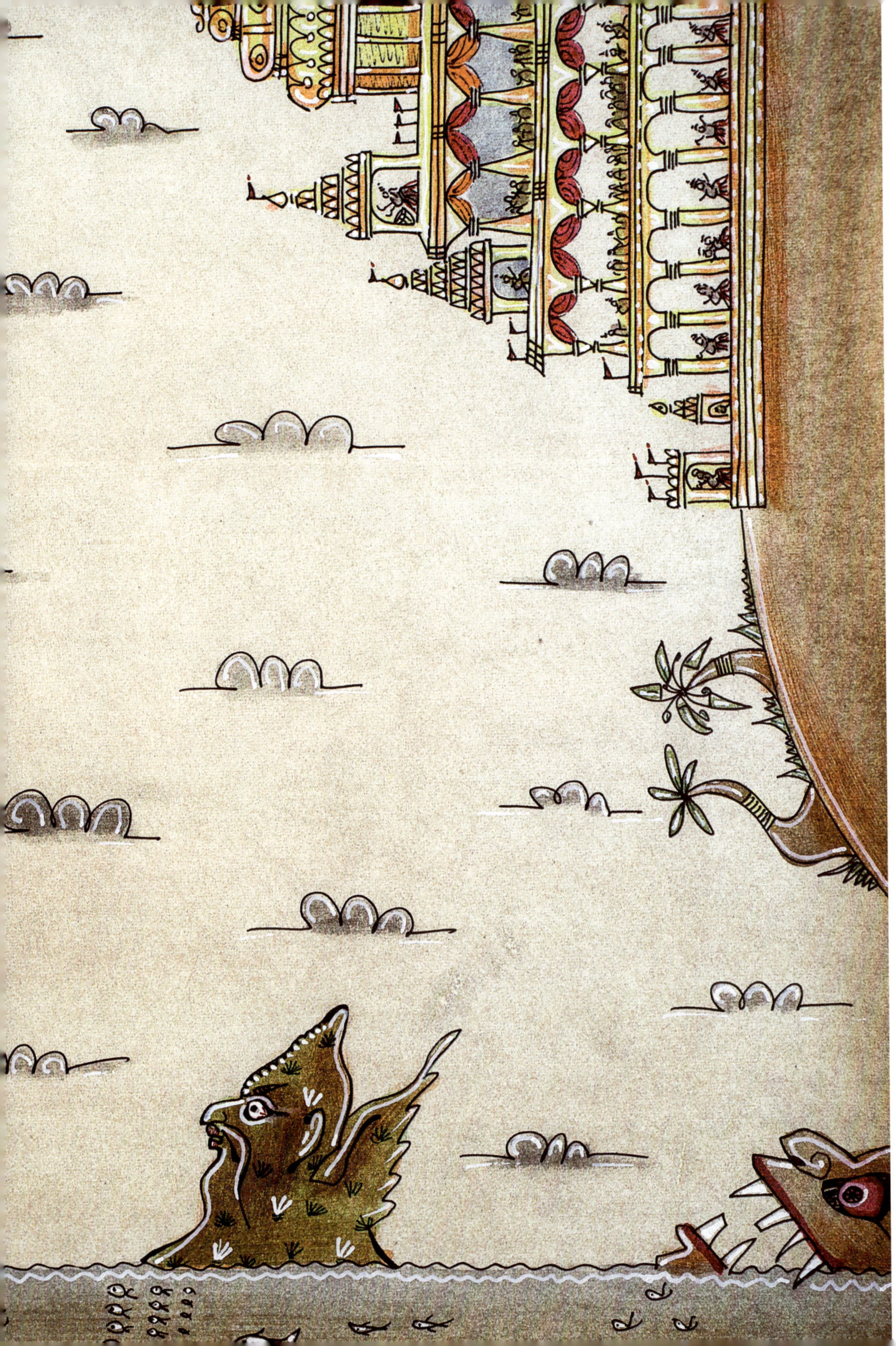

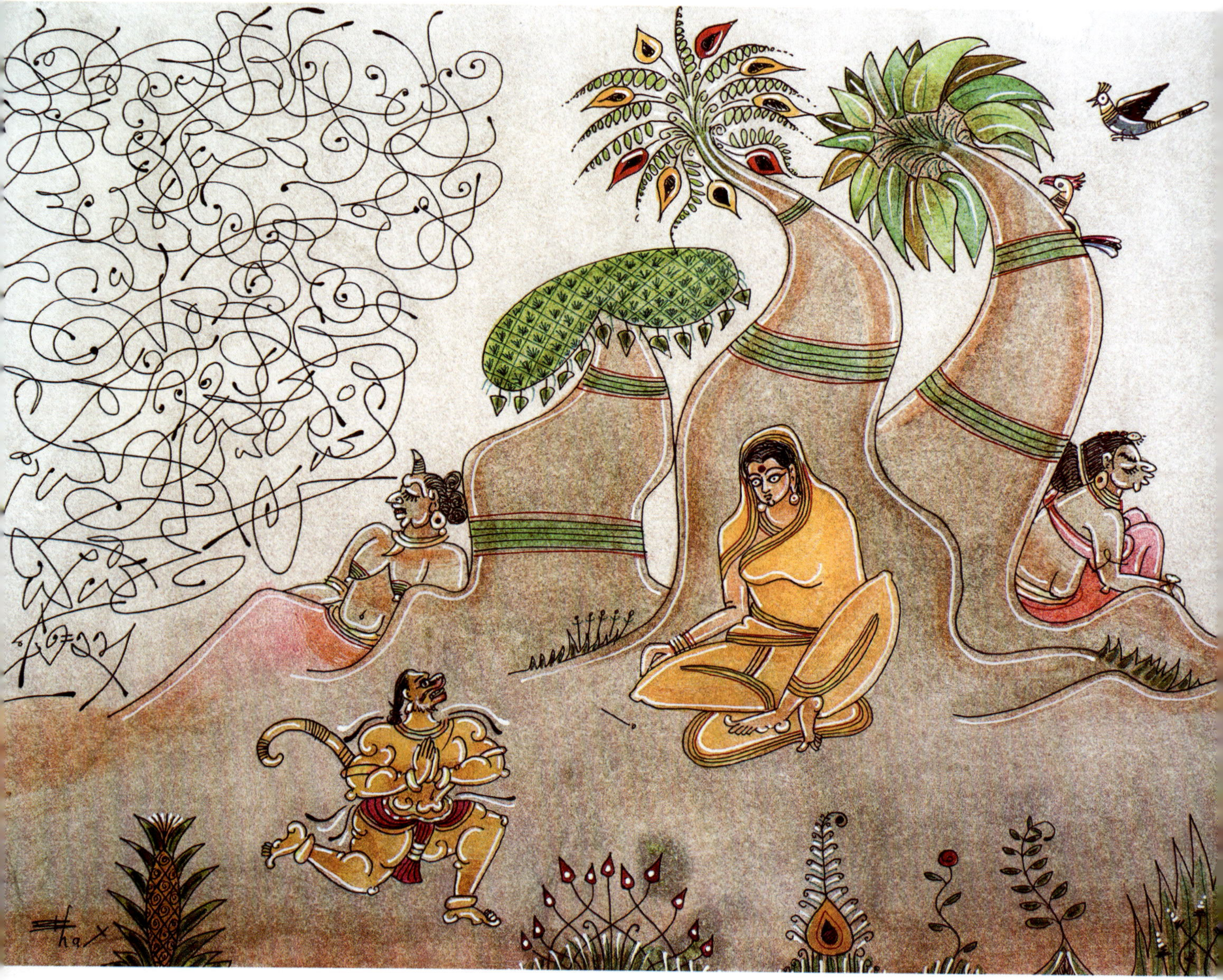

Hanuman finds Sita in Ashokavana
Watercolor and pen on paper, 36 x 27 cm

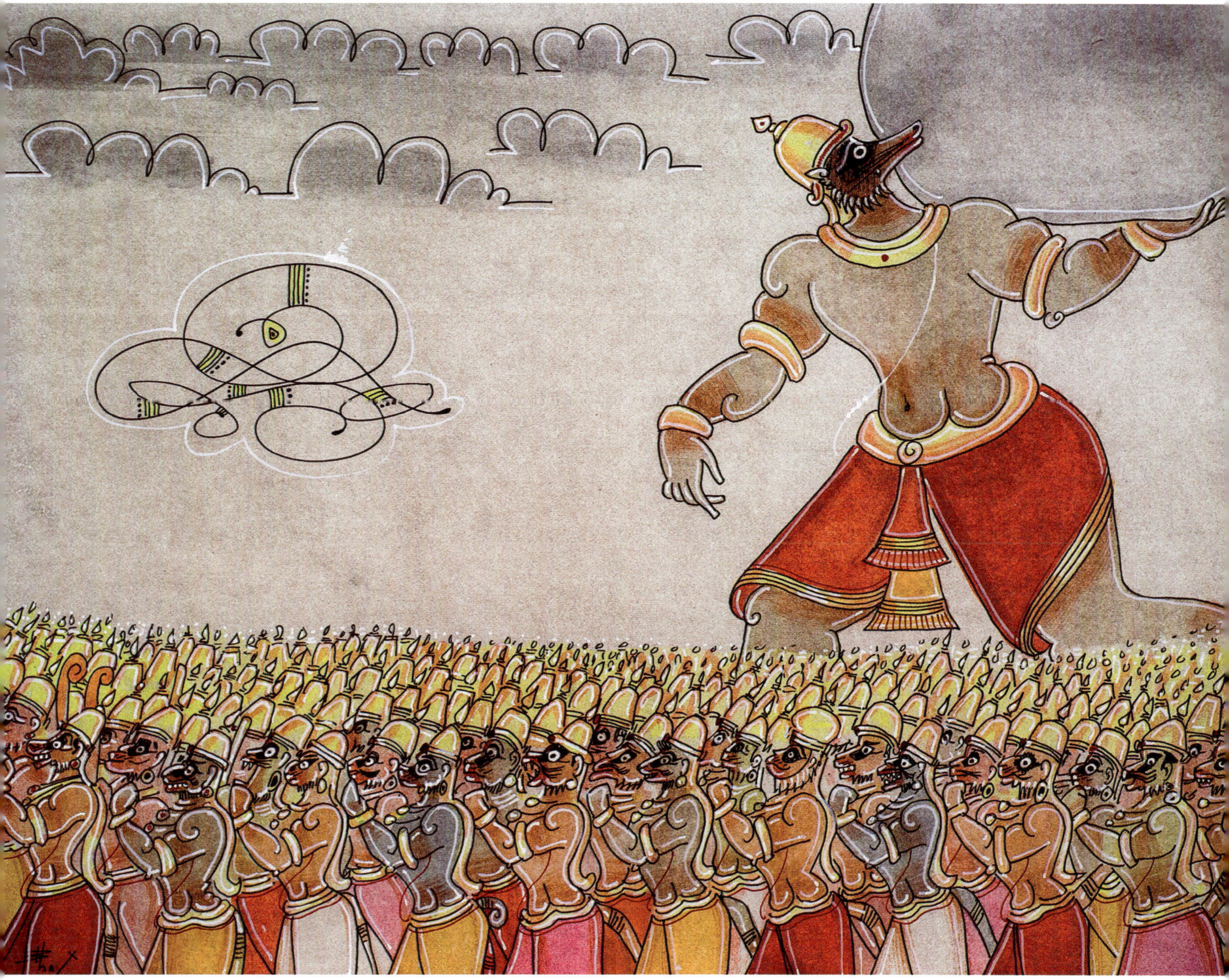

Jambavanta helps to build bridge
Watercolor and pen on paper, 36 x 27 cm

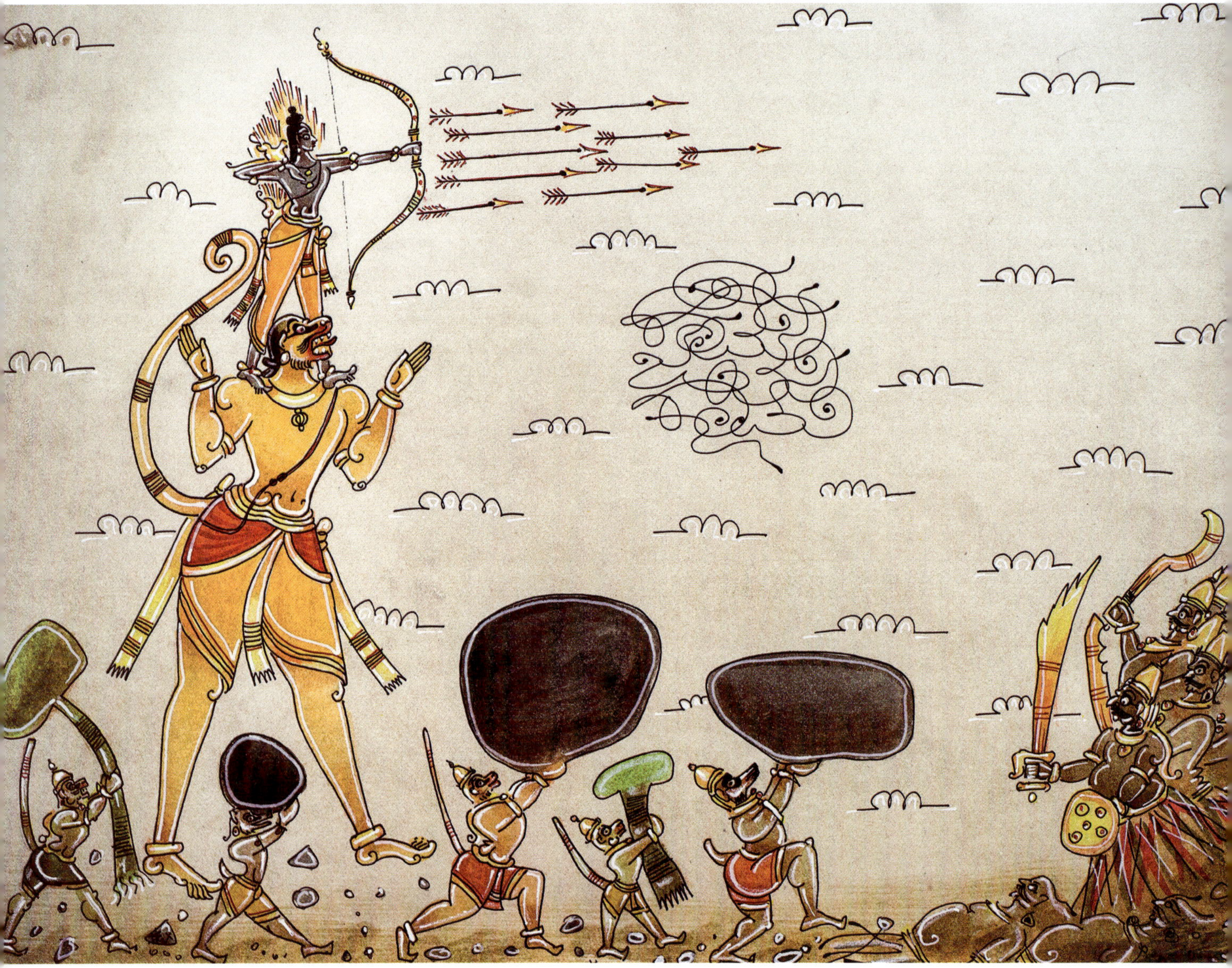

Rama and Ravana fight in Ayodha
Watercolor and pen on paper, 36 x 27 cm

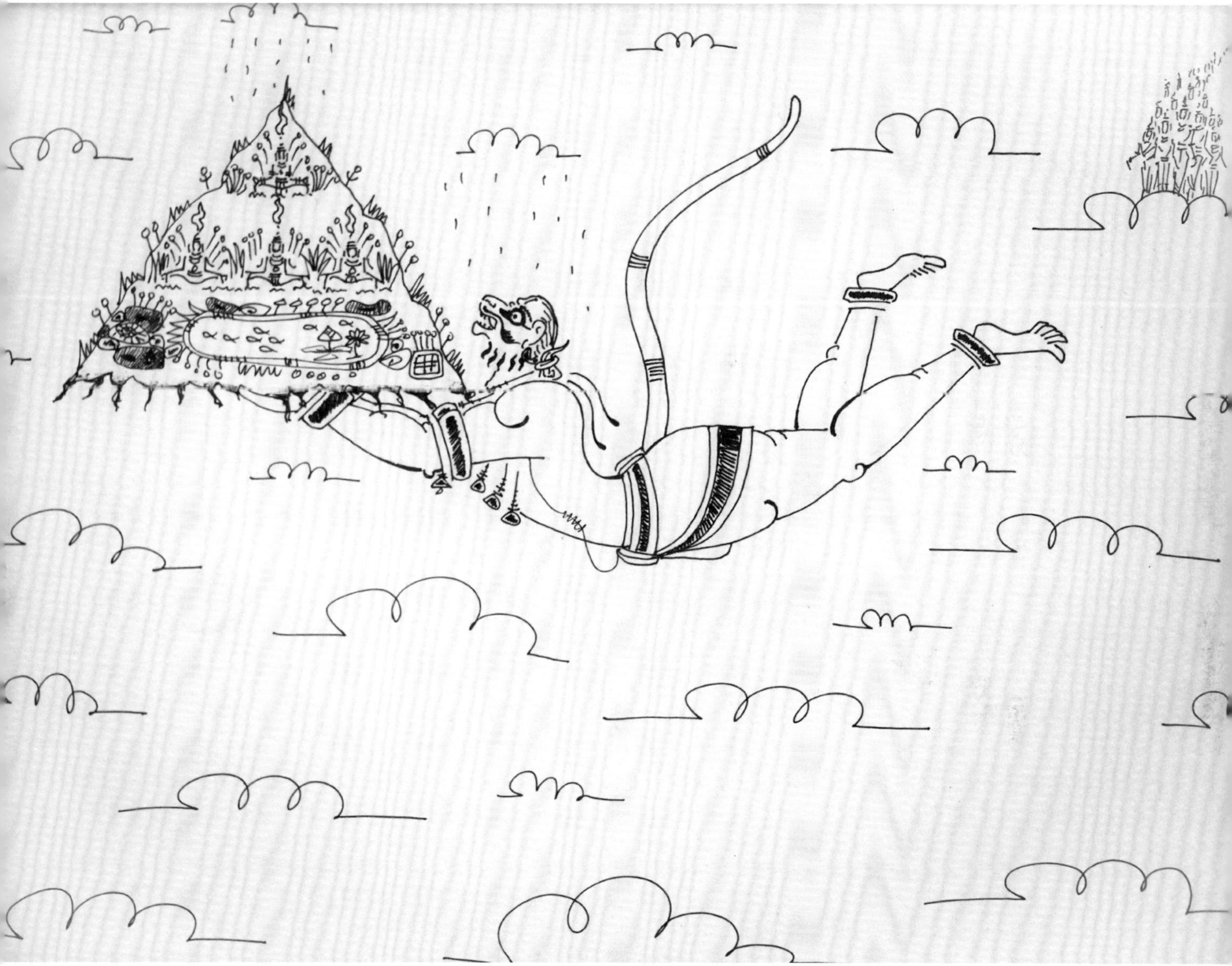

Hanuman carries Sanjivani
Pen on paper, 36 x 27 cm

Rama kills Ravana >
Watercolor and pen on paper, 36 x 27 cm

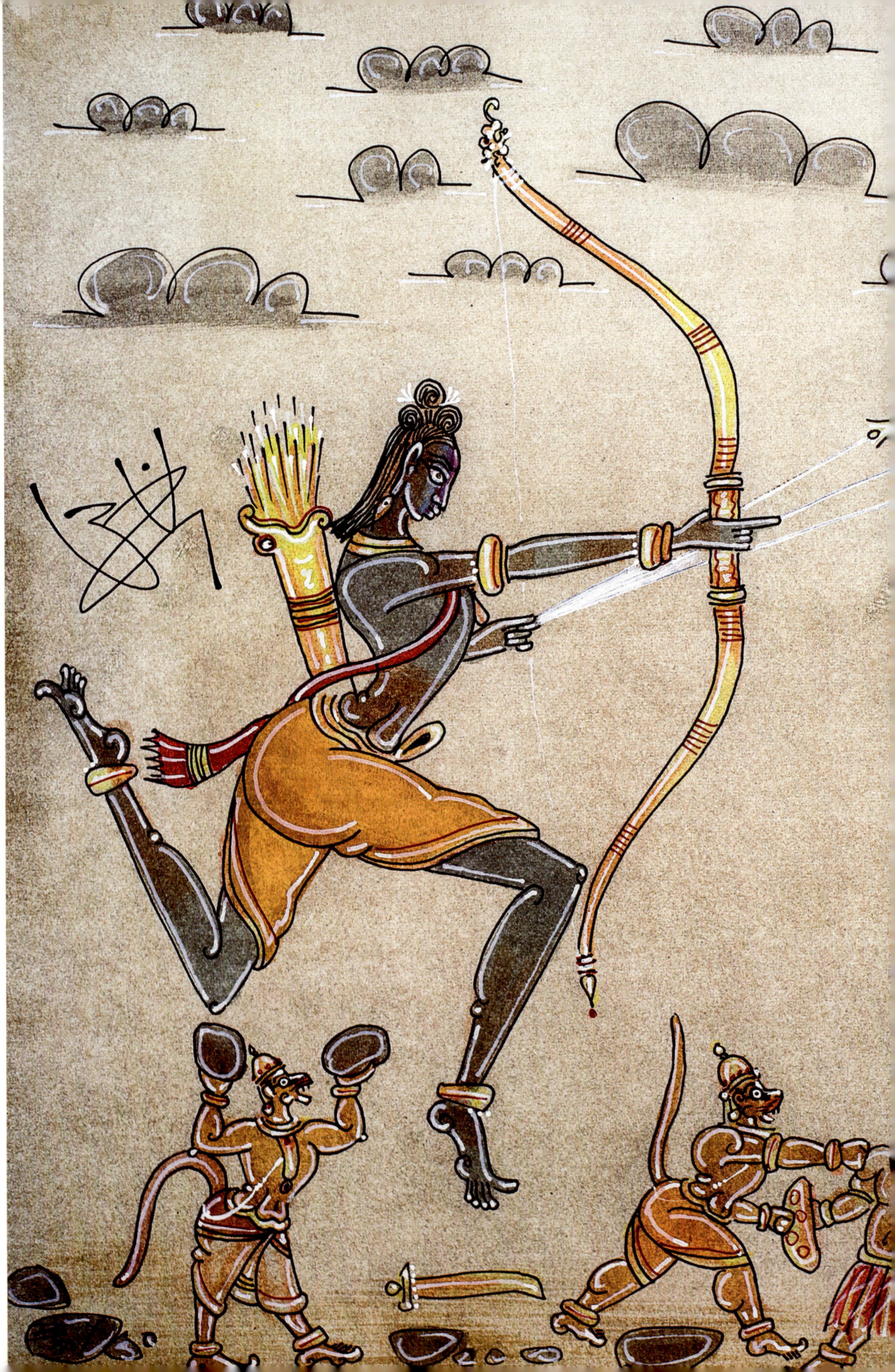

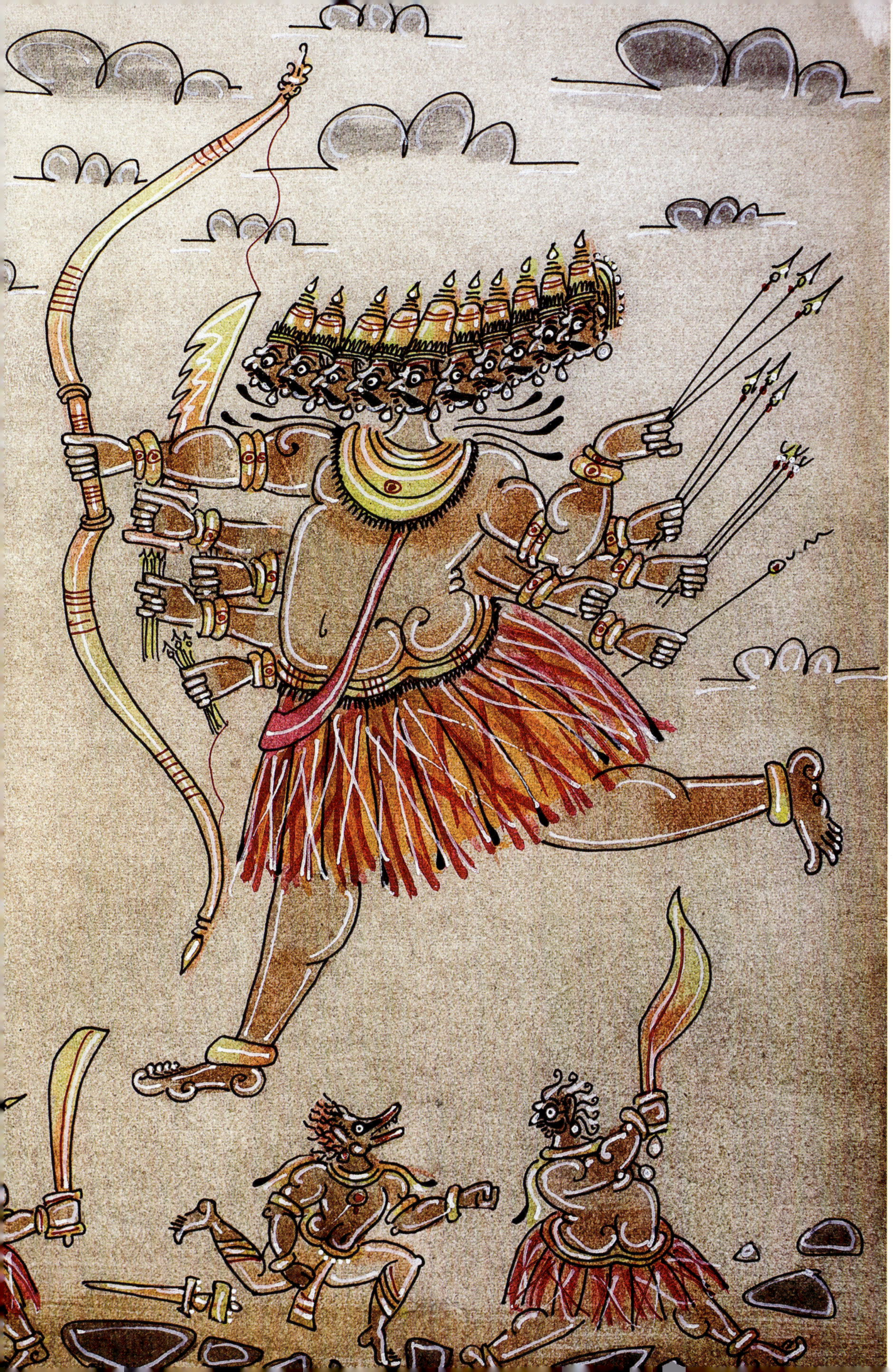

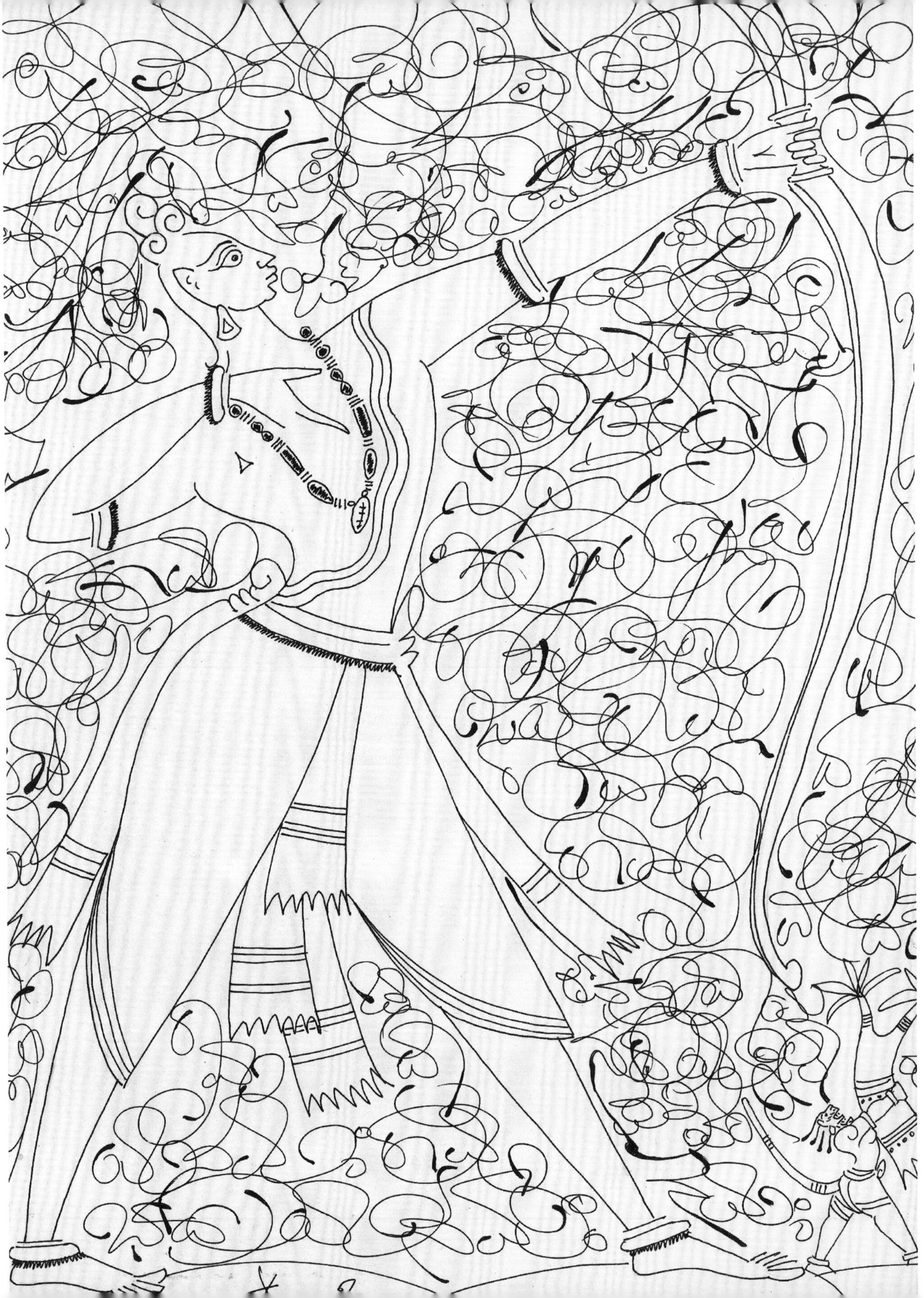

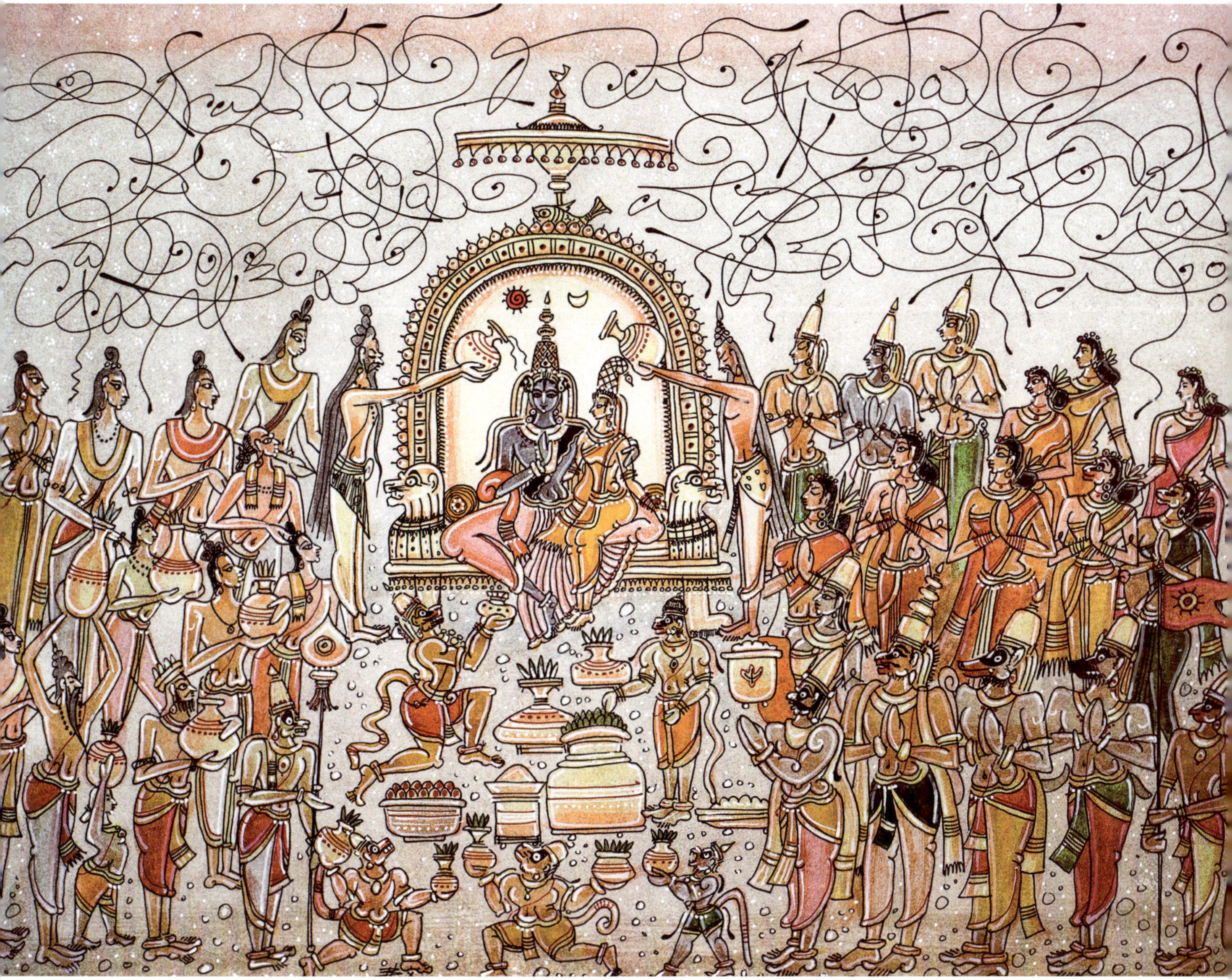

The coronation of Rama and Sita
Watercolor and pen on paper, 36 x 27 cm

< Rama wins the battle against Ravana
Pen on paper, 36 x 27 cm

Lava and Kusha singing Rama's glories >
Pen on paper, 36 x 27 cm

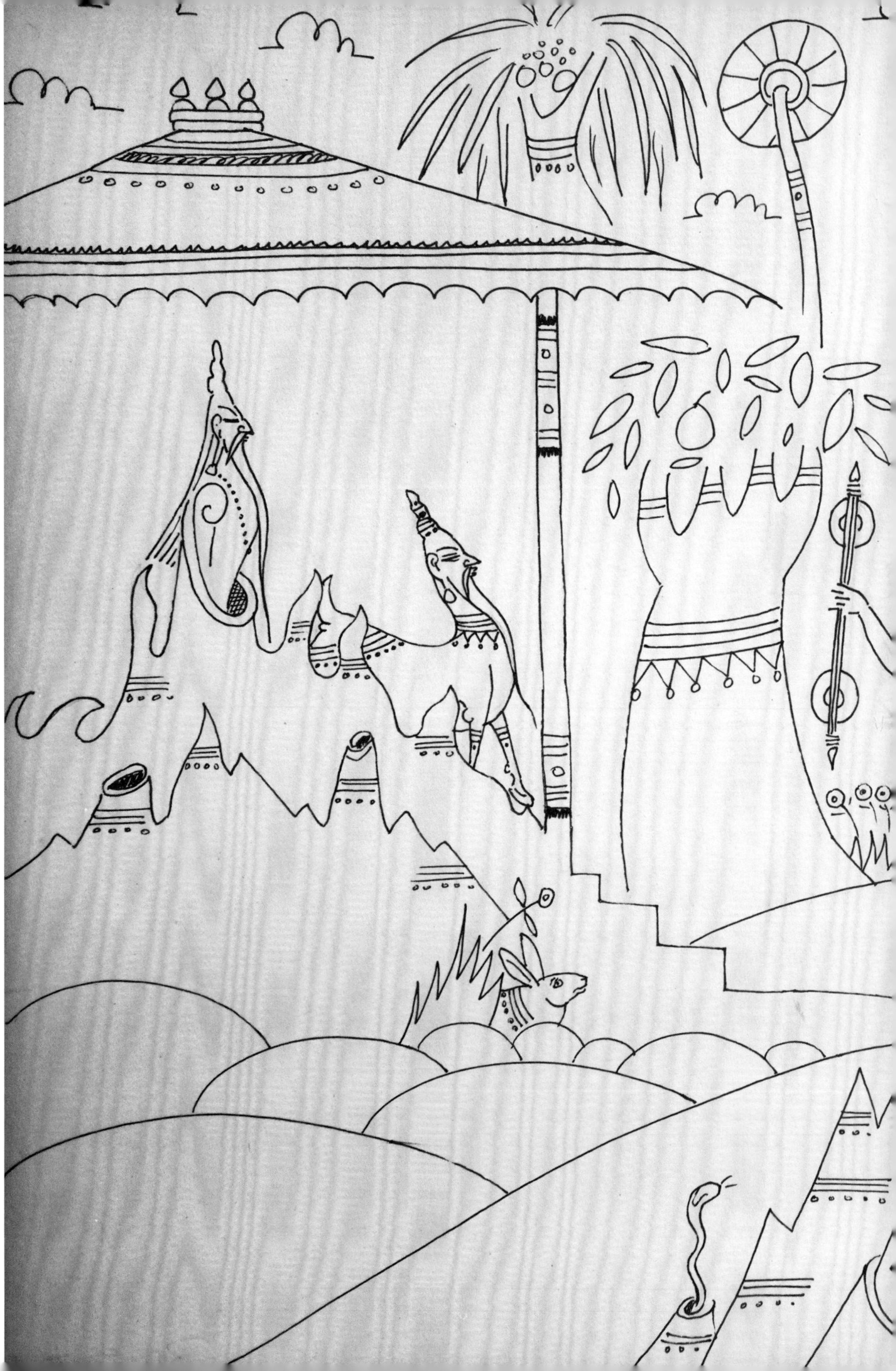

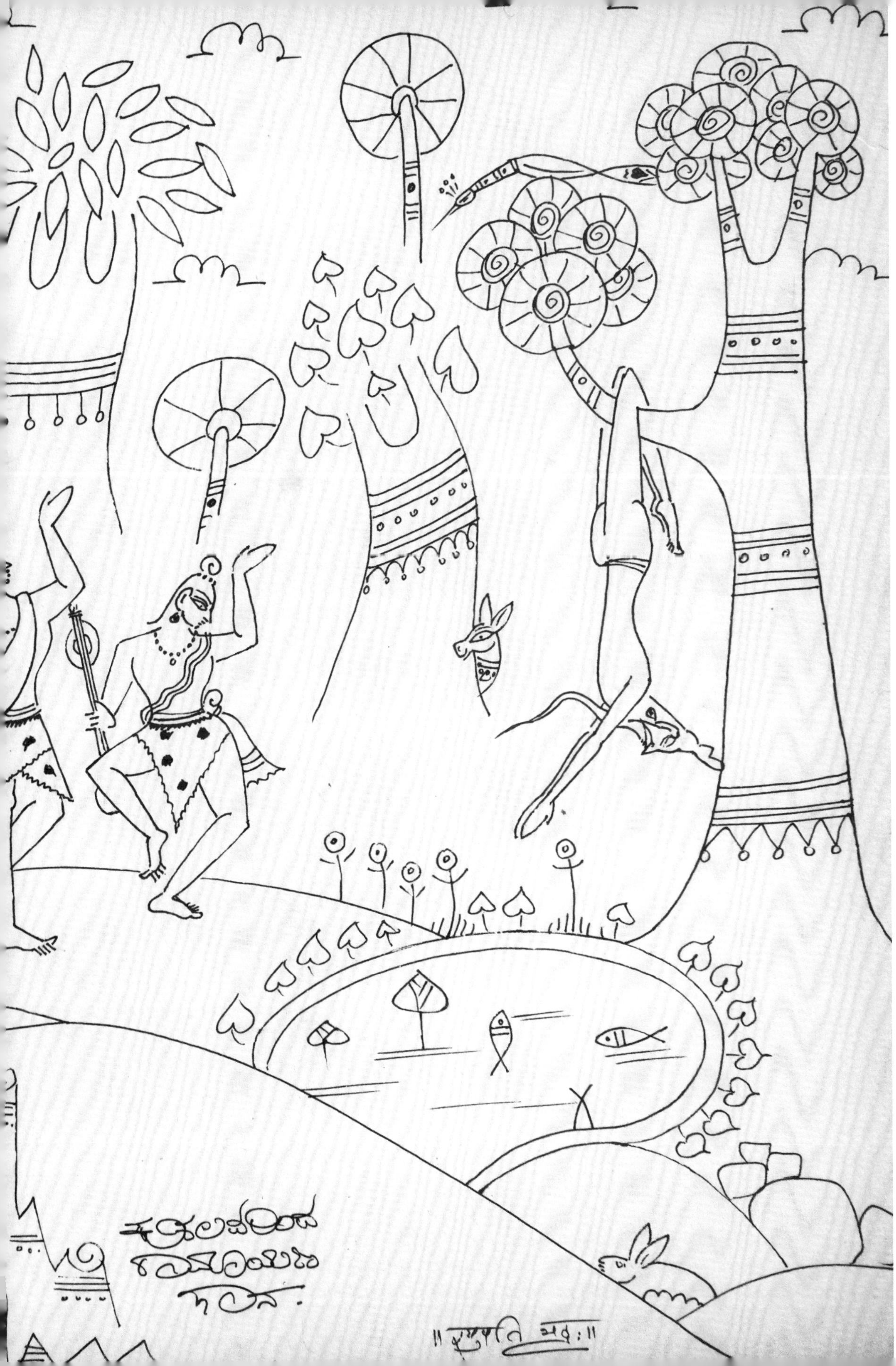

MAHABARATA

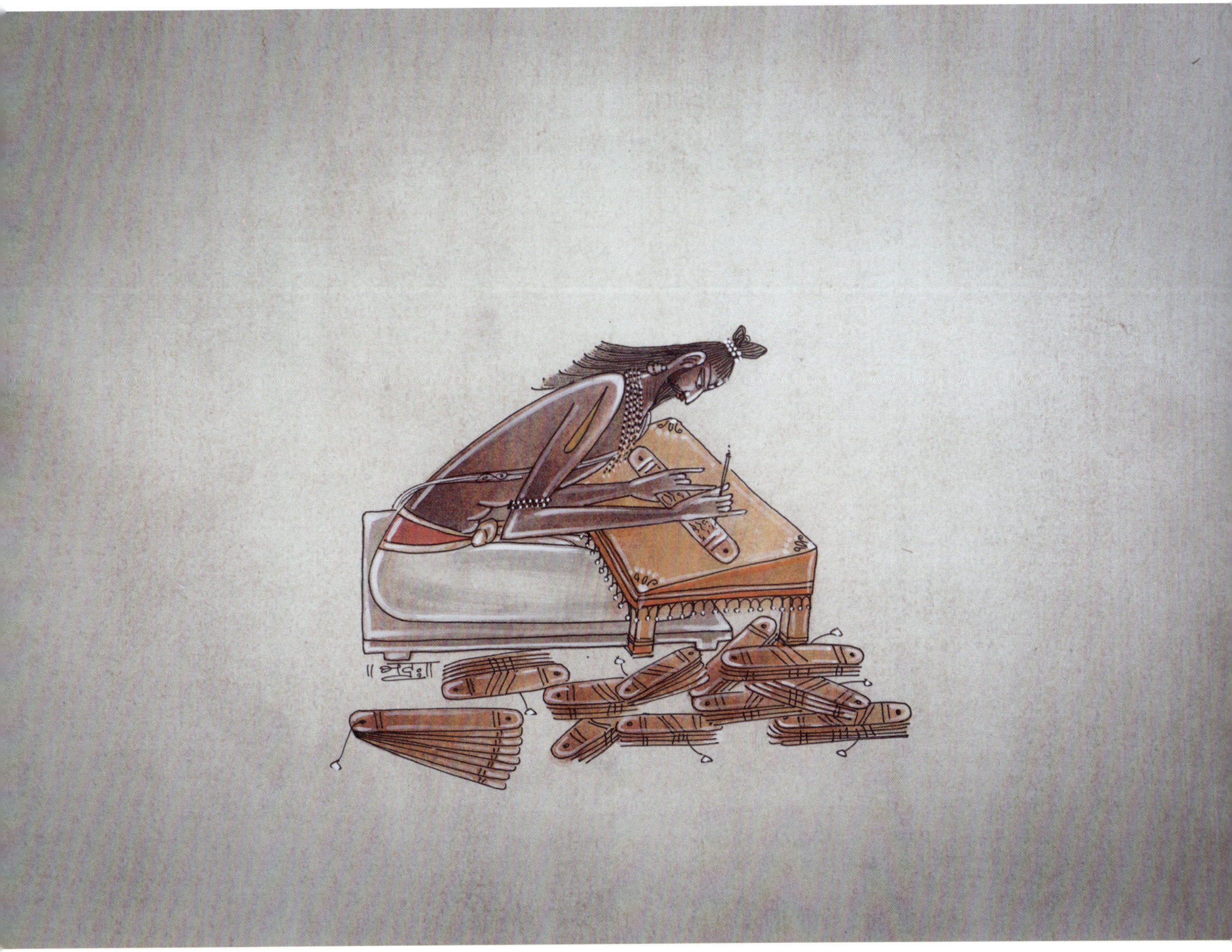

Vyasa writes the Mahabarata
Watercolor and pen on paper, 36 x 27 cm

Veda-vyasa blesses Ambika to bring about the next generation >
Watercolor and pen on paper, 36 x 27 cm

Janamejaya and Vyshampayana >>
Watercolor and pen on paper, 36 x 27 cm

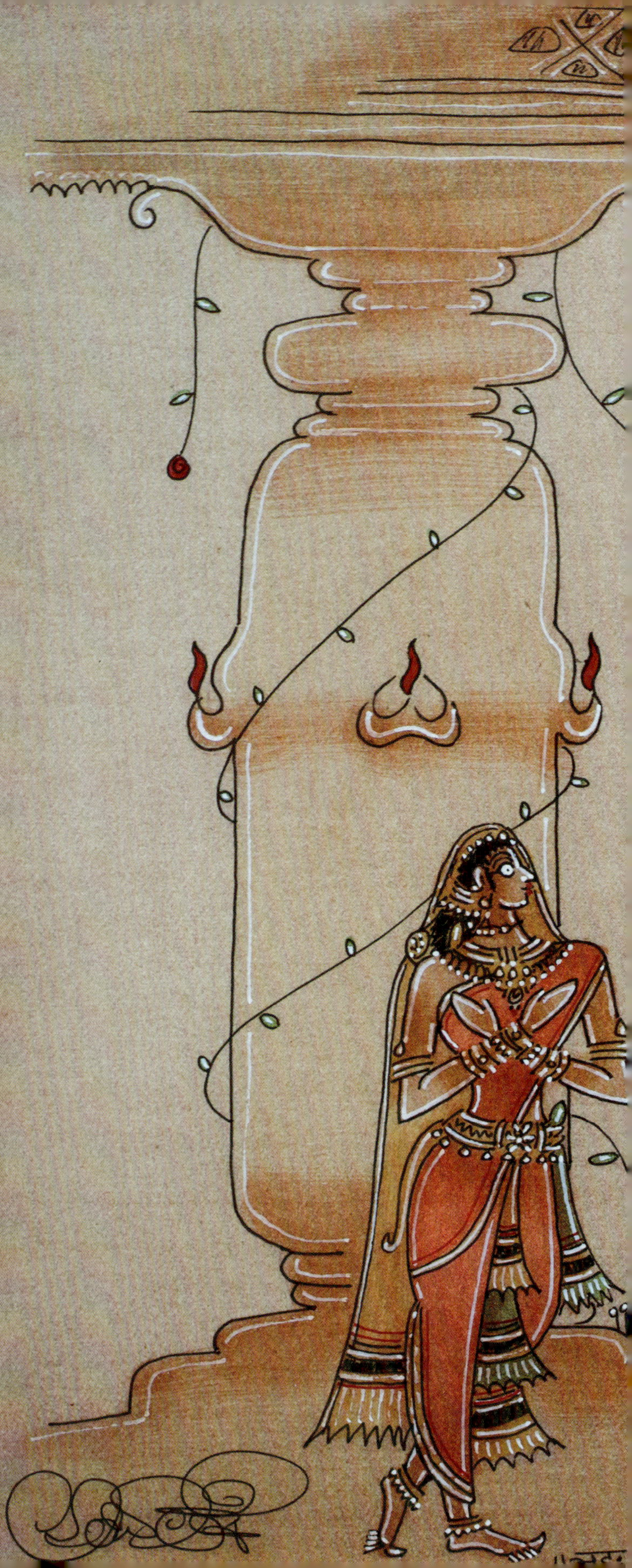

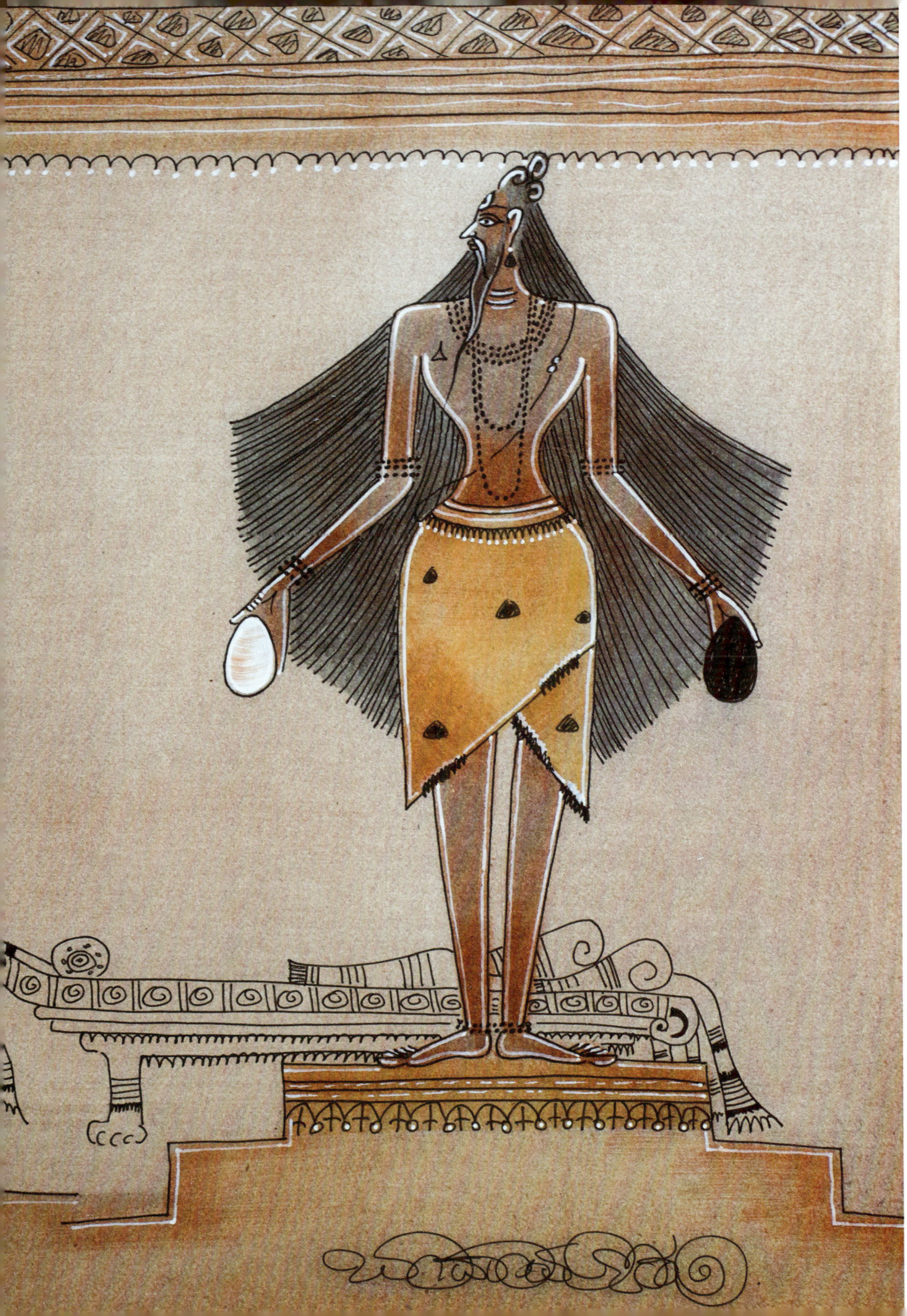

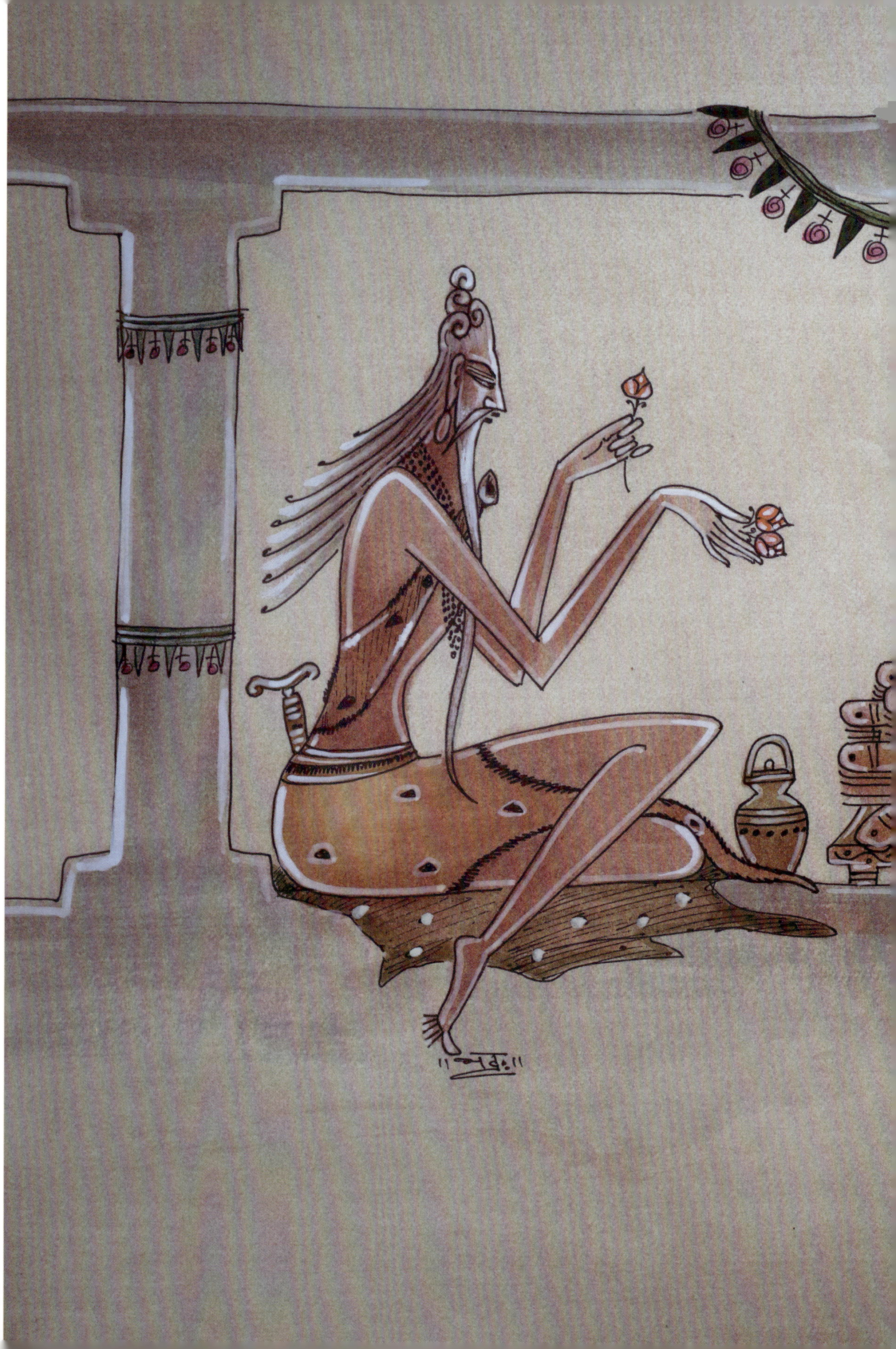

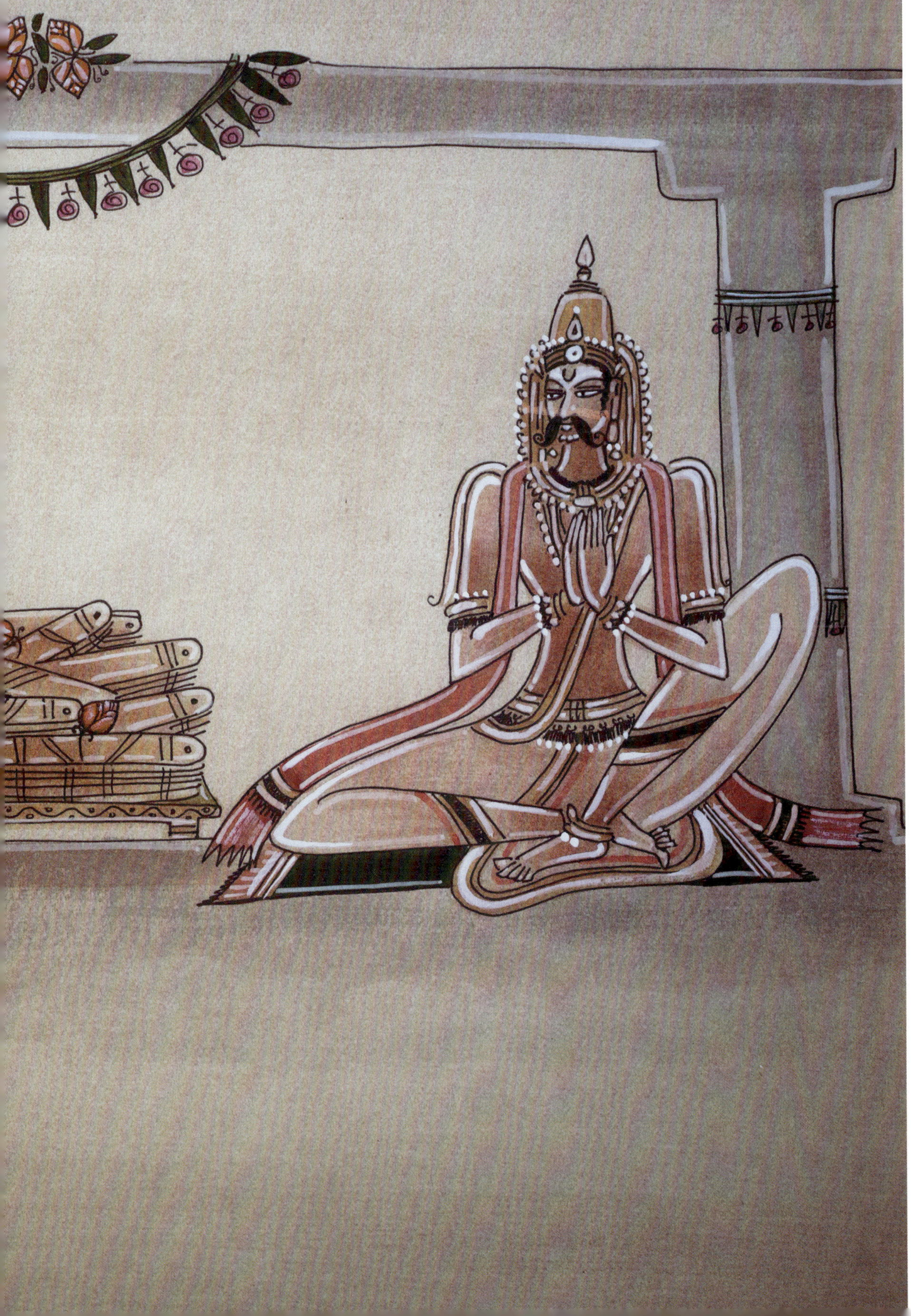

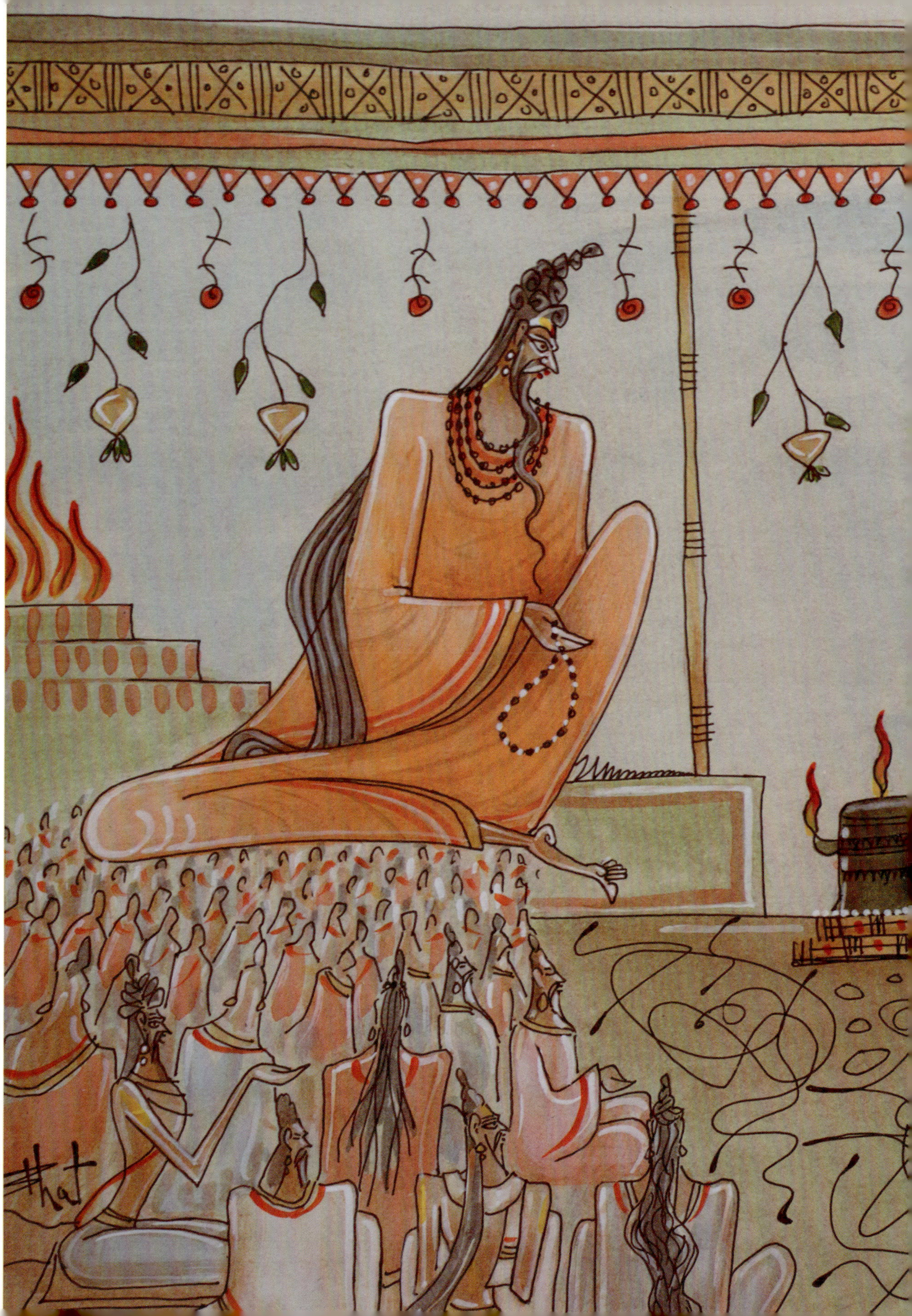

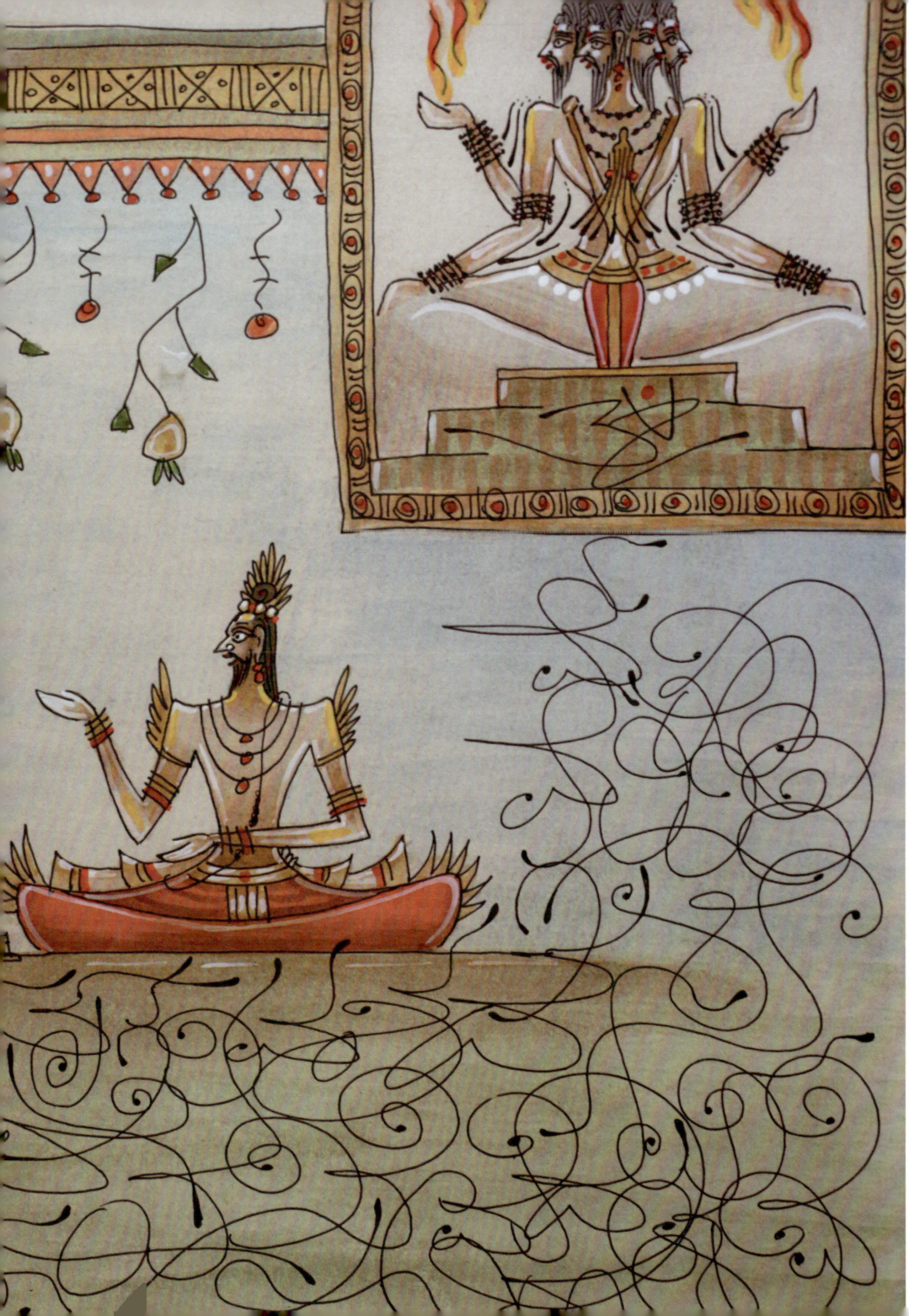

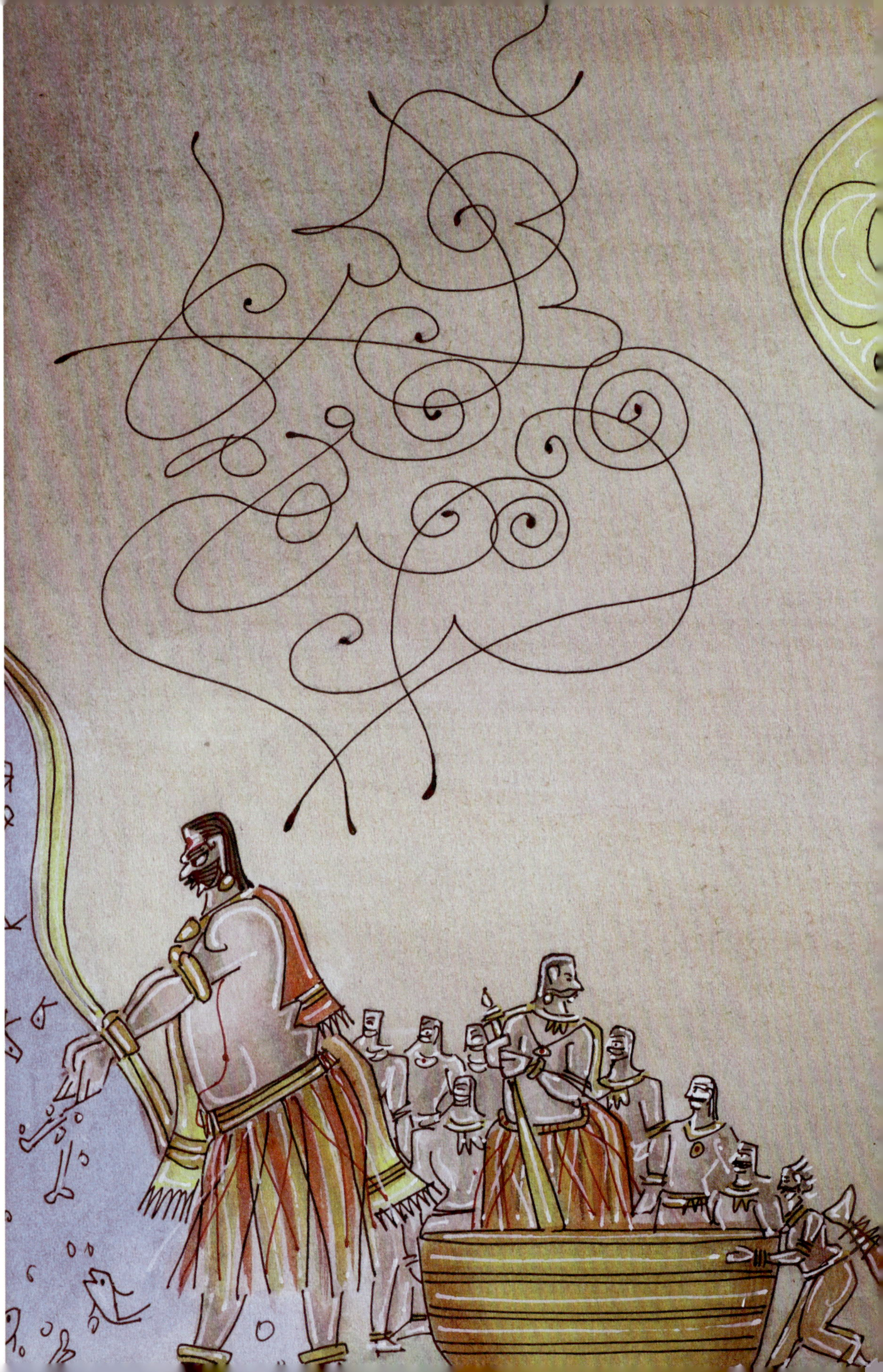

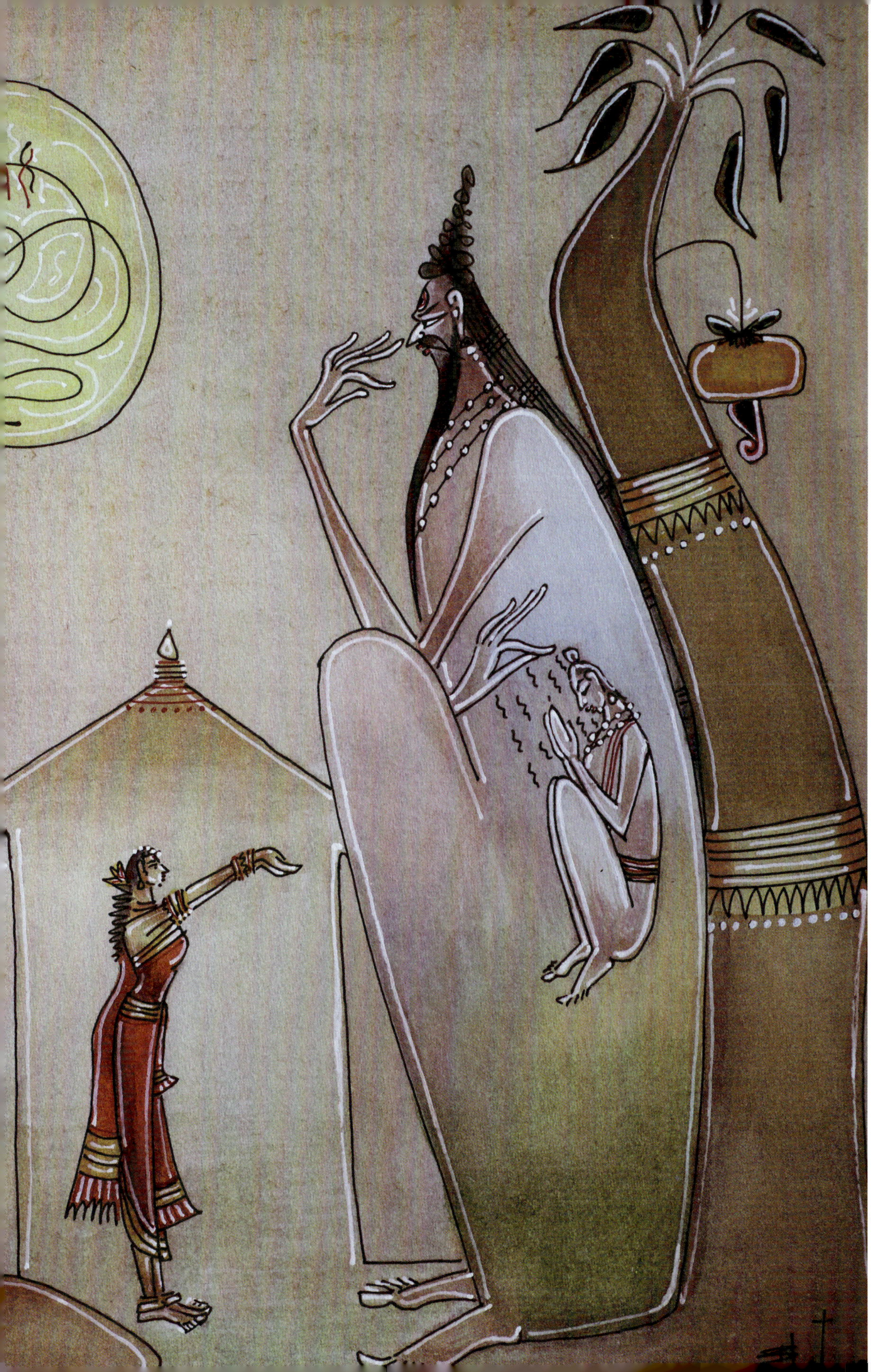

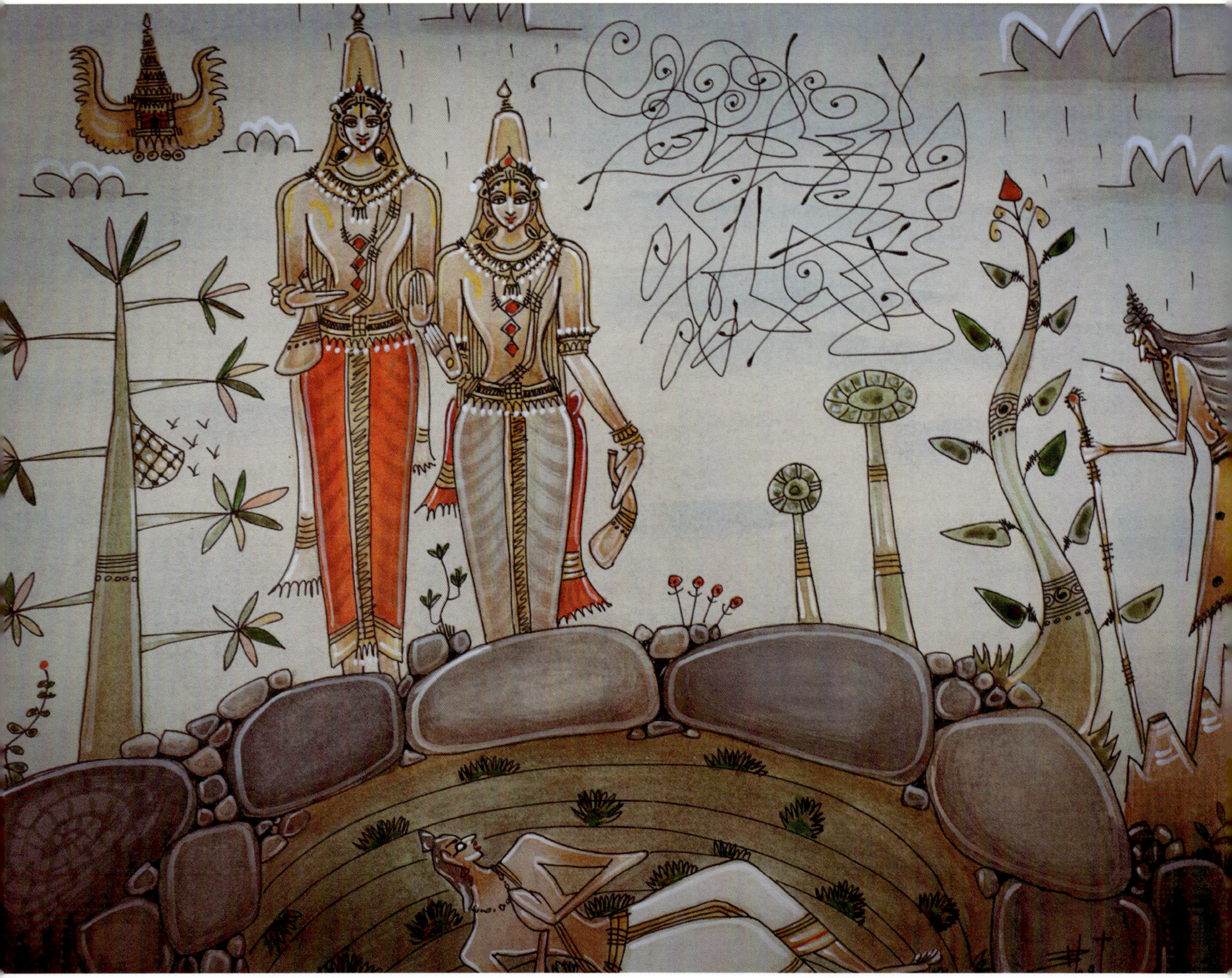

The Ashvini-devas give eyes to Utthamamanyu
Watercolor and pen on paper, 36 x 27 cm

< Mrita-sanjivani to Khacha by Shukracharya and Devayani
Watercolor and pen on paper, 36 x 27 cm

<< Sutapuranika's conversation
Watercolor and pen on paper, 36 x 27 cm

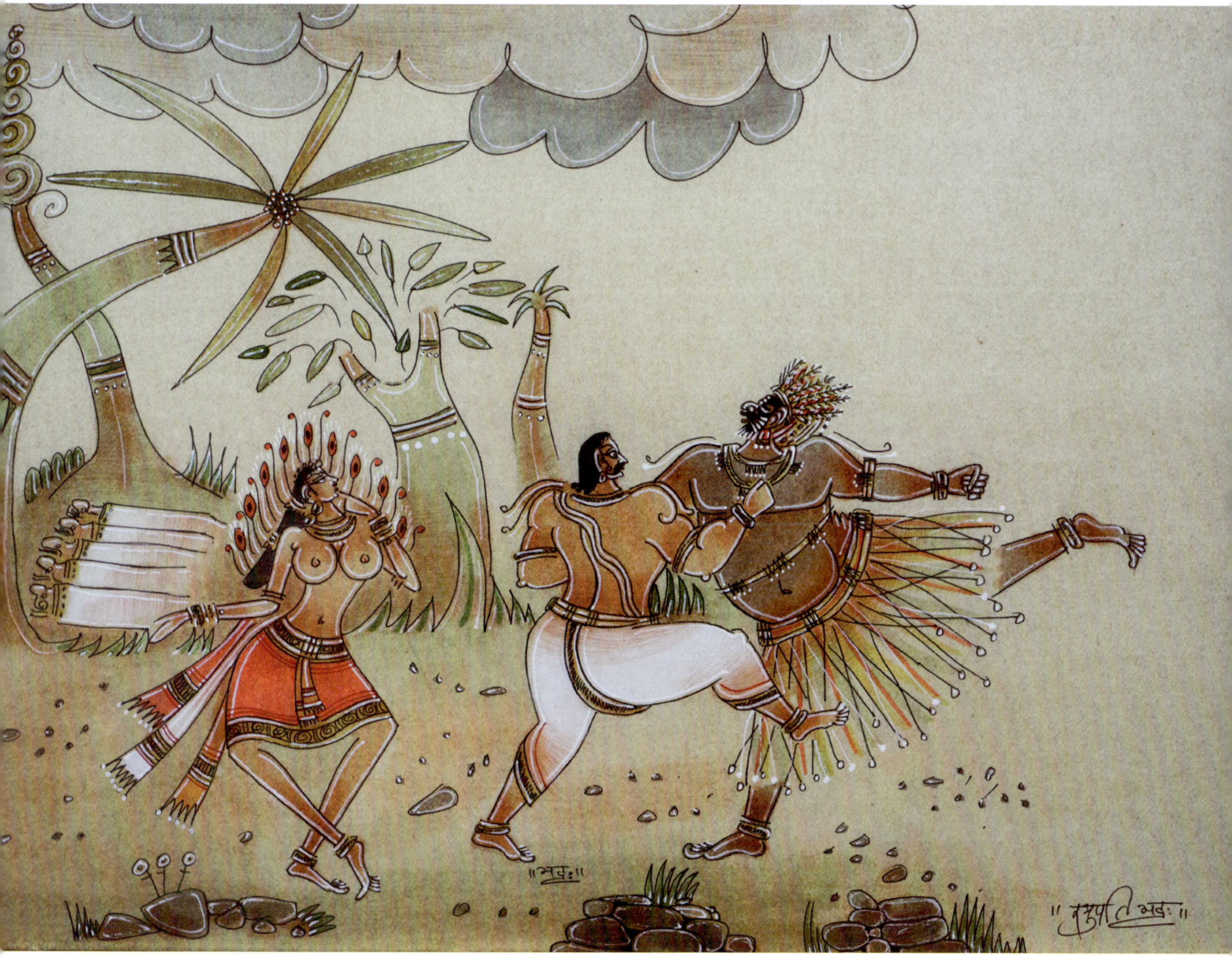

The defeat of the demon Hidimbasura
Watercolor and pen on paper, 36 x 27 cm

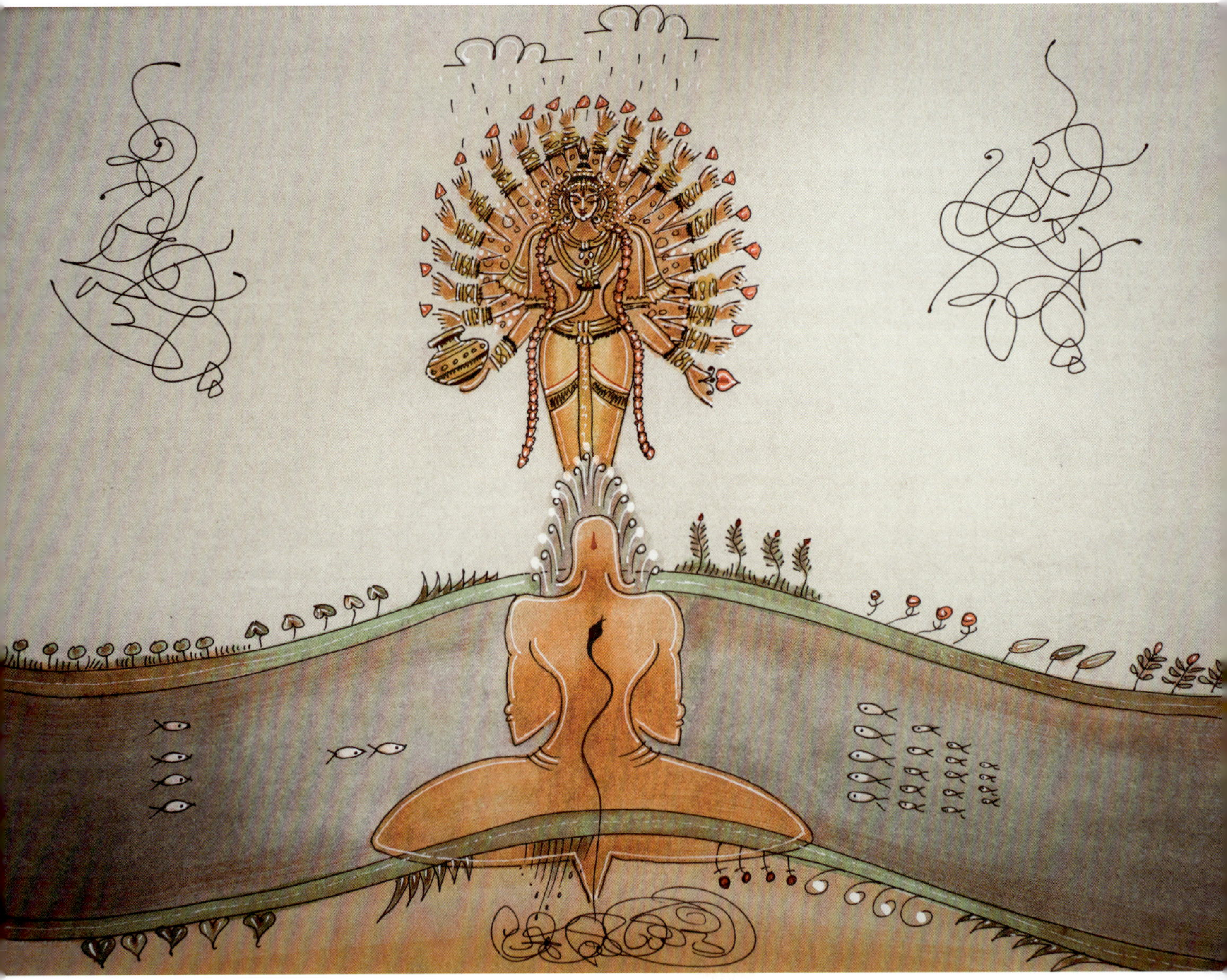

Dharmaraya receives Akshaya-patre from Surya-deva
Watercolor and pen on paper, 36 x 27 cm

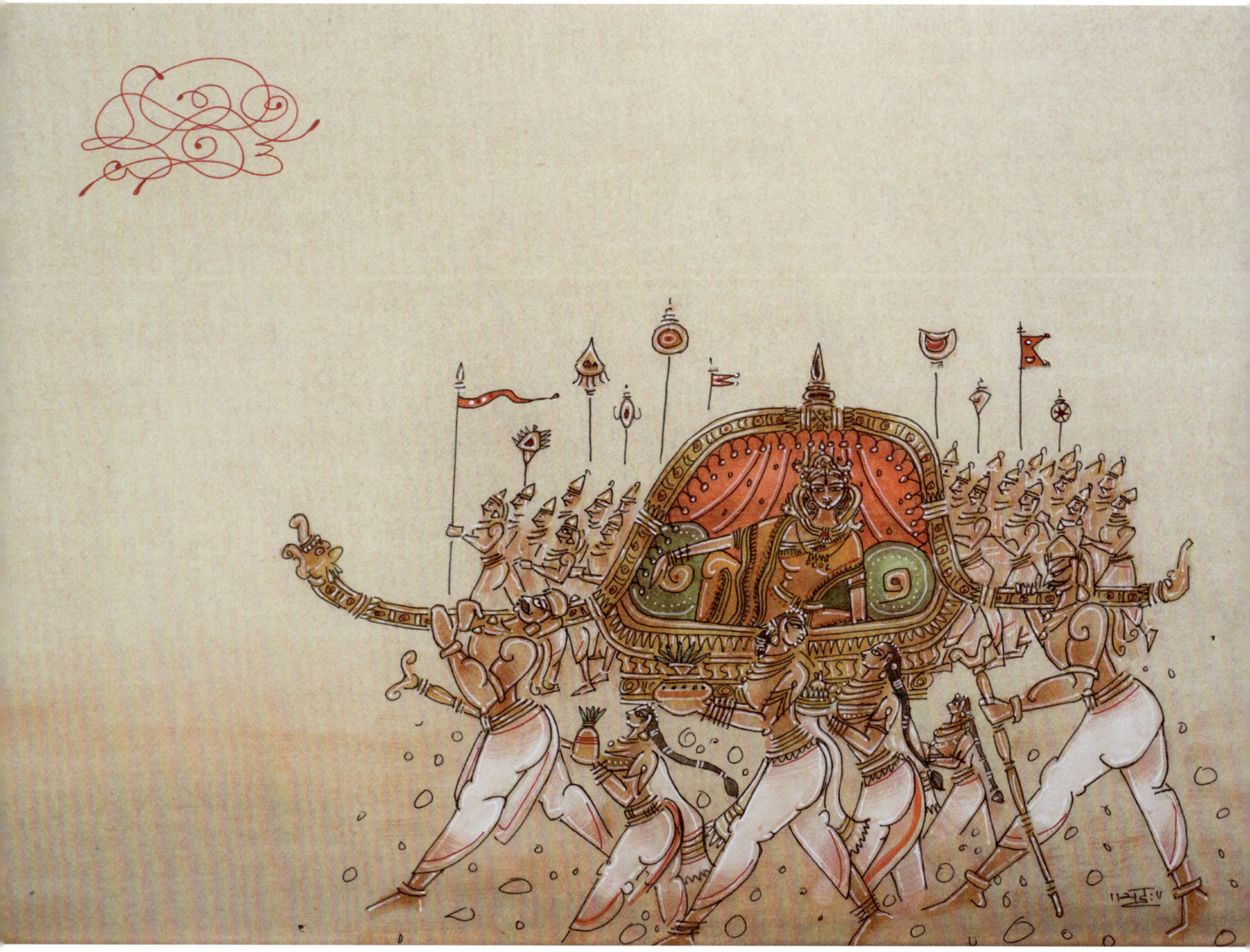

Draupadi on her way to Swayamvara
Watercolor and pen on paper, 36 x 27 cm

Karna offers his Kavacha and Kundala >
Watercolor and pen on paper, 36 x 27 cm

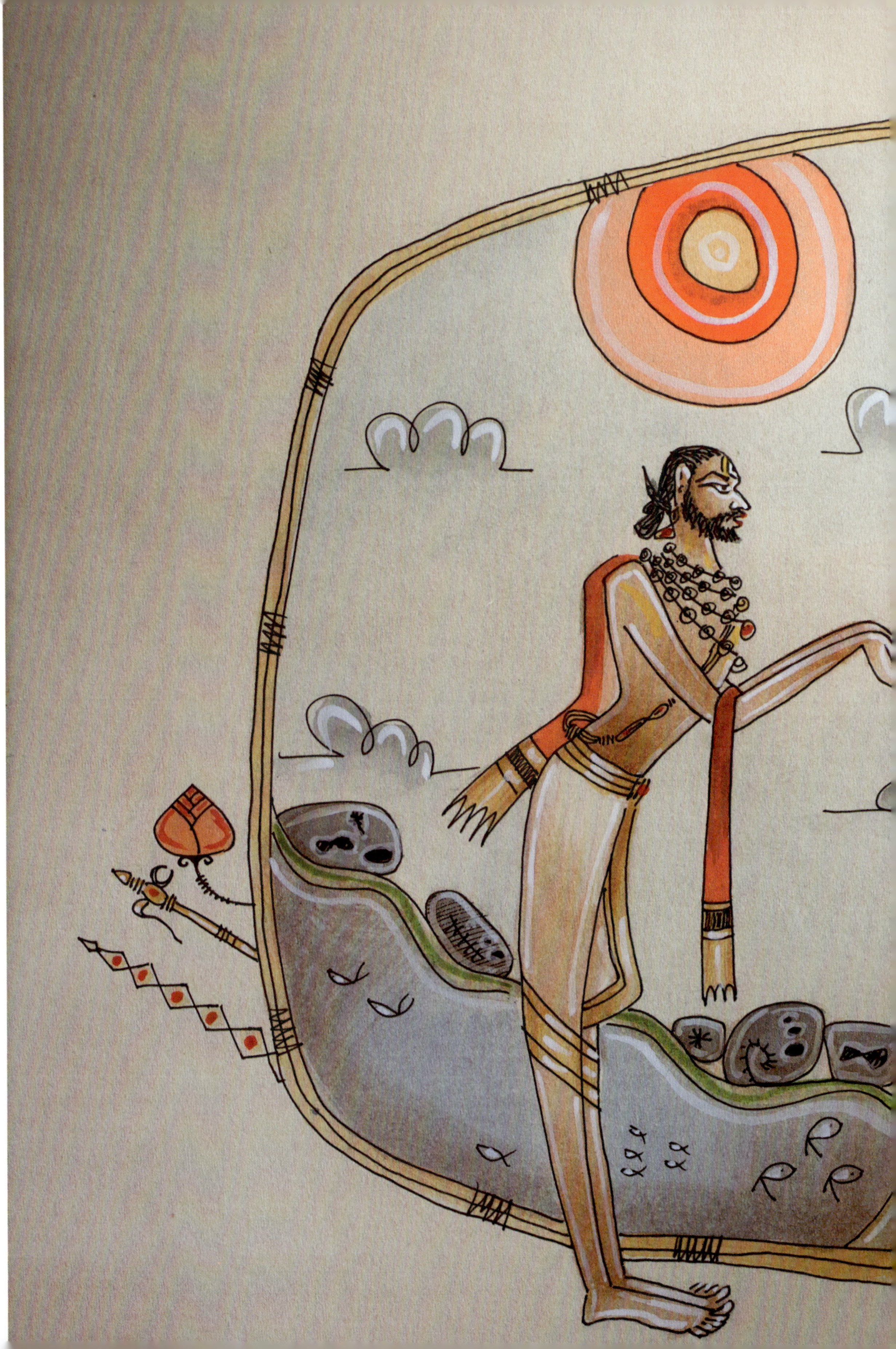

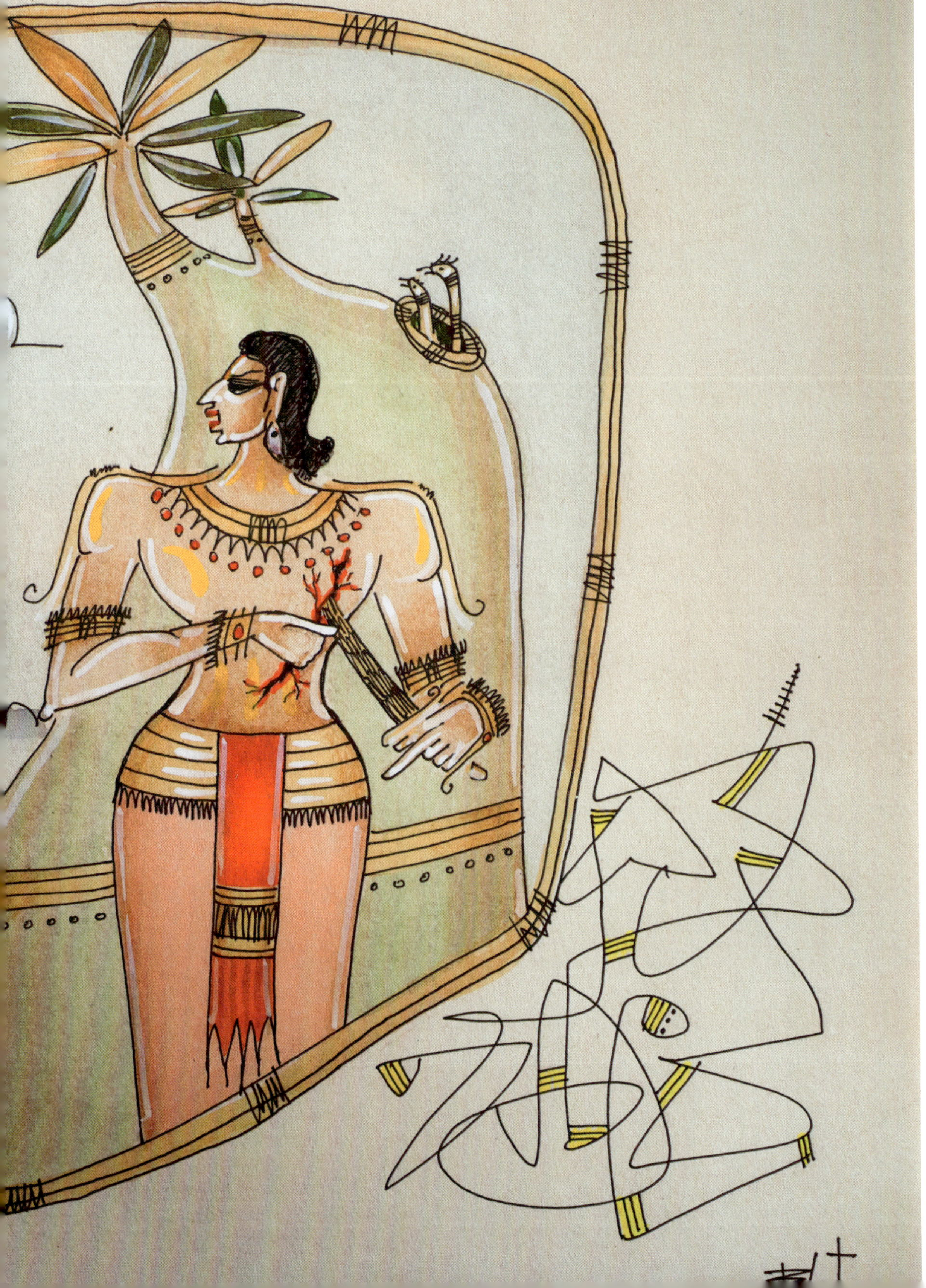

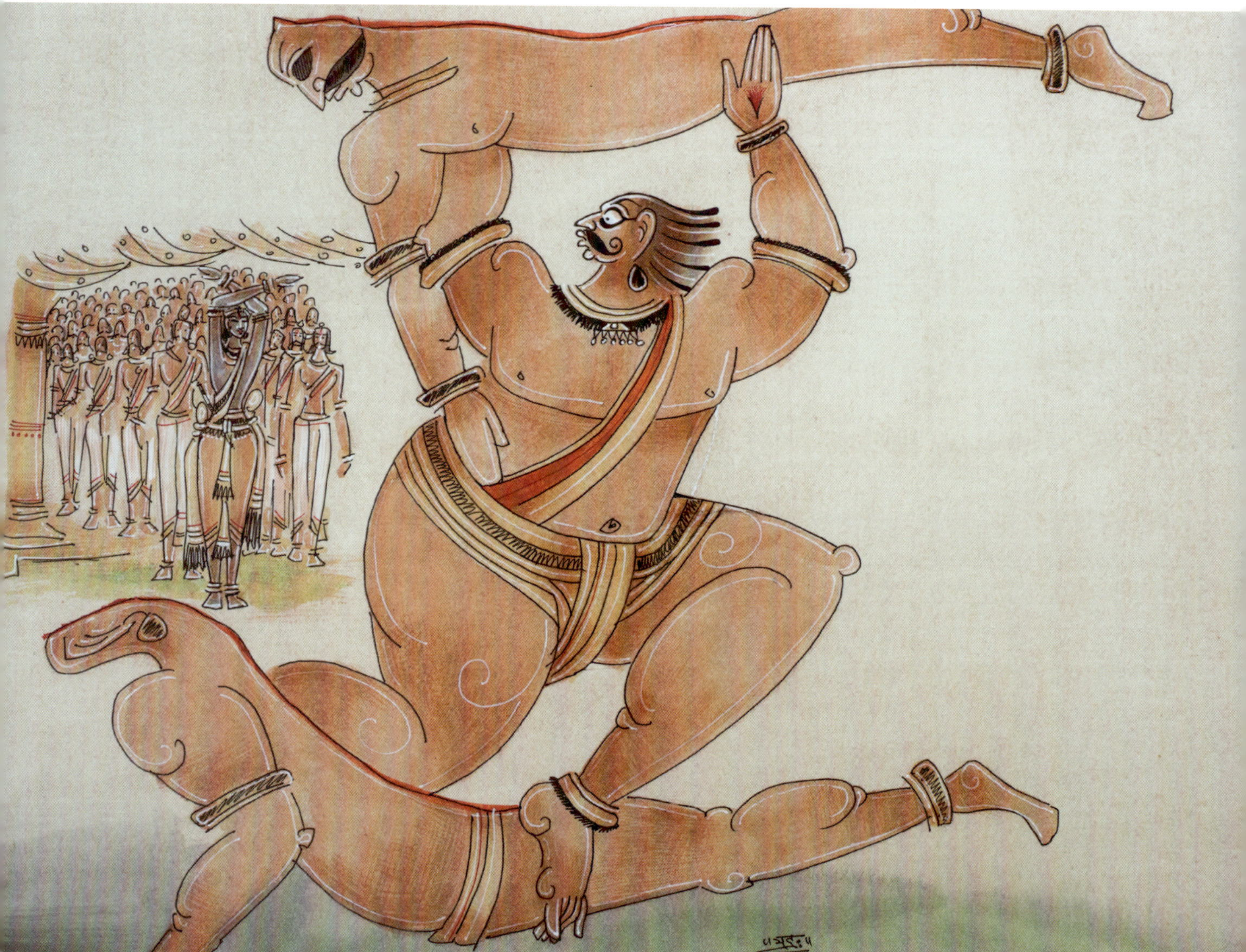

Bhima kills Jarasanda
Watercolor and pen on paper, 36 x 27 cm

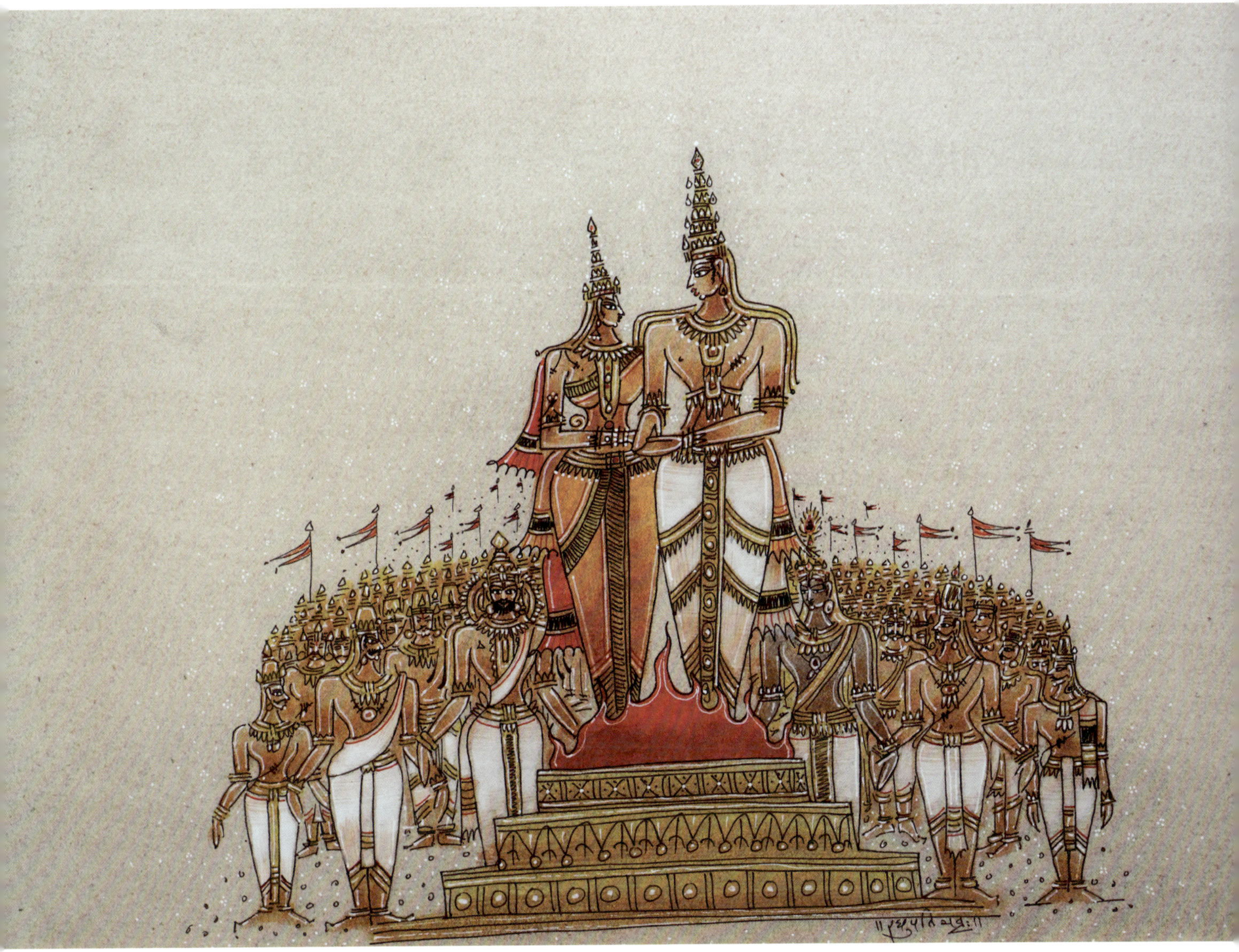

Abhimayu's wedding
Watercolor and pen on paper, 36 x 27 cm

Sanatsujata converses with Vidura and Drutarashtra >
Watercolor and pen on paper, 36 x 27 cm

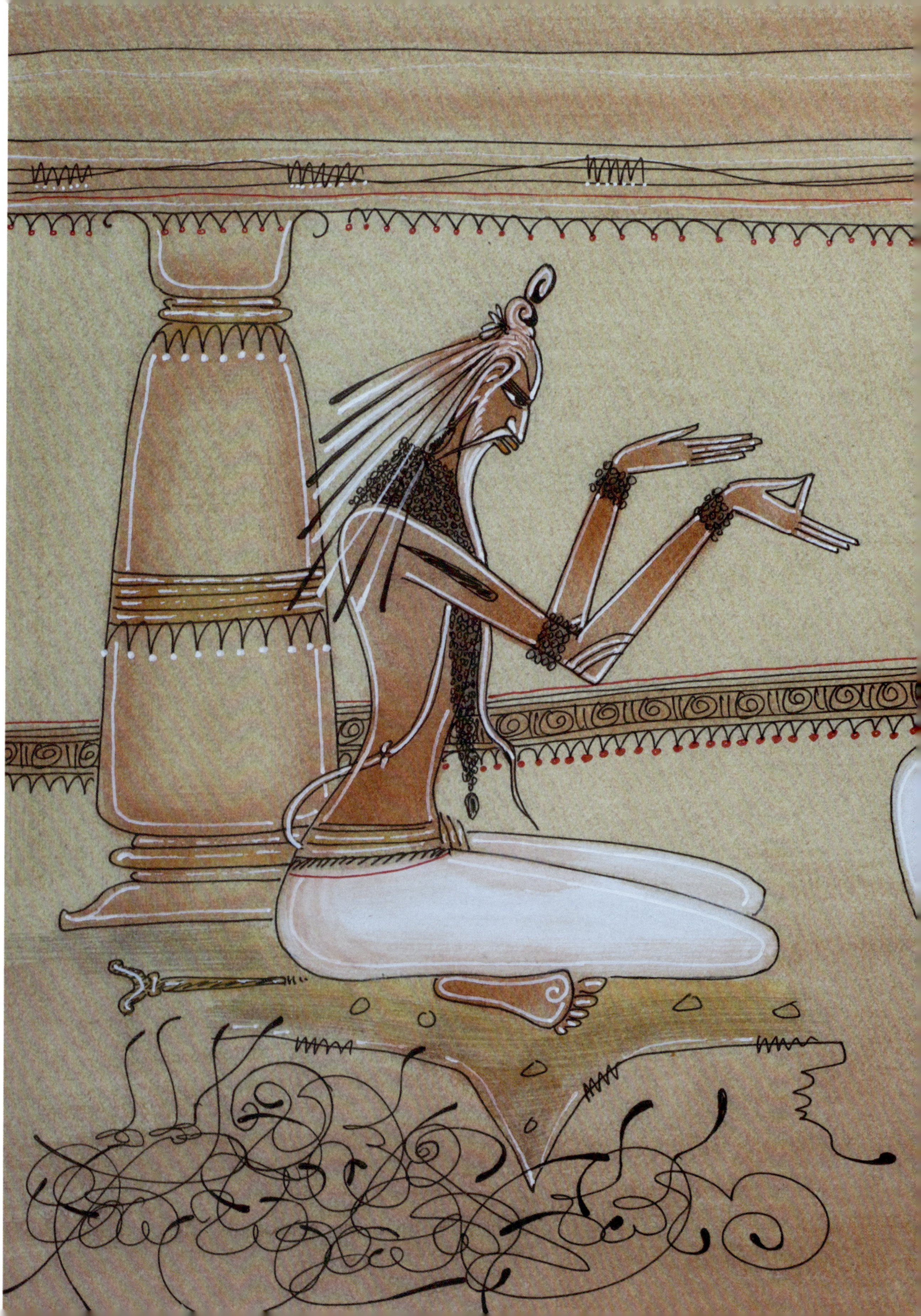

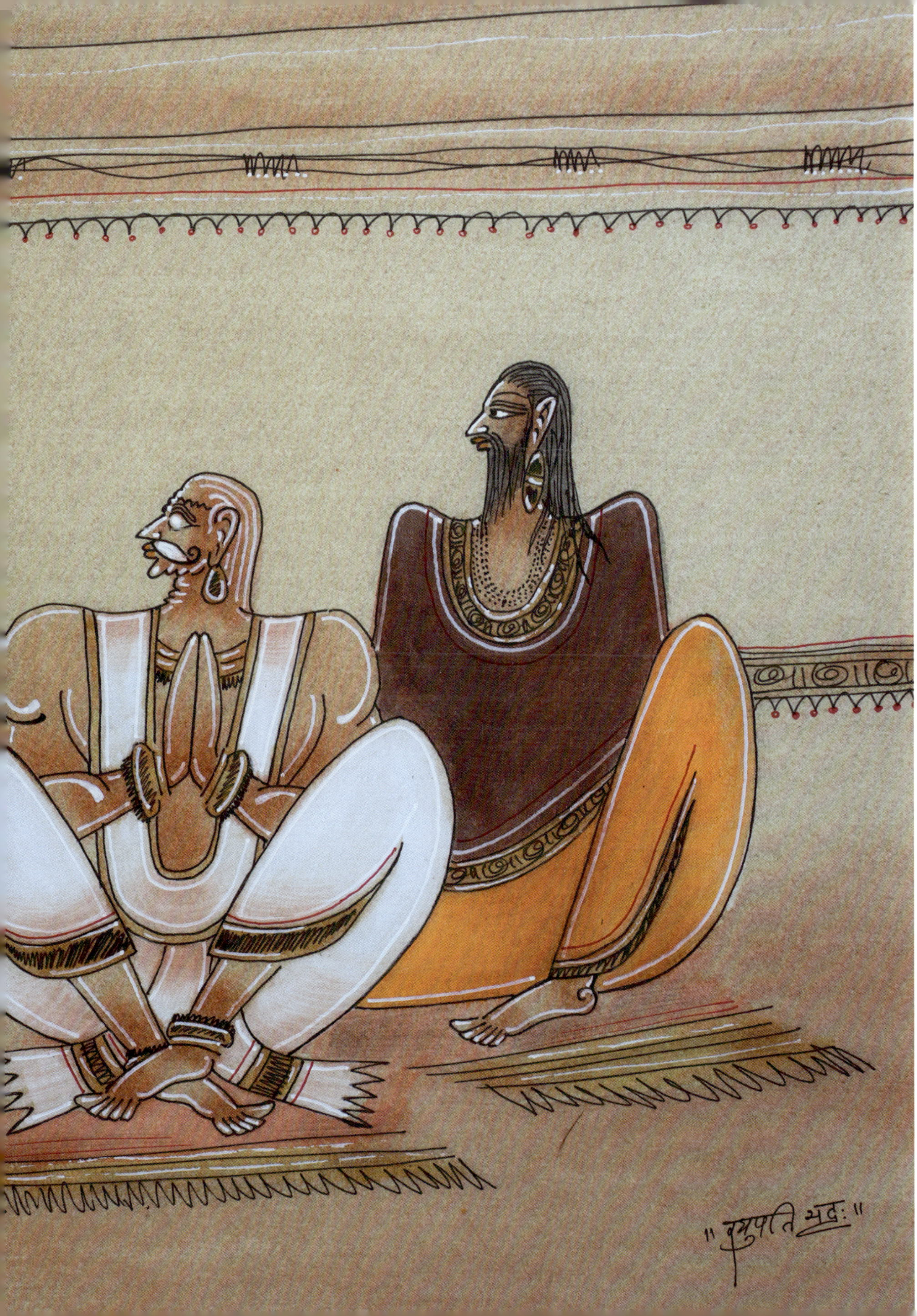

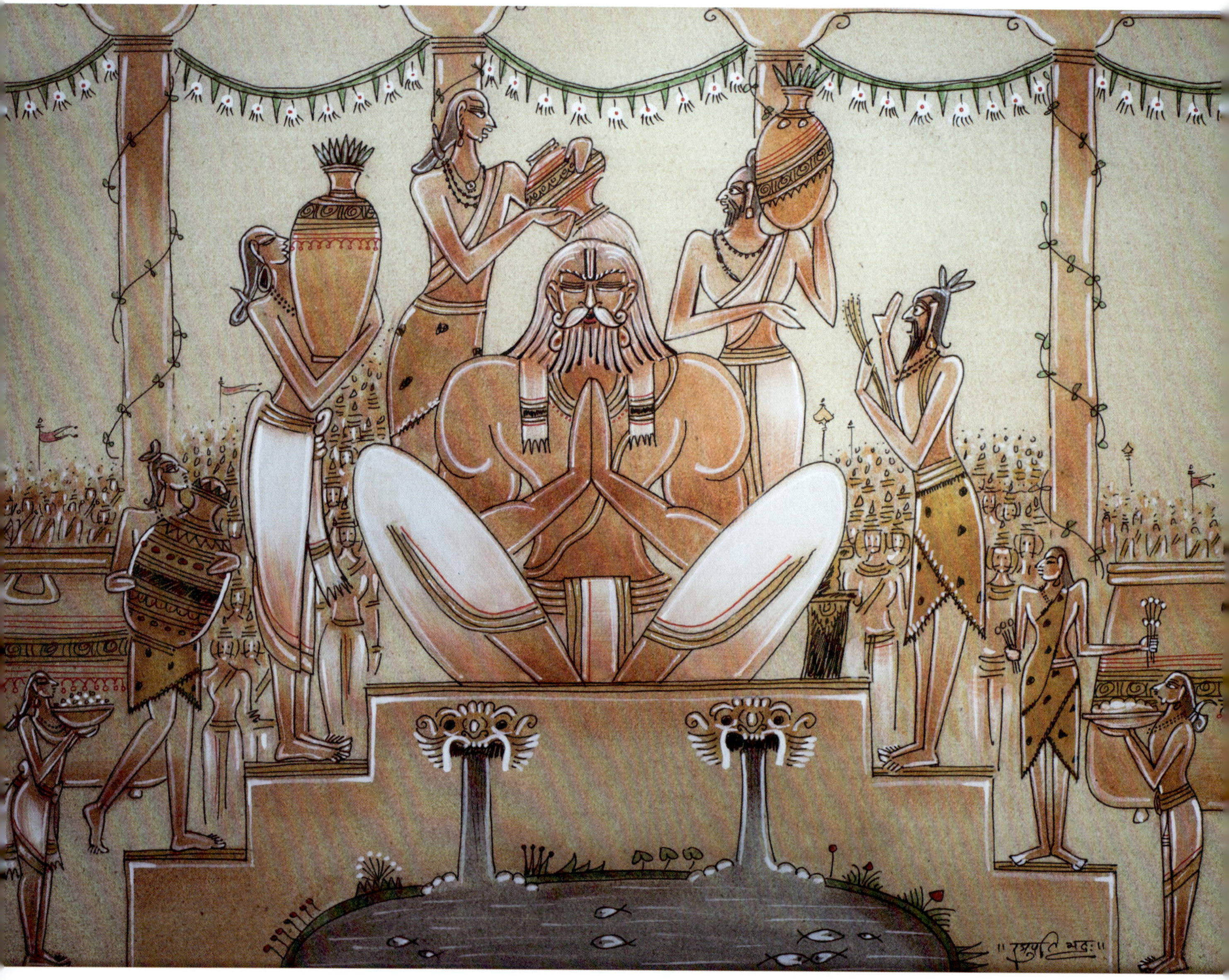

Bhishma's coronation
Watercolor and pen on paper, 36 x 27 cm

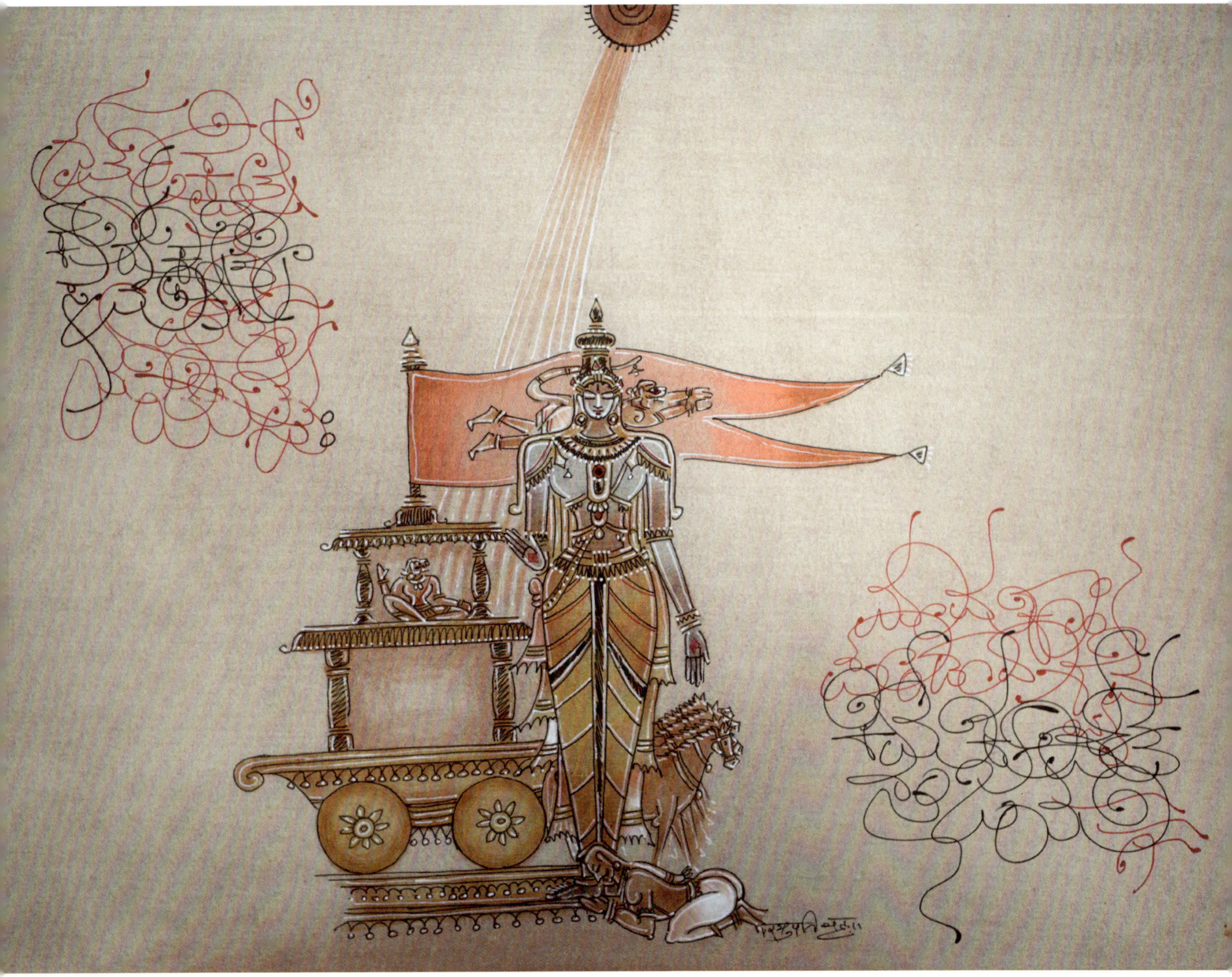

Krishna and Arjuna in the battlefield of Kurukshetra
Watercolor and pen on paper, 36 x 27 cm

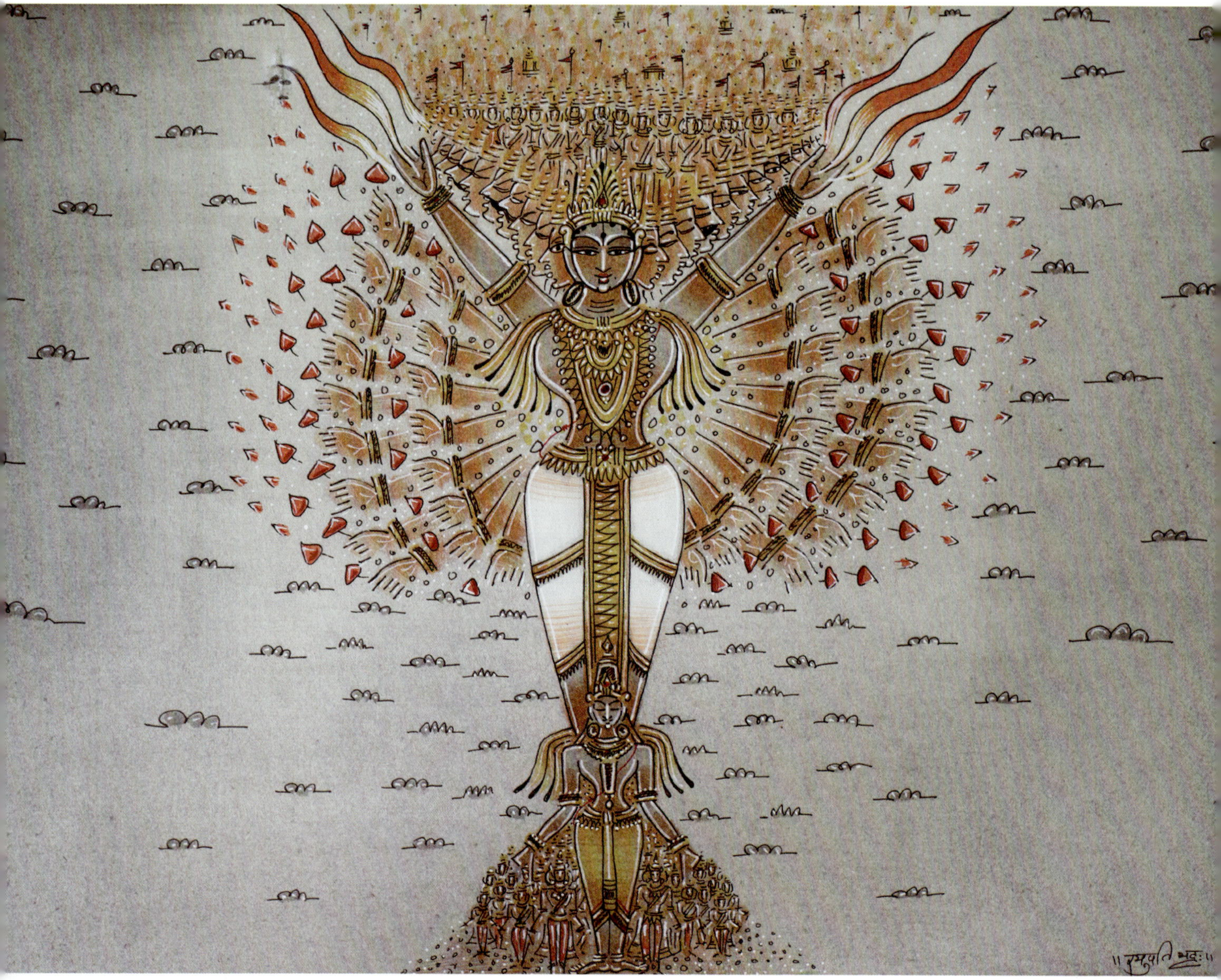

Vishwarupa
Watercolor and pen on paper, 36 x 27 cm

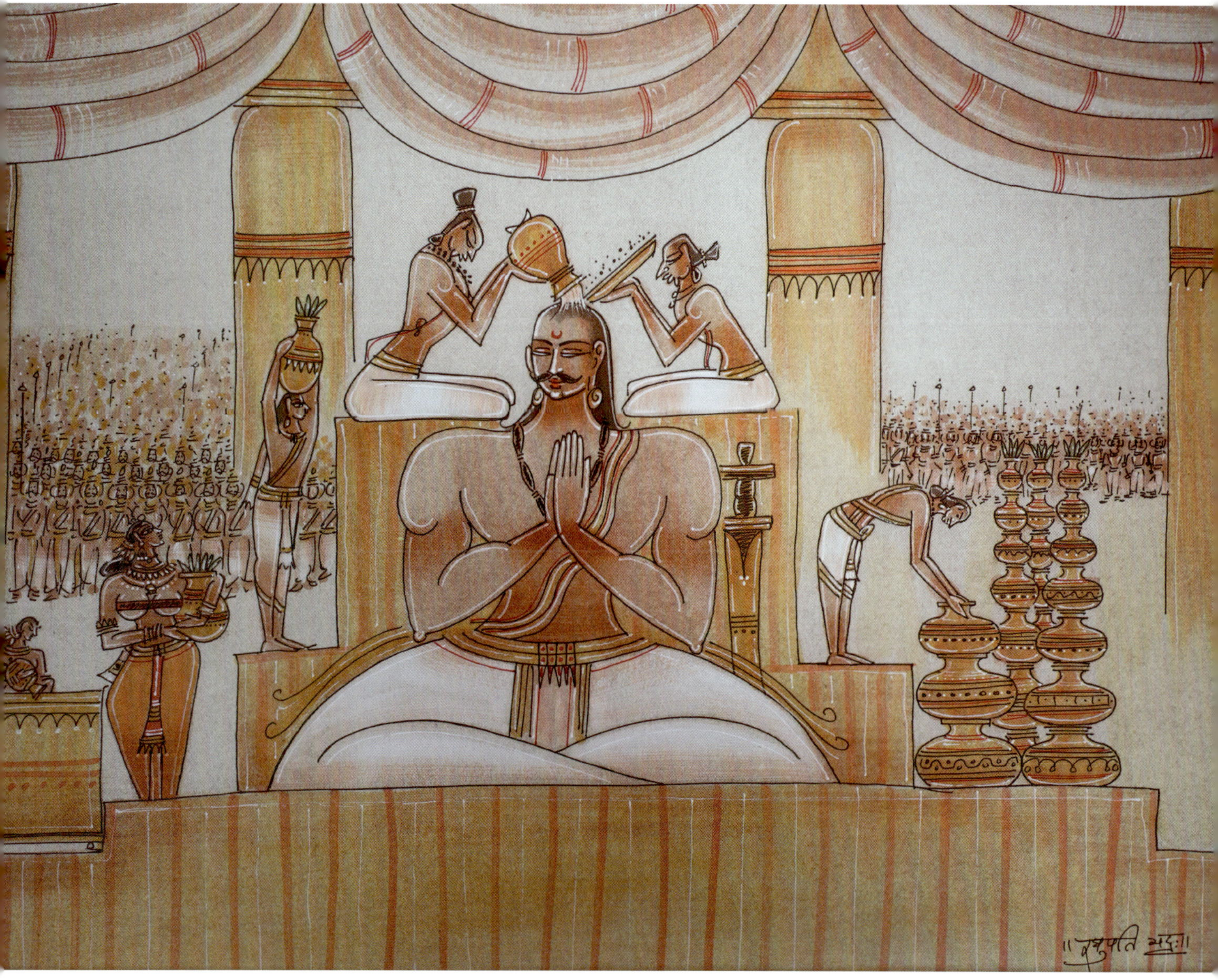

Karna's coronation
Watercolor and pen on paper, 36 x 27 cm

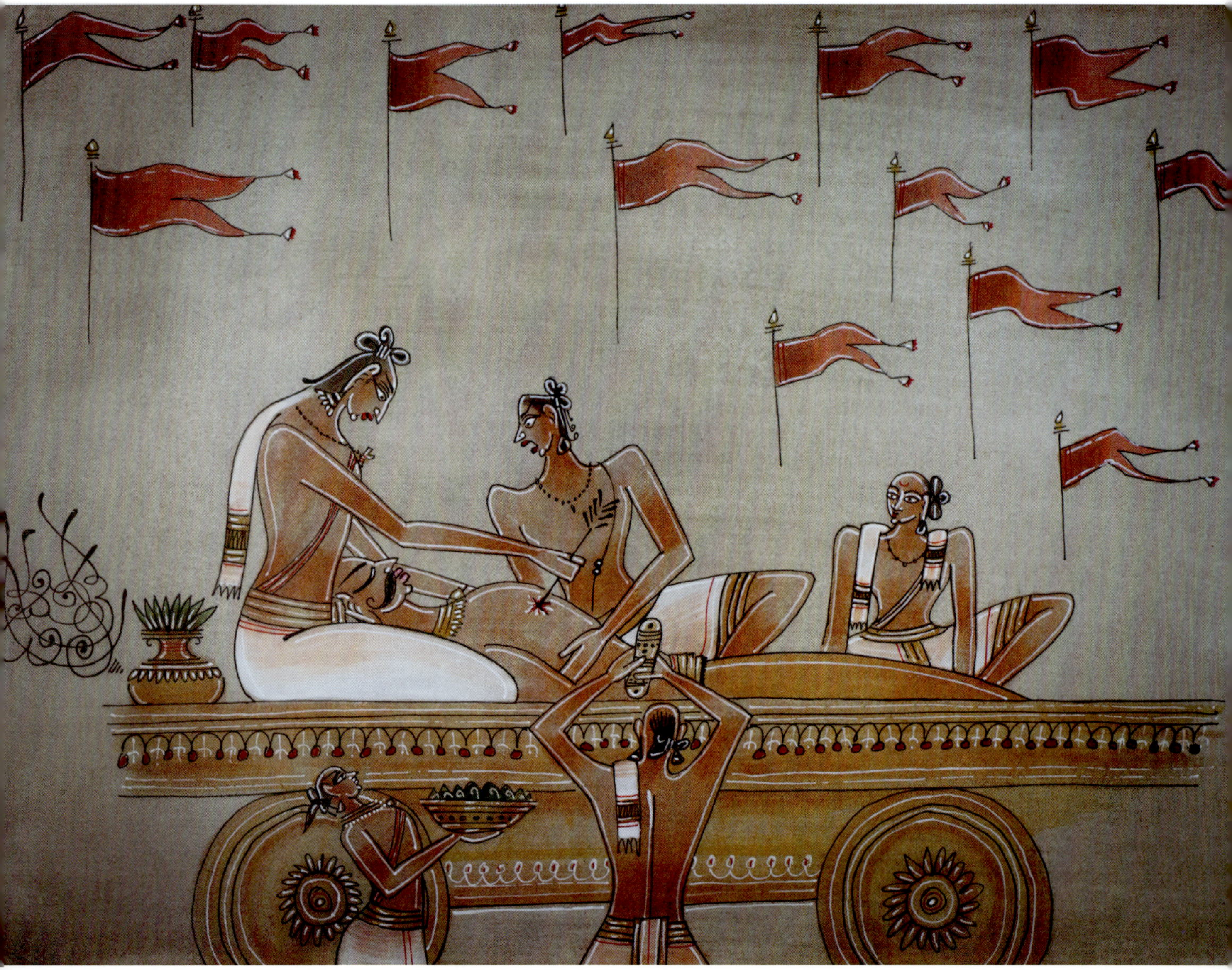

Dharmaraya receives Ayurvedic treatment
Watercolor and pen on paper, 36 x 27 cm

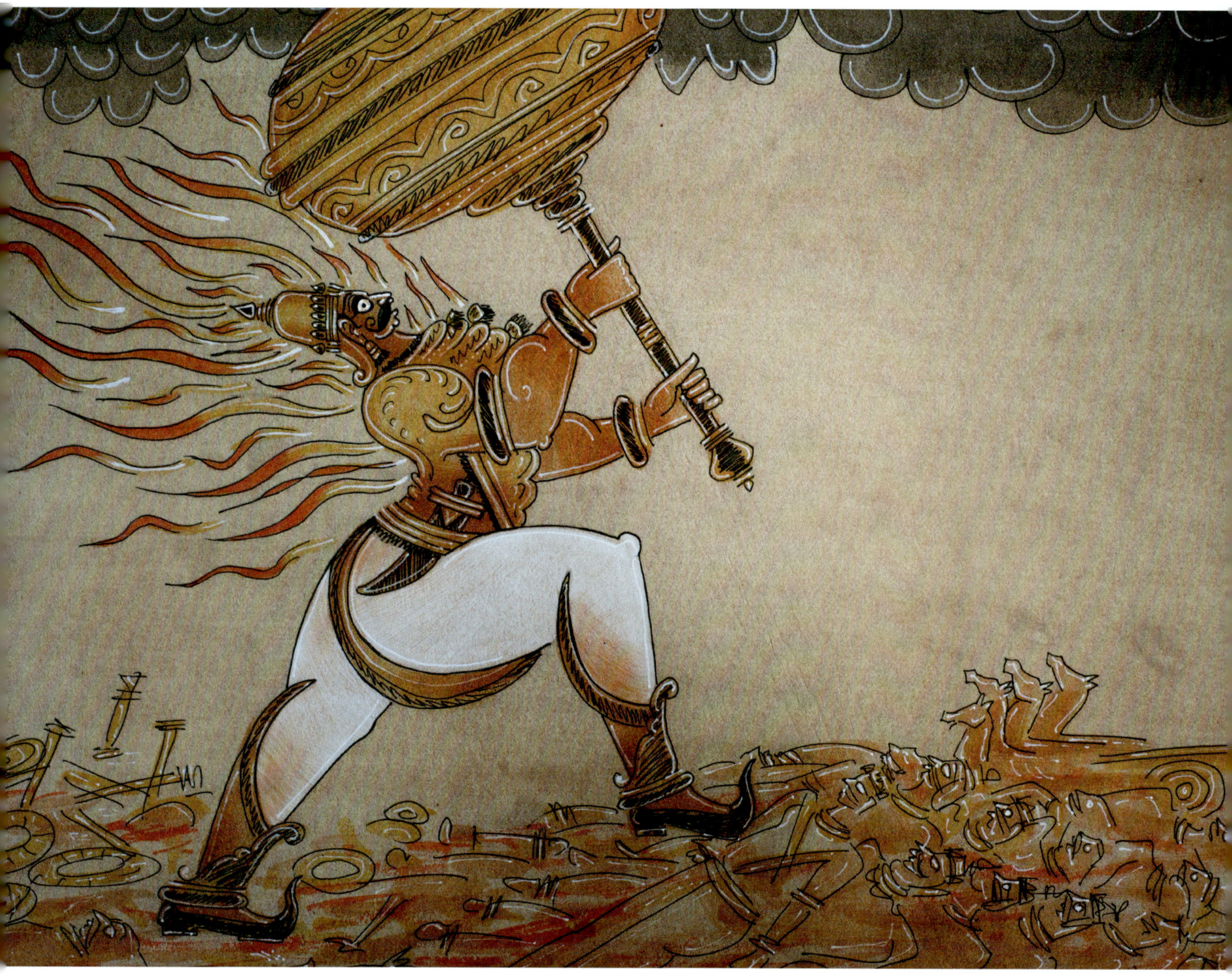

Bhima on the battlefield
Watercolor and pen on paper, 36 x 27 cm

The fight between Karna and Arjuna >
Watercolor and pen on paper, 36 x 27 cm

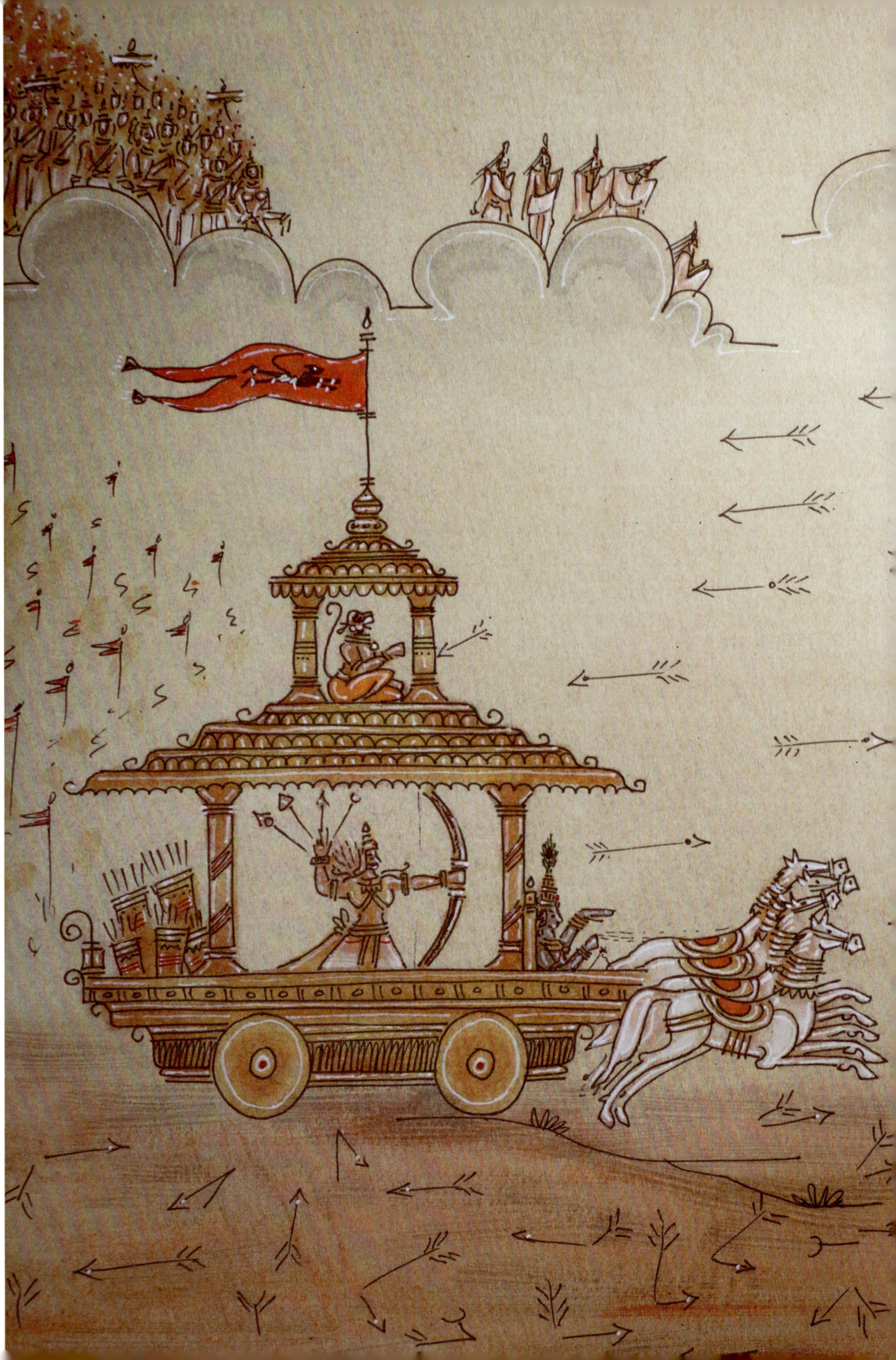

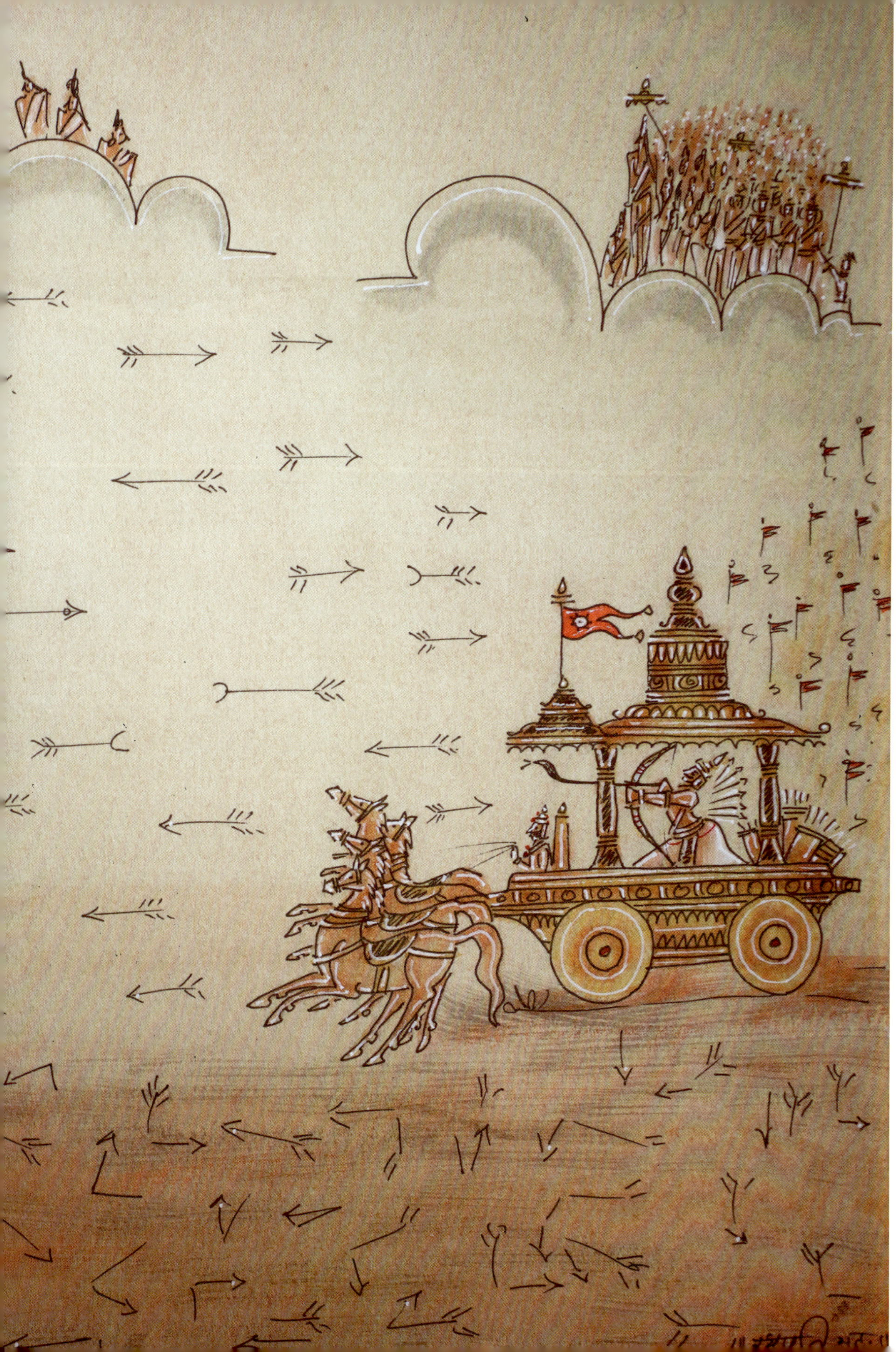

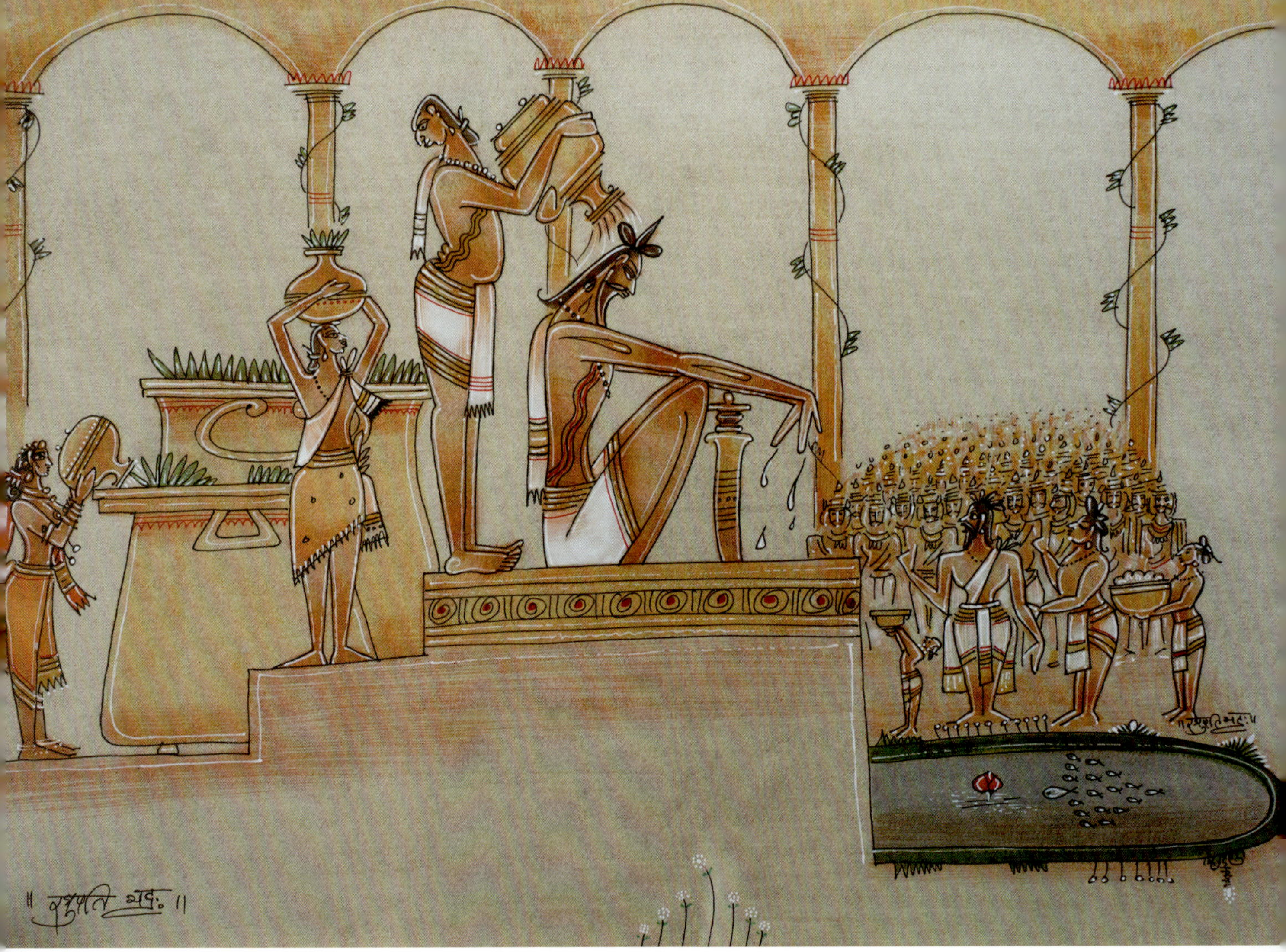

Drona's coronation
Watercolor and pen on paper, 36 x 27 cm

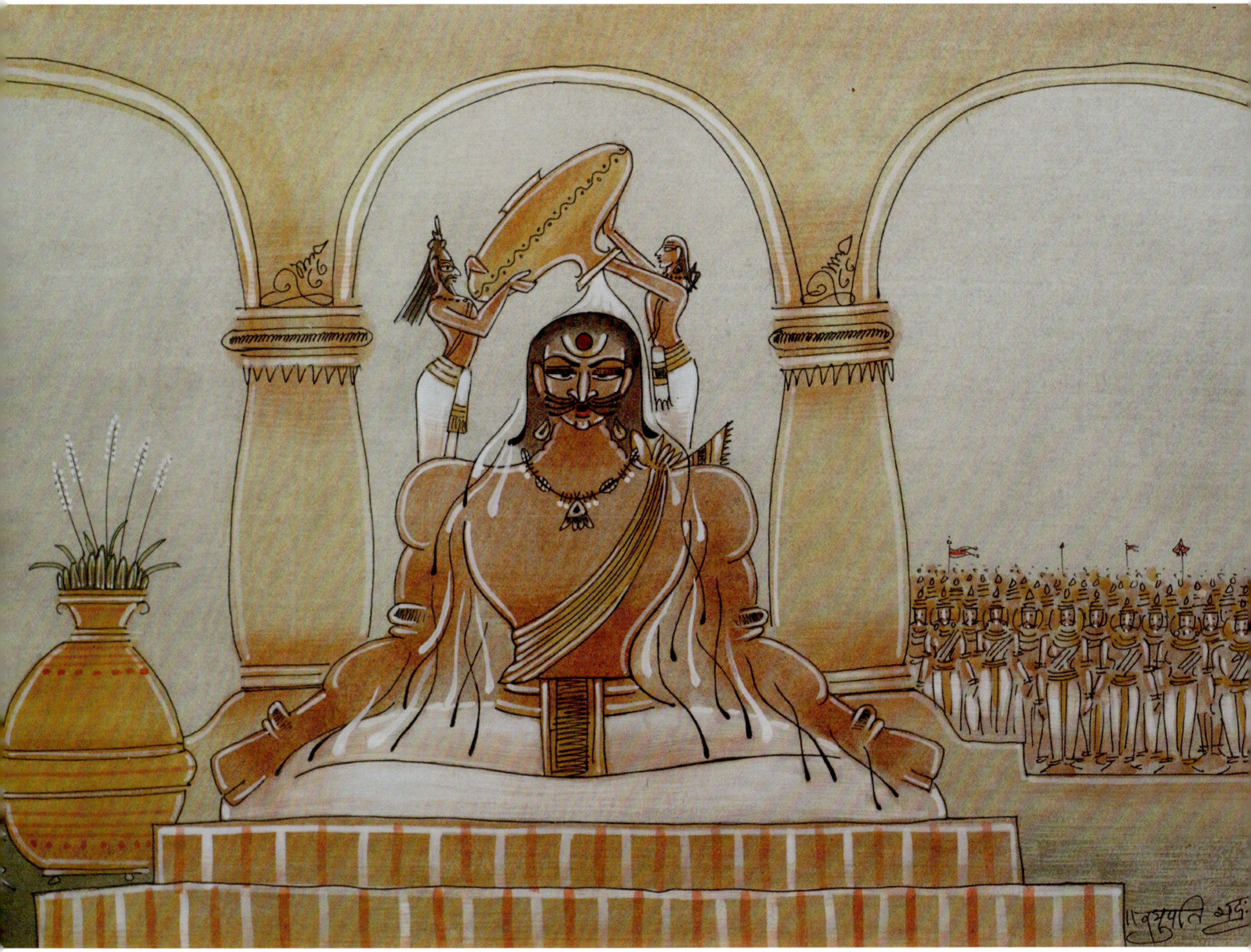

Shalya's coronation
Watercolor and pen on paper, 36 x 27 cm

The fight between Dhuryodhana and Bhima >
Watercolor and pen on paper, 36 x 27 cm

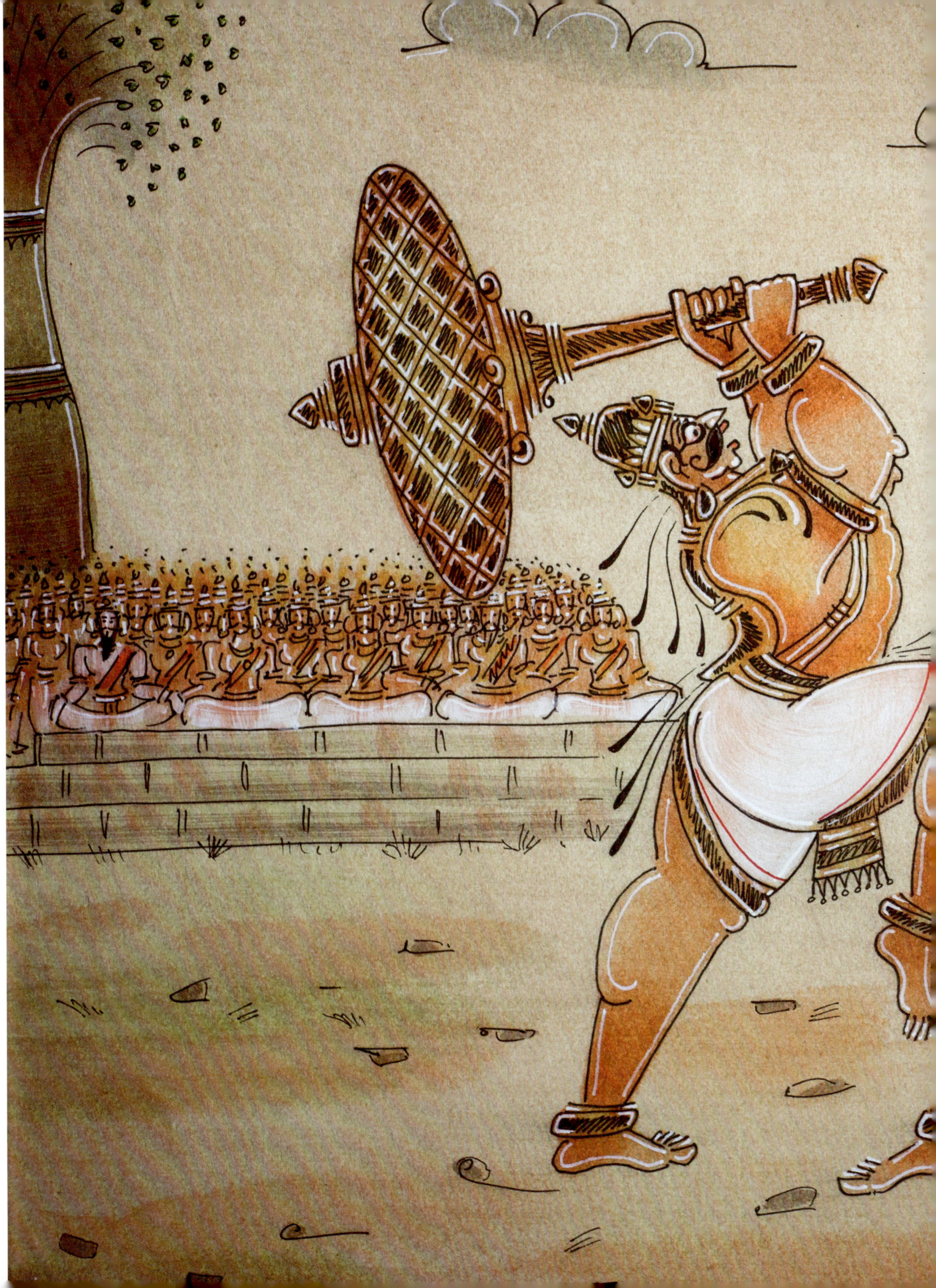

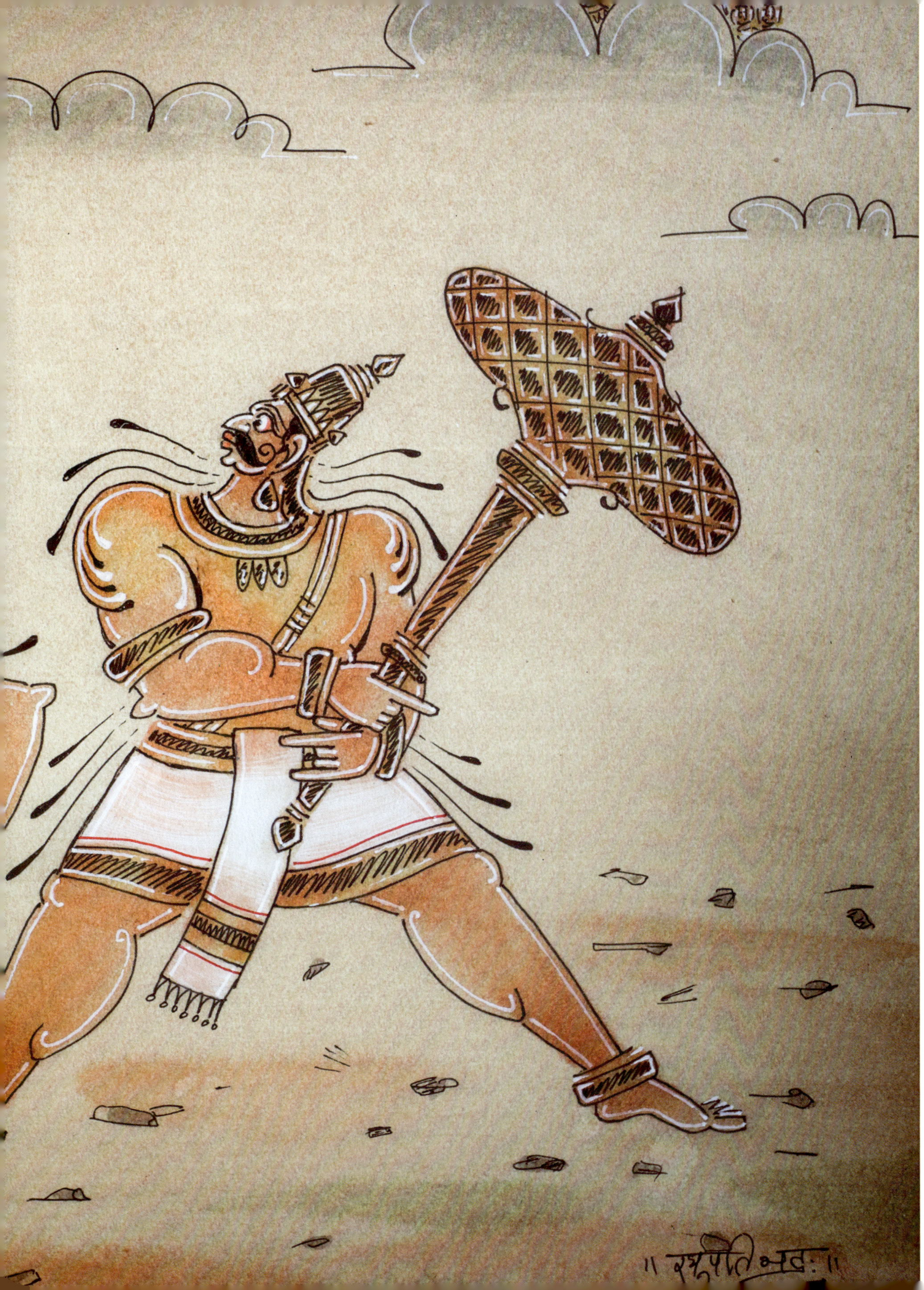
॥ रघुपति भट्टः ॥

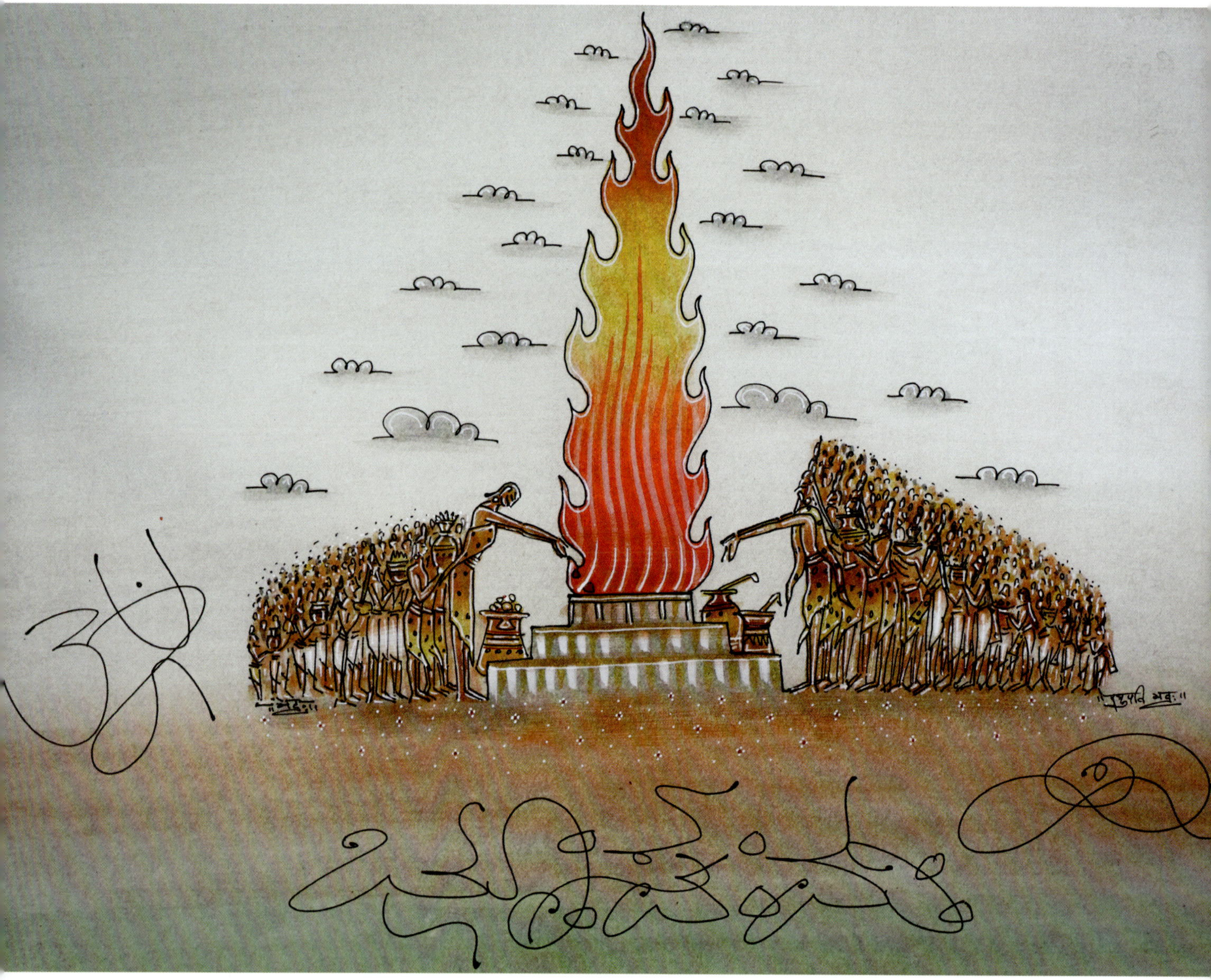

Rajasuya yaga
Watercolor and pen on paper, 36 x 27 cm

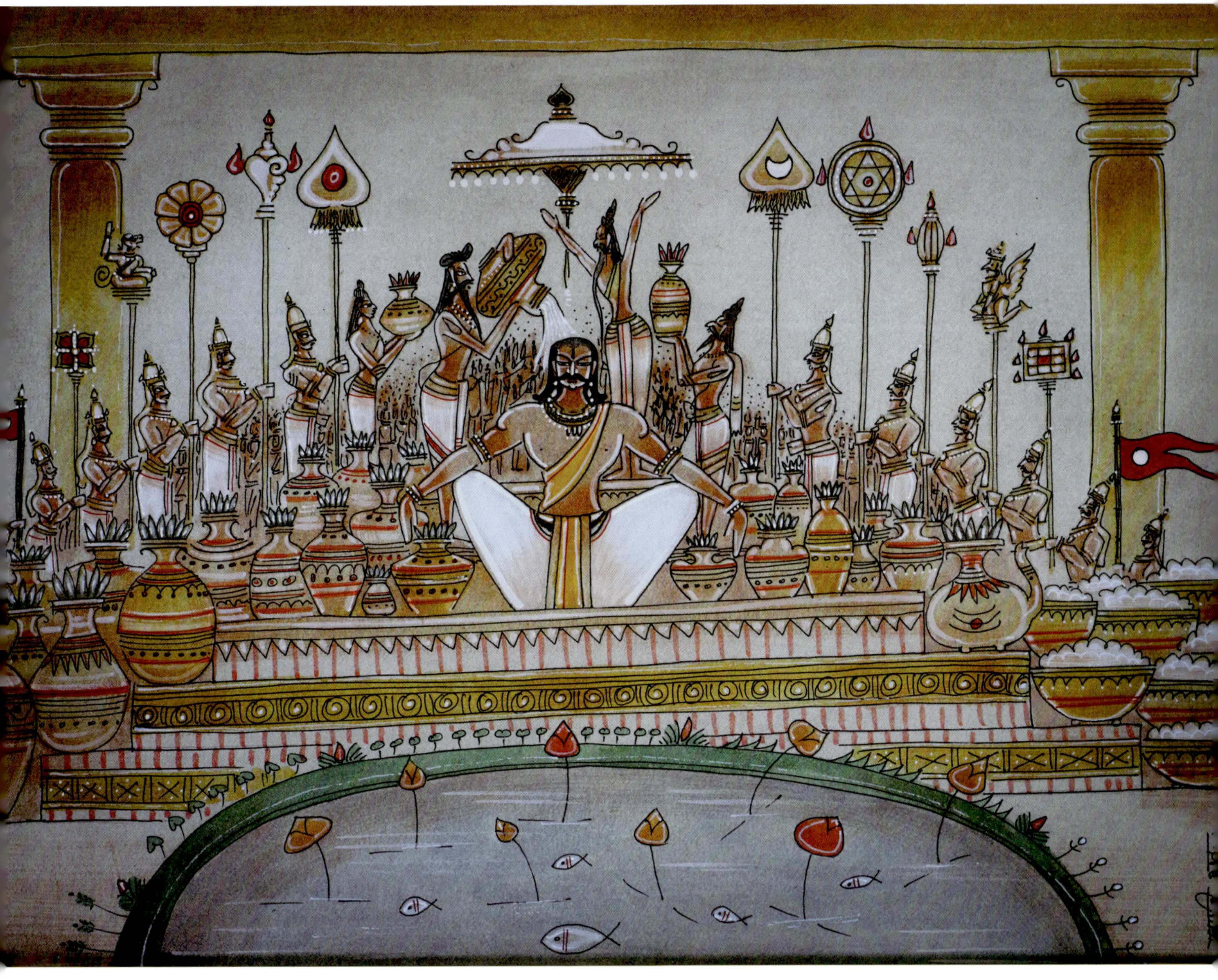

Yudhisthira's coronation
Watercolor and pen on paper, 36 x 27 cm

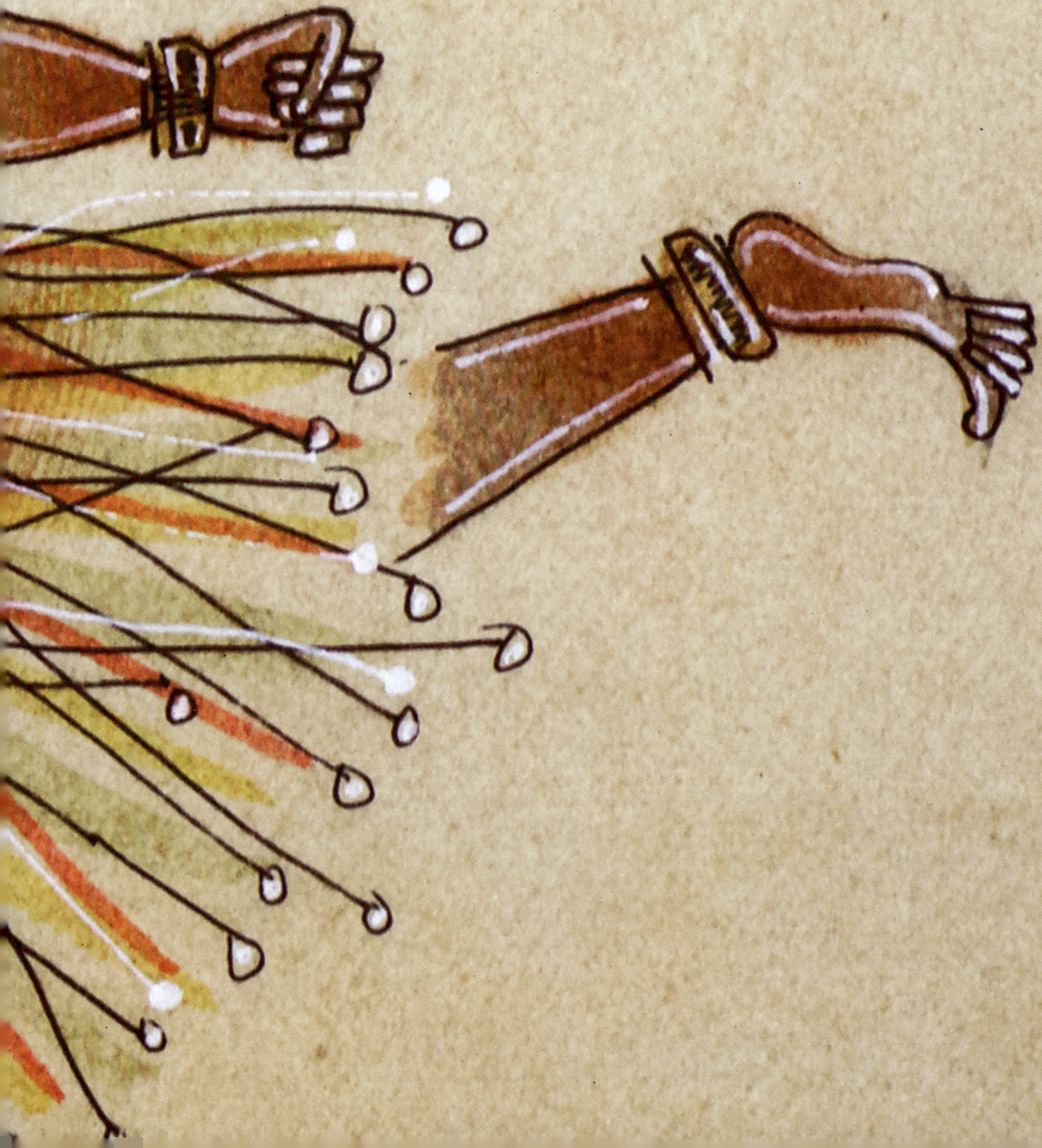

1997 Tunisia, organized by Handicraft Department, Govt of India

2001 Indian embassy to Tokyo, Chayamachi gallery Osaka, Hiroshima

2006 World peace Conference in Kyoto, Japan

2008 World Peace Conference, Kyoto

2010 Yoga Station, Ottowa, Canada

2010 Puttige Mutt, USA

2011 Attended world peace conference Tanzania, Africa

2012 Renovated wall paintings and gold leaf work in Durbar Hall of Mysore Palace

2013 Gold leaf work in Durbar Hall, Khasagi Darbar Hall and Kalyana Mantap, Mysore

COLLECTIONS

Sixty miniatures based on the Ramayana, Victoria & Albert Museum, London

Twenty-four wodeyar works, Lalith Mahal Palace Hotel, Mysore

Eighty-six works, MOSA, Belgium

Paintings in Manjusha Museum, Dharmasthala and several prestigious places around the world

MEMBERSHIP

Ex-president of Samskara Bharathi, Mysore

1993 - 1996 Karnataka Lalitha Academy member

2001 - 2003 Selection committee member, awards in Visual Arts, Government of India

BOOKS ABOUT HIS PAINTINGS

Dr. Sjoman, *Infinite Painted Worlds - The inner light of Ganjifa Raghupathi Bhatta*

Tomasz Poplaswski, *Brush with a Sage - The Soul of Yoga on Canvas*